D1617192

Biblical Interpretation and Middle East Policy

UNIVERSITY PRESS OF FLORIDA / STATE UNIVERSITY SYSTEM

Florida A&M University, Tallahassee
Florida Atlantic University, Boca Raton
Florida Gulf Coast University, Ft. Myers
Florida International University, Miami
Florida State University, Tallahassee
University of Central Florida, Orlando
University of Florida, Gainesville
University of North Florida, Jacksonville
University of South Florida , Tampa
University of West Florida , Pensacola

Biblical Interpretation
and
Middle East Policy

The Promised Land, America, and Israel, 1917–2002

Irvine H. Anderson

University Press of Florida

Gainesville Tallahassee Tampa Boca Raton

Pensacola Orlando Miami Jacksonville Ft. Myers

Copyright 2005 by Irvine H. Anderson
Printed in the United States of America on recycled, acid-free paper
All rights reserved

10 09 08 07 06 05   6 5 4 3 2 1

Library of Congress Cataloging-in-Publication Data
Anderson, Irvine H., 1928–
Biblical interpretation and Middle East policy : the promised land, America,
and Israel, 1917–2002 / Irvine H. Anderson.
p. cm.
Includes bibliographical references (p.) and index.
ISBN 0-8130-2798-5 (alk. paper)
1. Christianity and international affairs—History—20th century.
2. Middle East—Foreign relations—United States. 3. United States—Foreign
relations—Middle East. 4. Christian Zionism—United States—
History—20th century. I. Title.
BR115.I7A53 2005
261.8'7'0973—dc22   2004-054151

The University Press of Florida is the scholarly publishing agency for the State
University System of Florida, comprising Florida A&M University, Florida Atlantic
University, Florida Gulf Coast University, Florida International University, Florida
State University, University of Central Florida, University of Florida, University of
North Florida, University of South Florida, and University of West Florida.

University Press of Florida
15 Northwest 15th Street
Gainesville, Fl 32611-2079
http://www.upf.com

For my father and mother,
Irvine and Elizabeth Anderson

Contents

Tables

Acknowledgments

This is a case study of the influence of cultural tradition on international relations, specifically of the influence of the Christian Bible on British and American Middle Eastern policy in the twentieth century. In one sense it documents what has been obvious to many observers for a long time, but only in selected episodes. It draws on original research down a number of unexplored avenues and on the research of others in specific instances. I hope that it offers a coherent picture of how biblical influences have permeated British and American society and how those influences have created a cultural framework within which Zionist and pro-Israel lobbies could more easily function. This is an influence sometimes referred to as "Christian Zionism."

It is impossible to fully acknowledge the assistance of the scores of people who have made this study possible, some in small ways and some in large, but a few stand out. Dr. Henry R. Winkler, president emeritus of the University of Cincinnati, first suggested that I pursue a study such as this, and I was encouraged to undertake it by Rev. Dr. Donald Wagner, executive director of Evangelicals for Middle East Understanding; Rev. Walter Owensby, of the Washington Office of the Presbyterian Church (USA); and Professor Samuel P. Huntington of Harvard University.

Many people provided invaluable insights and kept me from straying too far afield. Among them were Dr. Peter Obermark, then of Hebrew Union College in Cincinnati, who provided considerable help with recent biblical scholarship, and Rev. Dr. Philip B. Cliff, of Birmingham, England, who greatly enhanced my understanding of the English Sunday school movement. Rev. Dr. Stephen R. Sizer of Surrey, England, gave me a better understanding of the phenomenon known as Christian Zionism. Dr. Andrew Semmel, then legislative assistant to Senator Richard Lugar, helped me to better understand the workings of Congress. Professor Yaakov Ariel, of the University of North Carolina, read the entire first version of this study and made a number of excellent suggestions. I, of course, remain responsible for any remaining errors of fact or interpretation.

When it comes to research, I must give high praise to the many archivists in England who helped me to explore their records, and to Michael Marten, who did research on my behalf in Scotland. Special thanks also goes to the staffs of the numerous American denominations that assisted in locating relevant material in this country. And I must note the unique aspect of the electronic age that makes possible an incredible amount of bibliographic research from the comfort of one's home. With the Internet I was able to research the catalogs of numerous libraries and through the medium of interlibrary loan obtain almost any volume that I needed. The staff of the Pleasant Ridge branch of the Public Library of Cincinnati and Hamilton County was extremely helpful in this regard. And this study would not have been possible without a generous travel grant from the Earhart Foundation in Ann Arbor, Michigan. I must also acknowledge the assistance of the University of Cincinnati Foundation in obtaining funds for the project. Finally, I am much appreciative of the efforts of three editors at the University Press of Florida—Amy Gorelick, Susan Albury, and Elaine Durham Otto—for seeing that this study saw the light of day in the form in which it now appears.

My loving wife, Donna, made this study possible by providing the encouragement and material support that I frequently overlooked or forgot during my five years of preoccupation.

Prologue

A Synopsis of the Study

Several months after leaving office, reflecting on his decision to give prompt recognition to the State of Israel under pressure from Zionists and against the adamant advice of his diplomatic and military advisors, Harry Truman was quoted as saying, "I am Cyrus. I am Cyrus."[1] There were obviously many factors involved in that decision, but the statement itself is significant. Cyrus was the Persian emperor who authorized the return of the Jews from Babylonian captivity to Palestine in 538 B.C.E. Truman, with his Baptist background and intimate knowledge of the Bible, clearly relished the parallel.

The interplay between Zionist lobbyists, national interests, and Christian teachings was intense in America's midwifery to the State of Israel, but the roots go well back into nineteenth-century England. And that interplay continued to influence American behavior throughout the twentieth century. The third element of that triumvirate—Christian teachings—is the focus of this study.

There is a considerable volume of material on British and American policy toward Palestine and Israel, but much of it focuses on key individuals and does not discuss the depth and breadth of Christian sentiment in both countries. The thesis here is that so many people in Britain and the United States have been influenced by childhood stories from the Bible about Abraham, Joshua, and the Promised Land and by what has come to be known as "End Times" or "Armageddon" theology that much of the electorate in both countries has been predisposed to support the return of the Jews to Palestine. This has made it relatively easy for Zionist and pro-Israel lobbies to be effective with both the executive and legislative branches of government in Great Britain and the United States.

The word *predisposed* is key. It does not imply that Christian orientation has been the principal reason that the British government and then the American government supported the return of the Jews to Palestine. It simply means that Christian familiarity with and interpretation of the Bible created the seedbed within which other factors could flourish.

With a widespread assumption among the electorate that God had promised the land to the Jews, other influences could come to bear more easily— the Zionist lobby in Britain in the early part of the century and the pro-Israel lobby in the United States after World War II; a sense of compassion and guilt among Americans about the Holocaust; a view of Israel as the only true democracy in the Middle East; and an assumption that Israel was a strategic ally in a dangerous part of the world. There was also no real countervailing force —no general knowledge of Islam, Arabs, or the Middle East among the electorate, no powerful Arab lobby, and limited understanding of the importance of maintaining healthy relations with friendly oil-producing Arab states in the region.

The analysis that follows is in two parts. Part I deals with the biblical background to Christian Zionism, starting with a split in twentieth-century approaches to biblical interpretation between the liberal "historical/critical" method and the fundamentalist "literal/prophetic" approach. It examines a few of the key texts that have been used to justify Christian support of a return of the Jews to Palestine, including portions of the books of Genesis, Joshua, Daniel, and Revelation, and looks at both ways in which those books may be interpreted.

This is followed by a chapter on the Sunday school movement and Armageddon theology in Britain and the United States. It includes examples of Sunday school lessons about Abraham and Joshua in major denominations in both countries. It also describes the growth of Armageddon theology, or dispensational premillennialism, from its origin in nineteenth-century England to its development in twentieth-century America, with emphasis on the individuals, books, and institutions through which it has been disseminated.

Part II moves to policy, with an initial chapter devoted to the origins of the Balfour Declaration, Woodrow Wilson's support for its issuance, and its reaffirmation during the Mandate period. Christian influence included Balfour's childhood grounding in the Old Testament, Wilson's Presbyterian background, and the subtle influence of William Blackstone's Bible-based memorial to Wilson advocating support of a return of the Jews to the Holy Land. This is where the interplay between Zionist lobbying, perceived national interests both in Britain and the United States, and Christian predisposition comes into full view.

The Mandate period is especially interesting, partly because of both Methodist and Jewish influence within the Labour Party, and partly because of attempts by the government to calm the area after a series of "disturbances" only to have it blocked by Jewish opposition and adamant protests in Parliament. Positions taken by some of the Nonconformist churches and church newspapers vis-à-vis those disturbances shed some light on general public attitudes toward the issues.

The next chapter moves to the United States and Truman's decision to hurriedly recognize the newly proclaimed State of Israel. The decision was clearly in opposition to the "national interest" as perceived by the American military and diplomatic leadership. Conventional wisdom has attributed the decision to Clark Clifford's influence and a desire to secure the New York Jewish vote in the upcoming presidential election. Not so, say other analysts: it was the effectiveness of the Zionist lobby. This study takes a slightly different approach and emphasizes a third influence—Truman's Baptist background and intimate knowledge of the Bible.

The final chapter is a complex one. It includes observations on the influence of the American Israel Public Affairs Committee (AIPAC) on congressional funding for Israel and on relevant congressional hearings in both the House and the Senate. There is a comparison of the positions taken on the subject of the Arab-Israel conflict by principal American religious denominations, and it reports on data from several polling organizations on American attitudes toward Israel. As a test of the "pro-Israel lobby/national interest/Christian predisposition" thesis, it examines the dynamics of the highly controversial 1995 congressional vote calling for the United States to move its embassy from Tel Aviv to Jerusalem. The evidence of Christian influence throughout this period is highly persuasive.

The epilogue is simply a comment on the fact that, even though the events of September 11 changed many of the dynamics of international affairs, the positions of the parties to this study initially remained very much the same. But as the American "war on terrorism" evolved, dissenting voices were overwhelmed and the American administration became increasingly vocal in its direct support of Israel—to the dismay of some of its allies and many in the Arab world. Future historians will have to assess the degree to which the determinants of American policy described in this study continue into the future. But if one can extrapolate from the past into the future, it is reasonable to assume that an American cultural predisposition to support Israel, based at least in part on the influence of the Christian Bible, will continue to be one of the factors in the dynamics of policy formulation.

I

The Bible in Anglo-American Culture

I

Biblical Criticism and the Rise of Fundamentalism

Until the end of the eighteenth century, most Protestants in the English-speaking world accepted the Bible as the authentic Word of God. That is, they saw it as a divinely inspired history of God's creation of the world and His interaction with His chosen people—the Hebrews first and then the Christians. One might, or might not, live by its precepts, but its authenticity was not subject to serious question. All of that changed in the course of the nineteenth century through developments in science, philosophy, and biblical criticism. Literalism was challenged not only by Charles Darwin's theory of evolution through natural selection but also by men such as British geologist Charles Lyell, who questioned the creation of the earth in the biblical six days in 4004 B.C.E.; German philosopher Immanuel Kant, who questioned man's ability to know "absolute realities" outside the human mind; and sociologist Emile Durkheim, who saw religion as purely a product of social forces.[1]

As serious as was the challenge of Darwin's theory of evolution to the popular mind, and that of other writers to the intellectual elite, a more profound challenge to biblical literalism originated in Germany. Known originally as "Higher Criticism" and later as the "historical/critical" method, it applied the emerging tools of archaeology, history, and literary analysis to the Bible itself. This development began to cast considerable doubt on the historical accuracy of biblical stories—from Noah and the Great Flood, to Joshua's trumpeting down the walls of Jericho, to the Israelites' sojourn in Egypt. Liberal theologians in Britain and the United States gradually accepted this approach, many by viewing the Bible as containing profound theological truth in the form of stories based loosely on historical events but not intended to be taken literally.

The reaction to all of this was a tremendous upsurge of religious fundamentalism in the United States around the idea that if one doesn't believe the Bible to be literally true, there is no moral anchor for the country. This was not a totally new development, because elements of this viewpoint had existed for a long time in English Puritanism and among the early Protestant settlers of New England. But it found new expression during the early twentieth century, in the Scopes "monkey trial" of the 1920s, and in reaction to the disquieting social changes following World War II.

A corollary to biblical literalism has been the emergence of what has sometimes been termed "Armageddon theology," or more correctly, "dispensational premillennialism." This involved predictions of an imminent "end times," including an ingathering of Jews to the Holy Land, a "wafting away" of true believers prior to the "tribulation," an earth-destroying battle of Armageddon, and the return of Christ to reign for 1,000 years of peace. Based primarily on the books of Daniel and Revelation, this particular interpretation dates back to England in the early part of the nineteenth century, but it has found considerable expression in post–World War II America.

We thus have two extremes of biblical interpretation. One is the historical/critical approach that views the Bible as containing theological truth but not intended to be taken literally or prophetically. This, or a variation of it, is the dominant approach in most American mainline seminaries and among most of the ministers of those denominations. The other is a literal/prophetic approach that is dominant in more fundamentalist seminaries and churches. Gallup poll data also suggest that many Americans subscribe to this interpretation. There are, of course, many shades of understanding between and around those two polar opposites. But it is useful to set them apart in order to understand the significance of the latter for British and American Middle East policy.

Certain passages in the Old and New Testaments in the Bible have been especially influential in predisposing much of the British and American electorate to support Israel. The story in Genesis of God promising the land to Abraham and his descendants and the story in the book of Joshua of his leading the Israelites in the conquest of that land have had considerable impact. Both stories have been widely used in Sunday school lessons for younger children in both countries, and both have been cited by fundamentalists who support the return of the Jews to the Holy Land. The principal, but not the only, sources for Armageddon or premillennial dispensational theology have been the book of Daniel in the Old Testament and the book of Revelation in the New. Additional material has been drawn from many parts of the Bible as "proof-texts" for this approach to interpretation.

As a basis for better understanding of what follows, this study begins with a concise examination of how those passages have been understood both by scholars of the liberal historical/critical school and by proponents of the fundamentalist literal/prophetic viewpoint. This summary will be very brief, and those who would like to pursue the subject in depth are referred to the works cited in the endnotes.

Strictly speaking, the historical/critical approach is not entirely new. Early versions of it can be found in the writings of English philosopher Thomas Hobbes (1588–1679) and the Dutch Jewish philosopher Benedict de Spinoza (1631–1677). In his *Leviathan,* published in 1651, Hobbes, the profound skeptic, argued *on the basis of internal evidence* that Moses could not possibly have authored the first five books of the Bible, as had traditionally been believed. This was a significant step toward critical analysis. Spinoza went further. He argued that the Bible was never written to provide a coherent philosophical or theological system or to recount the "true course of historical events." Instead, he viewed it as a narrative of events "in an order and style which [had] the most power to move men, especially uneducated men, to devotion." In other words, it was written to persuade and never meant to be taken as literal history.[2]

Such early writings had little impact on the popular mind, and it was the growth in scientific thinking and critical analysis in the nineteenth century that propelled this line of criticism forward. Much of what grew into the historical/ critical method of biblical scholarship originated in the universities of Germany, which were relatively free from church restraint and also centers of theological debate.[3] The studies were done by many people, but much of it was summarized and popularized by Julius Wellhausen (1844–1918) in his *Prolegomena to the History of Israel* in 1878.[4] Interest in the approach moved fairly soon to England and Scotland, and then to the United States, where biblical studies were just beginning to take hold.[5]

Many of the resulting conclusions are based on critical analysis of the texts themselves, but they are greatly influenced by a growing body of archaeological discoveries that have enabled scholars to obtain increasing insights into the history of the ancient Near East. Much of the evidence in writing comes from state and temple texts in the archives of Egypt, Sumer, Akkad, Babylonia, Assyria, the Hittite Kingdom, and Persia. Among other things, they reveal "a vast fund of writings in the wider world which used literary forms very much like the forms of biblical literature and that dealt with the same or similar historical and thematic concerns."[6] What follows is a summary of recent historical/critical scholarship on biblical passages relevant to this study, starting with selected verses from the book of Genesis.

The Promised Land

Since the idea of the Promised Land plays an important role in the development of Christian Zionism, it is well to start with several passages from Genesis where the promise is made to Abraham and his descendants plus references to the promise in Joshua. (All of the translations below are from the New Revised Standard Version of the Bible, which has been one of the two most widely used translations in the United States in the past decade.)[7]

The story of Abraham is well worth reading in its entirety, but what has been quoted below are the relevant portions—those pertaining directly to the Promised Land. The story begins with Abraham traveling with his father from Ur of the Chaldeans (in the southern part of present-day Iraq) to Haran (in present-day Turkey just north of the border with Syria). After his father's death, Abraham receives a commandment from the Lord:

Now the Lord said to Abram [whose name is changed to Abraham later in the story], "Go from your country and your kindred and your father's house to the land that I will show you. I will make of you a great nation, I will bless you, and make your name great, so that you will be a blessing. I will bless those who bless you, and the one who curses you I will curse; and in you all the families of the earth will be blessed."

So Abram went, as the Lord had told him; and Lot went with him. Abram was seventy-five years old when he departed from Haran. Abram took his wife, Sarai, and his brother's son Lot, and all the possessions they had gathered, and the persons whom they had acquired in Haran; and they set forth to go to the land of Canaan. Abram passed through the land to the place at Shechem [north of present-day Jerusalem], to the oak of Moreh. At that time the Canaanites were in the land. Then the Lord appeared to Abram, and said, "To your offspring I will give this land." So he built there an altar to the Lord, who had appeared to him. (Genesis 12:1–7)

As a result of a famine, Abraham then moves his flocks to Egypt. There follows an episode in which Abraham tells Pharaoh that Sarai is his sister and Pharaoh takes her into his house. When Pharaoh learns the truth, he gives Sarai

back to Abraham and Abraham returns to the land of Canaan. By this time
Abraham has become very rich in livestock, silver, and gold. He and Lot decide
to separate; Lot settles in the plain of Jordan, and Abraham stays in Canaan.

> The Lord said to Abram, after Lot had separated from him, "Raise up
> your eyes now, and look from the place where you are, northward and
> southward and eastward and westward; for all the land that you see I
> will give to you and to your offspring forever. I will make your offspring
> like the dust of the earth; so that if one can count the dust of the earth,
> your offspring also can be counted. Rise up, walk through the length
> and breadth of the land, for I will give it to you." So Abram moved his
> tent, and came and settled by the oaks of Mamre, which are at Hebron;
> and there he built an altar to the Lord. (Genesis 13:14–18)

Numerous other events occur, including the capture of Lot by his enemies
and his rescue by Abraham. At one point Abraham begins to question the promise. The Lord reassures him, asks for an animal sacrifice, and makes a covenant
with him.

> When the sun had gone down and it was dark, a smoking fire pot and a
> flaming torch passed between these pieces [of sacrifice]. On that day the
> Lord made a covenant with Abram, saying, "To your descendants I give
> this land, from the river of Egypt to the great river, the river Euphrates."
> (Genesis 17:18)

There is a dramatic sequence where Abraham, at Sarai's suggestion, has a son
by Sarai's slave girl, Hagar, and the son is named Ishmael (later understood by
the Arabs to be *their* ancestor). When Abraham is ninety-nine years old, the
Lord appears to him again and seals the covenant with the rite of circumcision.

> Then Abram fell on his face; and God said to him, "As for me, this is my
> covenant with you: You shall be the ancestor of a multitude of nations. No
> longer will your name be Abram; but your name shall be Abraham; for I
> have made you the ancestor of a multitude of nations. I will make you
> exceedingly fruitful; and I will make nations of you, and kings shall come
> from you. I will establish my covenant between me and you, and your
> offspring after you throughout their generations, for an everlasting cov-
> enant, to be God to you and to your offspring after you. And I will give to
> you, and to your offspring after you, the land where you are now an alien,
> all the land of Canaan, for a perpetual hold; and I will be their God. . . .

This is my covenant, which you shall keep between me and you and your offspring after you: Every male among you shall be circumcised." (Genesis 17:3–8, 10)

There is much more to the story. Sodom and Gomorrah are destroyed; Sarai bears Abraham a son, Isaac; Hagar and Ishmael are sent away into the desert; Abraham almost sacrifices Isaac at the Lord's command (by tradition at the Dome of the Rock in present-day Jerusalem); Sarai dies and is buried at the cave of Machpelah (in Hebron); Isaac marries Rebekah; Abraham takes another wife who bears him six sons; he dies and is also buried in the cave of Machpelah.

The story has had a powerful influence on the minds of many—Jews and Christians alike—for centuries. Of most relevance for this study is the fact that the story of Abraham and the Promised Land have been deeply imbedded in Christian Sunday school lessons, Bible reading, and ministers' sermons throughout the nineteenth and twentieth centuries in England and the United States.

In Deuteronomy 1:6–8, after the Israelites have come out of Egypt and are camped on the east side of the river Jordan, Moses reminds them of the promise God has made to them of "the land of the Canaanites and the Lebanon, as far as the . . . river Euphrates." And in Deuteronomy 11:22–25, the Lord says, "If you will diligently observe the entire commandment that I am commanding you . . . your territory shall extend from the wilderness [possibly the southern Negeb desert] to the Lebanon and from the . . . river Euphrates to the Western Sea." (This is approximately the hypothetical scope of David's rule in the tenth century B.C.E.)[8]

The passages in Deuteronomy, however, are not as widely known as are the stories of Abraham and Joshua. The book of Joshua opens with a reassertion of the promise:

After the death of Moses the servant of the Lord, the Lord spoke to Joshua son of Nun, Moses' assistant, saying, "My servant Moses is dead. Now proceed to cross the Jordan, you and all this people, into the land I am giving them, the Israelites. Every place that the sole of your feet will tread upon I have given to you, as I promised to Moses. From the wilderness and the Lebanon as far as the . . . river Euphrates, and the land of the Hittites, to the Great Sea in the west shall be yours. . . . Be strong and courageous; for you shall put the people in possession of the land that I swore to their ancestors to give them." (Joshua 1:1–6)

Joshua sends two scouts ahead, and they hide out in the home of Rahab, a prostitute, who saves them from discovery by the king of Jericho and is promised safety in return. After much ritual preparation, the Israelites cross the Jordan and camp just north of Jericho. As commanded by the Lord, for six days Joshua has his warriors march around the walls of the city, with priests blowing rams horns and followed by the ark of the covenant. On the seventh day, they repeat the procedure and end with a tremendous shout. The walls fall down, and the warriors rush in and put "to destruction by the edge of the sword all in the city, both men and women, young and old, oxen, sheep, and donkeys" (Joshua 6:21). Only Rahab and her family are saved. Joshua and his men go on to occupy the land that they have been promised—the land that becomes the ancient land of Israel. And this, of course, is the same land that, in the twentieth century, the Zionist movement claimed for the state of Israel.

Biblical scholars of the historical/critical school have challenged the literal interpretation of those, and many other, passages in the Old Testament as not representing actual historical events. This is not to say that they challenge the theological truth of God's creation of the world or the moral precepts taught in the Bible. Except for some recent challenges, most scholars accept the fact that Abraham and the other Patriarchs were historical figures. What they do argue is that the stories about Abraham and the Patriarchs were woven into legendary accounts over many years to justify Israel's existence "as a divinely chosen people who formed a small state clinging precariously to political existence on the arid land lying between the great fertile valleys of Egypt and Mesopotamia."[9] William F. Albright, especially, has argued that the Patriarchs "were indeed human beings who were the heroes of stories handed down," but there was "a good deal of ethnic tradition intermingled with the . . . narratives."[10]

There appear to have been good reasons for scholars to challenge the historical accuracy of the first six books of the Bible—Genesis, Exodus, Leviticus, Numbers, Deuteronomy, and Joshua, sometimes referred to as the Hexateuch —which include the Creation, Abraham, the great Flood, the Exodus, Moses, and capture of the Promised Land by Joshua.

There are two versions of the Creation in Genesis—put together in such a way that they appear to be a combination of two traditional stories.[11] There is similar evidence of more than one tradition having been combined, leaving contradictions intact. This alone is obviously not enough to challenge the accuracy of the stories; it could have been the result of careless copying down through the ages. But there are more questions.

The story of the Flood does not appear to have been original with the Bible. There is a remarkably similar version in the early Sumerian epic of *Gilgamesh,* which predates the compilation of the Bible by many years.[12] A clay cuneiform fragment of the *Gilgamesh* epic dating to c.1400 B.C.E. was found in Israel at Megiddo in 1955, suggesting that the story was widely known in the culture in which the ancient Hebrews participated.[13] It is quite possible that one or more catastrophic floods had, in fact, occurred in the ancient Near East, and mythological stories of it had been used to make theological points in both cases. The *Gilgamesh* version reinforces certain concepts in Sumerian religion,[14] and the biblical version reinforces certain concepts in Hebrew religion. The biblical version may be theologically sound but not historical fact.

Even more controversial has been an argument as to whether the Hebrew people were ever in Egypt at all. The question is raised by the complete absence of mention of the Hebrew people in the Egyptian archives that have been recovered and deciphered to date.[15] The Egyptians were meticulous record keepers, and it is surprising that they do not mention a people who, according to the Bible, spent several generations there and exited in a dramatic crossing of the Red Sea. The biblical story includes the destruction of the pursuing army, including the Pharaoh, when the waters of the Red Sea closed, and that certainly should have come to the attention of the Egyptian record keepers. On the other hand, the ancients were noted for recording their victories—not their defeats.

The only Egyptian mention of the name "Israel" occurs on a stela recording Egyptian military operations in the area now known as Palestine in about 1220 B.C.E.[16] There was, in fact, considerable movement of Semitic people into and out of Egypt during that period, and it has been conjectured that some of these people could very well have been one of the clans that coalesced around the worship of Yahweh to form what later became the Hebrew people.[17] If this were true, the story of the Exile could have been the mythologizing of that memory. Again, this does not say that the Hebrew people were not in Egypt. It simply says that archaeology has cast doubt in the minds of many scholars as to the historical accuracy of the story of the Exodus.

A further problem of historical accuracy lies in the story of Joshua and the battle of Jericho. This one has found its way firmly in the American mind in the folk song, "Joshua fit [*sic*] the battle of Jericho, and the walls came tumbling down." Archaeologists have determined that the walls of Jericho were destroyed no less than seventeen times between 3000 B.C.E. and 2300 B.C.E., and again no later than 1300 B.C.E., but not at the presumed time of Joshua's entry into the Promised Land. The city was already in ruins when the Israelite conquest occurred between 1250 and 1225 B.C.E. That discrepancy, of course, depends on the accuracy of the dating, but it is one more reason why scholars question the historical accuracy of the biblical account.

Based less on archaeology than on critical analysis of the texts themselves, many scholars have concluded that the first ten books of the Bible (called the Pentateuch) were produced by a combination of at least three separate traditions. These are known as "J" (Yahwist), "E" (Elohist), and "P" (Priestly), named, in part, for the frequent use of either Yahweh (translated as "Lord") or Elohim (translated as "God") in the text, or from texts with an emphasis believed to reflect the interests of the early Hebrew priests. The three sources probably originated in oral traditions, but are believed to have been recorded in about 950 for J, 750 for E, and after 539 for P.[18] These appear to have been combined with a further source, referred to as "D" (for Deuteronomic), by unknown editors into close to final form around 410 B.C.E., after the return of the Jews from captivity in Babylon.[19]

To repeat what has already been said, this view of the Bible appears to reflect the telling of the story of God and His caring for his chosen people in a manner appropriate to the age in which it was written. It incorporates a firm belief in God, a clear moral code, and a sense of identity, purpose, and place for the Hebrew people.[20] Whether or not the stories are historically accurate in every detail is not the point. The point is the power of the theological message transmitted to the Jewish people and later, through the advent of Christianity, to much of the Western world. But, as one scholar has put it, "People who have grown up in the religious and cultural traditions that derive from the Bible story may find it unpalatable that the Old Testament text, 'Holy Writ' as it were, should be questioned at all. But to look objectively at its historicity is in no way to impugn its literary greatness or its theological profundity."[21] While his point may be absolutely correct, this new way of looking at "Holy Writ" appalled many traditionalists. Furthermore, an overly intellectual approach to the Bible can diminish the sense of meaning, purpose, and hope in life that many find there. It was the emergence of the historical/critical school in the last part of the nineteenth century, coupled with unsettling social changes, that contributed directly to the development of fundamentalism as we know it. The challenge to traditional ways of reading the Bible was too great to be ignored. There had to be a rebuttal.

The Fundamentalist Reaction

The rebuttal began slowly and picked up intensity over time. An institution that was to become a bastion of conservative Christianity was the Moody Bible Institute of Chicago. It was founded by revivalist Dwight L. Moody in 1886 to combat the pernicious influence of the "Higher Criticism," as the historical/critical approach was called in those days.[22] Moody was more interested in saving souls than he was in theological debate, but he has been called the father of American fundamentalism, and the 1999 doctrinal statement of the Institute still contains the phrase "The Bible, including both the Old and New Testaments, is a divine revelation, the original autographs of which were verbally inspired by the Holy Spirit (2 Timothy 3:16; 2 Peter 1:21)."[23] We shall hear more of the Institute later.

The most spectacular episode of the period was the trial for heresy of Professor Charles A. Briggs (1841–1913) of Union Theological Seminary, then a Presbyterian institution. Briggs had given an address in 1891 in which he directly attacked the doctrine of the Scriptures as "the inerrant Word of God," as articulated by Princeton theologians Archibald Hodge (1823–1886) and Benjamin Warfield (1851–1921). Briggs was put on trial by the Presbyterian Church and suspended from the ministry. "The result, however, was that both he and his seminary left the Presbyterian Church."[24] The uproar split the denomination down the middle; when Presbyteries were polled on the issue, almost half of them stood by the doctrine of inerrancy.[25]

In 1910, the Presbyterians of Princeton Seminary, who had formulated the doctrine, issued a list of five dogmas that they considered essential for Christianity: "(1) the inerrancy of Scripture, (2) the Virgin Birth of Christ, (3) Christ's atonement for our sins on the cross, (4) his bodily resurrection, and (5) the objective reality of his miracles."[26] By the end of the twentieth century, Presbyterian theologians had become more liberal, but in the early part of the century they were staunchly on the side of inerrancy.[27] And that, of course, would have included the historical accuracy of the stories of Abraham and Joshua.

The probable origin of the term *fundamentalism* came in 1910–15, when oil millionaires Lyman and Milton Stewart, founders of the Bible Institute of Los Angeles, financed the publication of twelve volumes of pamphlets entitled *The Fundamentals: A Testimony to the Truth*. The project was supported by the Moody Bible Institute, and some 3 million copies of the pamphlets were distributed free of charge to every pastor, professor, and theology student in America, plus Protestant missionaries throughout the world. The pamphlets included short articles by a number of theologians and ministers, on subjects such as "Fallacies of the Higher Criticism," "Mosaic Authorship of the Pentateuch," "Decadence of Darwinism," and "Virgin Birth of Christ."[28]

One of the pieces in the series was especially bitter. Theologian Dyson Hague of London, Ontario, writing on "The History of the Higher Criticism," observed that "some of the most powerful exponents of the modern Higher Critical theories have been Germans, and it is notorious to what length the German fancy can go in the direction of the subjective and of the conjectural. For hypothesis-weaving and speculation, the German theological professor is unsurpassed." Hague went on to argue that a "serious consequence of the Higher Critical movement is that it threatens the Christian system of doctrine and the whole fabric of systematic theology. For up to the present time any text from any part of the Bible was accepted as a proof-text for the establishment of any truth of Christian teaching, and a statement from the Bible was considered an end of controversy. The doctrinal systems of the Anglican, the Presbyterian, the Methodist and other Churches are all based upon the view that the Bible contains the truth, the whole truth, and nothing but the truth. . . . But now the Higher Critics think they have changed all that."[29] This appears to have been the core of the problem. The new approach challenged all that its critics believed to be true.

The reaction did not end there. Another bastion of conservative Christianity, the Dallas Theological Seminary, was founded in 1924 "with a distinct Bible-centered curriculum that would equip students to be expositors of the Word of God."[30] The first article in its doctrinal statement includes affirmation that "divine inspiration extends equally to all parts of the writings—historical, poetical, doctrinal, and prophetical—as appeared in the original manuscripts. We believe that the whole Bible in the originals is therefore without error."[31] By 1999, more than 9,700 alumni, representing fifty states and ninety-three countries, had prepared for the ministry at the seminary. This is by no means the only institution adhering to the doctrine of inerrancy, but it has been one of the more influential.

The center of the debate, however, shifted in the 1920s from direct criticism of the historical/critical approach to an attack on Charles Darwin's theory of evolution, through what came to be known as "Creationism." The issue had been there all along, from the original publication in 1859 of Darwin's *Origin of Species,* but it was the Scopes trial in 1925 that brought the issue front and center. Tennessee had passed a law in early 1925 prohibiting the teaching of "any theory that denies the story of Divine Creation of man as taught in the Bible, and to teach instead that man has descended from a lower order of animals."[32] John Thomas Scopes had filled in one day for the principal of the Dayton, Tennessee, high school at a biology review session based on the state's official textbook, George William Hunter's 1919 *Civic Biology,* which included a discussion of evolution. He was drafted to be a test case, and his trial drew national attention through the pyrotechnics of defense attorney Clarence Darrow and high-profile prosecuting attorney William Jennings Bryan. Scopes was convicted and fined $100, but the fine was later revoked by the Tennessee Supreme Court on a technicality.[33]

The real effect of the trial, however, was to galvanize believers into a focus on the biblical story of Creation as a linchpin for belief in the Bible itself. This was an issue that could be more easily understood than arcane theological debates, and the result was further reinforcement of a literal interpretation of the Bible. Going into the twenty-first century, the debate was still alive and well. A 1997 Gallup poll revealed that 44 percent of Americans could be considered creationists,[34] and there was an attempt to build a museum in northern Kentucky, across the Ohio River from Cincinnati, to demonstrate how God created the world in its present form 6,000 years ago.[35] At the opposite end of the scale is a book by paleontologist Niles Eldredge with the title *The Triumph of Evolution and the End of Creationism.* Eldredge attempted to refute all of the arguments in what has been called "creation science."[36]

To sum it up, despite a century and a half of debate over the historical accuracy of the Bible, the argument continues, and the doctrine of inerrancy is widely held by millions of Americans. Nancy Ammerman, in her study of fundamentalism, has noted inerrancy as one of its hallmarks. "Fundamentalists ... claim that the only sure path to salvation is through a faith in Jesus Christ that is grounded in unwavering faith in an inerrant Bible.... [If] but one error of fact or principle is admitted in Scripture, nothing—not even the redemptive work of Christ—is certain."[37] And she pointed out that in 1985 39 percent of Americans believed that the Bible should be taken literally.[38] A 1999 Gallup poll revealed a slight decrease to 33 percent of Americans who believed that it should be read literally, but this is still a substantial number.[39]

The significance of this study is the inference that the stories of Abraham, Joshua, and God's promise of the land to the Hebrew people are taken to be literally true by millions of Americans. Even some who do not take the Bible to be literal in every aspect believe in the story of the promise. A 1996 study by the National Opinion Research Center at the University of Chicago revealed that 46 percent of Americans believe that "God promised the land to the Jews."[40] As will be seen later in this study, that belief appears to have been a major contributing factor to "a cultural predisposition" on the part of the American electorate to support the State of Israel. But this belief in God's promise of the land to the Jews has not been the only factor. There is another belief that has had considerable influence.

Dispensational Premillennialism

Dispensational premillennialism is a complex and deeply believed interpretation of scripture as prophecy regarding the Second Coming of Christ and the End Times. The term *dispensation* refers to a belief that God deals with humankind in a series of different periods or "dispensations," usually seven, of which the millennium will be the last.[41] In each dispensation, "man is tested in respect of obedience to some *specific* revelation of the will of God."[42] Identification of these dispensations varies among conservative theologians, but the most common sequence is Garden of Eden, Adam to Noah, Noah to Abraham, Abraham to Moses, Moses to Christ, Christ's First to Second Coming, and the millennium.[43] The term *premillennial* refers to the coming of Christ *before* a prophesied 1,000 years of peace, as opposed to a postmillennial Second Coming *after* 1,000 years of peace. While there are considerable variations in belief on this subject, the dominant version is premillennialism.

The doctrine is exceptionally detailed, based on multiple references in the Bible, including Mark 13, Matthew 24, and Luke 21,[44] but it relies heavily on the books of Daniel and Revelation. It holds that, as forewarning of the End Times, there will be an ingathering of Jews from around the world to the Holy Land, followed by creation of a Jewish state. Since this has already happened, believers are encouraged to believe that the prophecies are, in fact, true. There is also a belief that God has a special role for the Jews in the End Times and that 144,000 will be converted to Christianity and play an important role as apostles of the Christian faith during the Tribulation.[45]

The initial event in the End Times will be the Rapture—the "wafting away" of all born-again Christians to meet Christ in the sky. They will simply disappear, leaving everyone else totally confused by their sudden absence. This will be followed by the Great Tribulation, a period of incomprehensible horror on earth. During this period, a revived Roman Empire, with its capital in Jerusalem and headed by the Antichrist, will rule most of the world. The Antichrist (also called "the Beast") will make a pact with the Israelites but then revoke it and persecute them as well. A coalition led by the King of the North (sometimes identified as Russia), the King of the South (possibly an Arab-African confederacy), and King of the East (possibly China) will converge on Palestine, intent on wiping out the Antichrist and the remnant of God's chosen people—the Israelites.

The armies from both sides assemble at *har megiddo* (Hebrew for Mount Megiddo, often rendered in English as Armageddon), a site north of Jerusalem, and the final battle takes place. Christ descends from the heavens and defeats all of his enemies in the bloodiest battle in all history. He regathers the remnants of the Jews, who now receive their Messiah, and judges them along with the Gentile nations. This is followed by 1,000 years of peace, with Satan bound and placed in the Abyss. At the end of the millennium, Satan escapes from captivity and leads a brief and unsuccessful rebellion. All of the dead are then resurrected and judged, with the sinners sentenced to eternal damnation, and the faithful living for eternity in a heavenly New Jerusalem.

This, in very brief outline, is the image of the End Times believed by many fundamentalist Christians. The part of most concern to us is the first phase— the ingathering of Jews to the Holy Land as prelude to the events that follow, and the special role that they are destined to play in those events. It is this aspect of dispensational premillennialism that has led many of the more fundamentalist Christians to support the return of the Jews to the Holy Land and whatever is required to defend the new State of Israel.

But the liberal historical/critical school and the fundamentalist literal/ prophetic school part company on how to interpret the texts on which this worldview is based. They *really* part company. There are far too many passages cited by fundamentalists as the basis for their interpretation to be included here, but a representative few should suffice to illustrate the differences. The ingathering of the Jews to Palestine is inferred from numerous sayings of Jesus regarding the End Times wherein the Jews are spoken of as being *in* Palestine, but one passage from Ezekiel is cited by Hal Lindsey in *The Late Great Planet Earth* as a specific prophecy of the return.[46] Ezekiel wrote as both a priest and a prophet, and among other things, he reported a vision regarding the future in which the Lord promised the Jews a return to the land of their forefathers:

[The Lord said] I will bring you back to the land of Israel. And you shall know that I am the Lord. . . . I will put my spirit within you, and you shall live, and I will place you on your own soil; then you shall know that I, the Lord, have spoken and will act, says the Lord. (Ezekiel 37:12–14)

In the New Testament, the Apostle Paul, writing to the Thessalonians, encouraged them to live a life "pleasing to God," and went on to say (in words resembling the Rapture) that in the End Times:

[T]he Lord himself, with a cry of command, with the archangel's call and with the sound of God's trumpet, will descend from heaven, and the dead in Christ will rise first. Then we who are alive, who are left, will be caught up in the clouds together with them to meet the Lord in the air; and so we will be with the Lord forever. (1 Thessalonians 4:16–17)

Much of the book of Revelation describes the horrors of what has come to be known as the Great Tribulation, the period that follows the Rapture. Writing from the island of Patmos in the eastern Aegean toward the end of the first century C.E., John spoke of a vision that included the opening of "seven seals."

Then I saw the Lamb [presumably Christ] open one of the seven seals, and I heard one of the four living creatures call out, as with a voice of thunder, "Come!" I looked and there was a white horse! Its rider . . . came out conquering and to conquer.

When he opened the second seal . . . out came another horse, bright red; its rider was permitted to take peace from the earth, so that people would slaughter one another. . . .

When he opened the fourth seal . . . I looked and there was a pale green horse! Its rider's name was Death, and Hades followed with him; they were given authority over a fourth of the earth, to kill with sword, famine, and pestilence, and by the wild animals of the earth. . . .

When he opened the sixth seal, I looked, and there came a great earthquake; the sun became black as sackcloth, and the full moon became like blood, and the stars of the sky fell to the earth as a fig tree drops its winter fruit when shaken by a gale. (Revelation 6:1–13)

A truly horrendous picture, and there is more, much more. But early in the period of the Great Tribulation, 144,000 Jews are singled out for special protection. John says:

I saw another angel ascending from the rising of the sun, having the seal of the living God, and he called with a loud voice to the four angels who had been given power to damage the earth and sea, saying, "Do not damage the earth or the sea or the trees, until we have marked the servants of our God with a seal on their foreheads." And I heard the number of those who were sealed, one hundred forty-four thousand, sealed out of every tribe of the people of Israel. (Revelation 7:2–4)

Further on, there arises the Beast, also called the Antichrist and identified with the numbers 666, to rule most of the world:

And I saw a beast rising out of the sea, having ten horns and seven heads; and on its horns were seven diadems, and on its heads were blasphemous names. . . . The beast was given a mouth uttering haughty and blasphemous words, and it was allowed to exercise authority for forty-two months. . . . [I]t was allowed to make war on the saints and to conquer them. It was given authority over every tribe and people and language and nation. (Revelation 13:1, 5–8)

The roles of the Kings of the North, South, and East in the End Times are drawn from the eleventh chapter of Daniel, which deals with the ultimate fate of an evil ruler (understood by fundamentalists to mean the Beast). The relevant passages predict:

At the time of the end the king of the south shall attack him. [And][47] the king of the north will rush upon him like a whirlwind, with chariots and horsemen and many ships. . . . But reports from the east . . . will alarm him, and he shall go out in great fury to bring ruin and complete destruction to many. He shall pitch his palatial tents between the sea and the beautiful holy mountain. Yet he shall come to his end, with no one to help him. (Daniel 11:40–45)

The location of the final battle is identified as Armageddon in the sixteenth chapter of Revelation—the only place in the Bible where that word appears.

The sixth angel poured his bowl on the great river Euphrates, and its waters were dried up in order to prepare the way for the kings of the east. [And the kings of the world] assemble . . . for battle on the Great Day of the Almighty . . . at a place that in Hebrew is called Harmageddon.[48]

As the battle is joined, the heavens open, and there appears a white horse, whose rider is assumed to be Christ, leading "the armies of heaven" (Revelation 16:12–16)

> Then I saw the beast and the kings of the earth with their armies gathered to make war on the rider on the horse and against his army. And the beast was captured, and . . . thrown alive into the lake of fire that burns with sulfur. And the rest were killed by the sword of the rider on the horse. (Revelation 19:19–21)

The devil is also captured, and he is thrown into a bottomless pit, and Christ rules for 1,000 years of peace—the millennium. At the end of 1,000 years, the devil escapes and gathers an army to challenge Christ.

> [Then] fire came down from heaven and consumed them. And the devil . . . was thrown into the lake of fire and sulfur, where the beast and the false prophet were, and they will be tormented day and night forever and ever. (Revelation 20:9–10)

After the final triumph, John saw a vision of a New Jerusalem, the blessed eternity for all the saints.

> Then I saw a new heaven and a new earth; for the first heaven and the first earth had passed away, and the sea was no more. And I saw the holy city, the new Jerusalem, coming down out of heaven from God, prepared as a bride adorned for her husband. (Revelation 21:1–2)

The imagery in these passages is incredible, and it has inspired artists for hundreds of years. But there has been a tremendous divergence of opinion on how to interpret them. It is almost as though liberal scholars and fundamentalists were living in two different worlds. The one understands the texts as literary messages of hope for the generation in which they were written, while the other sees them as prophecies of things to come in the distant future. It is the latter view that has been the foundation of dispensational premillennialism, but it would be well to examine the mainline scholarly interpretation before dealing with how the material has been understood by fundamentalists.

In brief, Daniel and Revelation are seen as representative of Jewish Apocalyptic literature, which flourished during the period of 165 B.C.E. to 135 C.E. This style of writing was intended as a source of hope for contemporaries of the authors during periods of terrible crisis. Readers were encouraged to stand firm during days of testing, because God's purposes could not be thwarted and would ultimately prevail against the machinations of wicked men. A character-

istic of the genre that has caused considerable confusion among later generations was the fact that it was generally written under another person's name—
a practice known as "pseudonymous." The material generally purported to
come from the pen of an ancient or highly respected hero in order to make it
more convincing to the general masses—though probably not to the well educated. Other writings of this sort—not included in the biblical canon—were
Enoch, the Secrets of Enoch, the Apocalypse of Baruch, and the Assumption of
Moses, to name a few.[49]

The book of Ezekiel was an exception, in the sense that it was not attributed
to someone other than Ezekiel himself, but it did contain apocalyptic passages,
and it has been cited as a reference by dispensational premillennialists. Ezekiel
was both a priest and a prophet, living at the time of the captivity of the Hebrew
elite in Babylon, between 597 and 538 B.C.E. He was highly critical of the Hebrews, as having fallen away from the precepts of God and deserving the pun-
ishment they were experiencing in captivity. But at one point, he has a vision of
the Lord saying to the people that He would revive them, put His "spirit within
[them]," and return them to their land. (This is the famous passage on the "dry
bones" of Israel being reconstituted, from which the "return to the land" phrase
is quoted by fundamentalists.) Mainline scholars have understood this passage
as intended to give hope to people then in captivity—not as prophecy of the End
Times.[50]

Unlike Ezekiel, the book of Daniel is full-fledged Apocalyptic literature,
written to give courage and hope to a people under great stress. It includes
stories of Daniel and his companions in Babylon, including Daniel interpreting
Nebuchadnezzar's dreams, Daniel's companions thrown into a fiery furnace,
and Daniel thrown into a lion's den—literary devices purporting to place
Daniel in the sixth century B.C.E. during the Babylonian captivity. Then the
book reports Daniel's vision of things to come—many events leading up to the
ultimate triumph of God at the end of time.

After much debate, scholars have placed the book as having actually been
written between 167 and 164 B.C.E., when the Jews were undergoing great
persecution under Antiochus IV Epiphanes, the Seleucid ruler from Syria, and
shortly before the Maccabean revolt against that persecution. The dating is
based in large part on the fact that the events which Daniel "foresaw" from the
sixth century down through 167 had happened exactly as he described them,
but did not happen as he described them from the middle of the period 167 to
164 onward. And the book appears to have been ascribed to an ancient hero
named Daniel in order to give it authenticity.[51]

The thrust of the book is clear. God protects those who are faithful to Him, and He will triumph in the end. Jesus himself used parables to make a point, and few worry about whether the parables record actual events. Many mainline Christian theologians see the book of Daniel in the same light; they do not view Daniel as prophecy related to the End Times.

Then there is the book of Revelation, which has puzzled and disturbed Christians for centuries. It departs from the traditional Apocalyptic format in several ways. Authorship is not attributed to an ancient hero; it is clearly John, living on the island of Patmos. Scholars are not sure, but some believe that this was John, the son of Zebedee, a disciple of Jesus, and that he may have been a prisoner, since Patmos housed a Roman penal colony. It does not depend on a long series of events that have already transpired to give it authenticity; it simply reports a vision of things to come in the very near future. And it opens in the form of a letter to seven churches in Asia Minor before it moves into the vision. The content, however, is in the full Apocalyptic tradition.[52]

Scholars have concluded that it was written during the reign of the Roman emperor Domitian, between 81 and 96 C.E., probably about 93 C.E. Domitian attempted to force all within his empire to worship him as a god, which Christians refused to do. This appears to have been the persecution through which Christians were being encouraged to stand firm. But it was written in symbolic code so that the Romans would not know what it meant, while recipients of the letter would.

A curious detail was the identification of the number 666 with the Beast, or the Antichrist, who would rise from the sea to rule much of the world. By matching numbers with the Hebrew system of assigning numbers to letters of their alphabet, scholars have conjectured that this was code for Nero, who had presided over an earlier persecution of Christians in Rome, and who had committed suicide in 68 C.E. There was a rumor that he was really alive and would return to seize Rome and perpetrate more horrors in the near future. Thus he was "the Beast," and Babylon in the text stood for Rome.

To Christians living in Asia Minor, the message would have been clear. Terrible things are about to happen, but Christ will return soon, and those who stand firm in their faith, even though it means death, will reap the reward of eternal bliss. The message was an important one; those charged with being a Christian were frequently "tried" by demanding that they worship an image of the emperor and curse Jesus. If they refused, the sentence was death. The message of Revelation was to stand firm in hope of salvation in the immediate future. It spoke to a generation then living under Roman persecution. By this interpretation, it is clear that Revelation was *not* prophecy of a distant End Times.

To those who are convinced that the Bible is the inerrant Word of God and that it contains the story of God's dealing with humankind in a series of dispensations with clear prophecies of things to come, what has just been said would appear to be speculative nonsense, or heresy. Some would say that even though the text may reflect the age in which it was written, that does not invalidate the message for the long run—*if correctly understood.* And there are many who hold to this view.

By itself, the belief in the Second Coming of Christ has long been an element of Christian thought: not the full-blown doctrine of dispensational premillennialism, but the basic idea of a Second Coming.[53] The belief appears in the writings of one of the earliest Christian theologians—Irenaeus (c. 130–c. 200 C.E.), bishop in southern Gaul (modern-day France) in the second century.[54] St. Augustine (354–430) denied a literal reign of Christ on earth for 1,000 years, but he anticipated a Second Coming at some point in the future.[55] Martin Luther (1483–1546) was not a strict millennialist, but he was more literal than Augustine in his understanding of the Bible. He foresaw a Second Coming and viewed Revelation as a prophetic history of the church with the pope as the Antichrist.[56] In more recent times, Jonathan Edwards (1703–1758), one of the most brilliant of American theologians, kept a journal on the book of Revelation, recording signs of the times that he believed were leading to the millennium and the return of Christ.[57] There were many others, but none of their predictions were as detailed as those that emerged in the nineteenth century.

The version of dispensational premillennialism that we know today originated in Great Britain in the 1830s with John Nelson Darby (1800–1882) and a group that he led, the Plymouth Brethren. Darby was born in London to well-educated upper-middle-class parents. His family moved to Ireland, and he studied law in Trinity College, Dublin, and practiced law for several years. As a result of a conversion experience, however, he left the law and became a curate in a county parish of the established church. He developed the theories that eventually became dispensational premillennialism, and resigned from the church to form a group for devotional meetings devoid of vestments, choir, musical instruments, and ordained clergy.[58]

Similar small dissenting groups had formed in England in the social ferment following the French Revolution and the Napoleonic Wars, and in 1831 Darby was invited to join and lead one of them in Plymouth, England. He named the group the Plymouth Brethren, and its membership was elitist, including judges, members of Parliament, and high-ranking army officers. Darby was exceptionally energetic and charismatic, and his knowledge of French and German made it possible for him to carry his evangelical mission to the continent as well as the English-speaking world.[59] He visited America six times between 1859 and 1874, and at his death he left forty volumes of writings and 1,500 assemblies around the world.[60] Partly due to internal infighting in England, the Darbyite Brethren never became a mass movement in Great Britain, but their anti-institutional ideas fell on fertile ground among laissez-faire evangelicals in nineteenth-century America. His ideas clearly exerted a powerful influence on men such as Dwight L. Moody, William E. Blackstone, and Cyrus Scofield.[61]

While strictly speaking not a dispensational premillennialist, one other nineteenth-century individual should be noted for his influence in Britain on the idea of returning the Jews to the Holy Land—Lord Ashley, after 1851 the seventh Earl of Shaftsbury (1801–1885). Since the turn of the century there had been growing interest among British Dissenters and Evangelical Anglicans in returning the Jews to Palestine—partly as a result of interpreting the French Revolution as the beginning of the End Times.[62] Ashley was an ardent believer in and supporter of this movement. The idea was to facilitate the return of the Jews *and convert them* in order to speed the Second Coming. To promote this idea, the London Society for Promoting Christianity Among the Jews was founded in 1808, and by midcentury, it had seventy-eight missionaries in thirty-two branch offices from London to Jerusalem. In addition to trying to convert Jews, the society's chief project was to create an Anglican bishopric in Jerusalem, and Ashley was a key figure in this effort.[63]

Ashley's place in history, however, stems largely from his efforts to persuade the British foreign secretary, Lord Palmerston, to establish a British consulate in Jerusalem as part of an overall plan to facilitate the return of the Jews. Historians have debated over just how much influence Ashley had on Palmerston when the two discussed the matter, but this at least appears to be an early case where Christian influence and perceived national interest coincided. Palmerston was clearly influenced by a desire to establish strategically located consulates to counter growing Russian influence in the decaying Ottoman empire.[64] At any rate, a consulate was established in 1840, and the Society's chief goal—the establishment of an Anglican bishopric in Jerusalem—was accomplished shortly thereafter. The Jerusalem bishopric, incidentally, was not a roaring success. A visitor to the bishop's church in 1844 reported that the total congregation included eight converted Jews and one or two tourists.[65]

One of the towering figures of the millennialist movement in the late nineteenth century and the early twentieth century was William E. Blackstone (1841–1935), a Chicago businessman and lay Methodist preacher.[66] Blackstone was a confirmed dispensational premillennialist who considered it his Christian duty to advocate the conversion and return of the Jews to their homeland in anticipation of the Second Coming. He was one of the founders in 1889 of the Bible House in Chicago, whose name was changed to the Moody Bible Institute in 1901 after the death of Dwight L. Moody. Blackstone was also active in the founding of the Bible Institute of Los Angeles.

Perhaps his best known effort was publication in 1878 of a treatise entitled *Jesus Is Coming*, primarily to persuade people of the imminent coming of Christ. A second edition came out in 1888, and an expanded edition in 1908. The thrust of the book followed closely the eschatological scheme of John Darby and paralleled that of Cyrus Scofield.[67] The book became one of the most popular on the subject and was ultimately translated into forty-two languages, including Yiddish and Hebrew (for use in missionary work with the Jews). Perhaps indicative of his sincerity, he had thousands of copies of his book in various languages stored in Petra in Trans-Jordan, so that during the time of troubles Jews who fled there would be able to discover the truth and be saved.[68]

Of most relevance for this study are the two memorials that Blackstone addressed to presidents of the United States advocating support for returning Jews to their homeland in Palestine. The first was addressed to President Benjamin Harrison in 1891. It did not dwell on Blackstone's millennialist concerns; instead, it focused on humanitarian concerns for the plight of Jews in Russia, and petitioned the president to call a conference of all the powers of Europe to "consider the conditions of the Israelites and their claims to Palestine as their ancient home."[69] With this wording he was able to personally obtain the signatures of 413 prominent Americans in Chicago, New York, Boston, Baltimore, Washington, and Philadelphia. This, incidentally, was five years before Theodor Herzl, the father of political Zionism, published *Der Judenstaat* and six years before he convened the first Zionist congress in Basel, Switzerland.[70]

The second memorial was perhaps the more significant. It was addressed to President Woodrow Wilson in 1916 at the time Wilson was considering a British request to approve issuance of what became known as the Balfour Declaration. Blackstone had developed a close relationship with a number of active American Zionists, including Louis Brandeis and Nathan Straus, the owner of R. H. Macy. The idea of a second memorial came from Straus, but it was warmly adopted by Blackstone.[71] The story of this memorial and the impact that it may have had will be taken up in chapter 3.

A friend of Blackstone and Moody was Cyrus I. Scofield (1843–1921), the originator of the Scofield Study Bible. Scofield was raised an Episcopalian, served in the Confederate army, started life as an attorney, fell on hard times, and turned to premillennialism as a result of a conversion experience. He was not formally trained as a clergyman, but he served as a Congregationalist minister in Dallas, Texas, and Northfield, Massachusetts, and then as a Southern Presbyterian minister in New York. He was actively engaged as a preacher in Bible conferences and was cofounder of the Philadelphia School of Bible.[72]

Scofield's major contribution was his Study Bible, first published in 1909 by Oxford University Press, revised and expanded in 1917, and further revised by others in 1967. It uses the Authorized King James Version of the Bible, embellished with an extensive system of footnotes and cross-references that expound the dispensational premillennialist interpretation. As one commentator has put it, "The notes were printed in a manner that a person would read them as he or she studied the Bible . . . [and it] gave millions of readers a sense of authority as they learned to view the Scriptures through the dispensational system."[73] Over the years, more than 10 million copies have been sold, and it is still very much in print.

Dispensational premillennialist theology has become deeply imbedded in American conservative religious circles. The 1999–2000 undergraduate catalog of the Moody Bible Institute states, "The church is an elect company of believers baptized by the Holy Spirit into one body . . . [and] it will be caught up to meet the Lord in the air ere He appears to set up His Kingdom."[74] There are much longer passages in the doctrinal statement of Dallas Theological Seminary, *We Believe.* Article V contains an extensive section on "The Dispensations," and Article XVIII deals with "the coming of the Lord in the air to receive to Himself into heaven both his own who are alive . . . and also those who have fallen asleep in Jesus." And there is an especially long passage in Article XX relative to the subject of this study:

> We believe that the period of great tribulation in the earth will be climaxed by the return of the Lord Jesus Christ to the earth as He went, in person on the clouds of heaven, and with power and great glory to intro-

duce the millennial age, to bind Satan and place him in the abyss, to lift the curse which now rests upon the whole creation, to restore Israel to her own land and to give her the realization of God's covenant promises, and to bring the whole world to the knowledge of God.

Belief in the Second Coming apparently goes well beyond people who would consider themselves fundamentalists. A 1997 Associated Press poll revealed that 65.9 percent of Americans believed that "Jesus Christ will return to Earth at some time in the future." The concentration was heaviest in the South. The percentage believing in a Second Coming was 74.1 percent in the South, 63.9 percent in the North Central area, 60.1 percent in the West, and 59.1 percent in the North East. Furthermore, 35.7 percent of the total believed that Christ would return within the next century.[75] A separate study in 1996 by the National Opinion Research Center at the University of Chicago found that among people who could be identified as supporters of the Religious Right 74 percent agreed that "the world will end in the battle of Armageddon between Jesus and Satan."[76] Polls such as these are obviously not that precise or definitive, but they do indicate that a substantial number of Americans have been influenced by a literal/prophetic interpretation of the Bible.

Summation

The theme of this study is the argument that there has existed a "cultural predisposition" on the part of many British and Americans to support the return of the Jews to Palestine, derived from several portions of the Christian Bible. One is stories of Abraham, Joshua, and the Promised Land in Genesis and Joshua. Another is an understanding of a number of passages—especially those in Daniel and Revelation—which have been understood to predict a Second Coming of Christ, preceded by a return of the Jews to the Holy Land, and followed by a Great Tribulation during which 144,000 converted Jews will serve as apostles of the Christian message.

There are many variations in belief about the historical accuracy and predictive certainty of all this, but they have formed around two general poles. One is a liberal historical/critical viewpoint, which sees the Bible containing profound theological truths about the sovereignty of God and the moral precepts by which we should live—but not intended as factual history. The other, the fundamentalist literal/prophetic view, considers the whole Bible to be the inerrant

Word of God, including the promise of the land to the Jewish people in the books of Genesis and Joshua.

A second factor has been a literal/prophetic interpretation of Daniel and Revelation, which predicts a return of the Jews to Palestine as preceding—and essential to—the Second Coming. Liberal theologians have interpreted those books as written solely to give comfort and hope to people living in terrible times—Daniel for the Jews under the persecution of Antiochus IV Epiphanes of the Seleucid empire, and Christians living under the persecution of the Roman emperor Domitian. But dating at least as far back as John Darby in Britain in the nineteenth century, those books and other passages have been interpreted by fundamentalist theologians as prophesying the drama of an End Times that included the return of the Jews to Palestine. This has clearly been the foundation of support for Israel by the Religious Right in recent times. The next chapter will examine how these viewpoints on the Promised Land and the End Times have been widely disseminated in Britain and the United States.

2

The Promised Land and Armageddon Theology

There is considerable evidence that knowledge of Palestine as the ancestral home of the Jews became deeply imbedded in British and especially American culture in the nineteenth and twentieth centuries. A 1917 editorial in a British newspaper, the *Christian World*, commenting on the Balfour Declaration, declared, "In the days of Cromwell, and ever since, the vision of a restoration of Palestine to the Jews has been continually before British eyes, and repeatedly in the nineteenth century its realization has been treated as a practical question."[1] The 1966 *Random House Dictionary* even defines the Promised Land as "Canaan, the land promised by God to Abraham and his descendants." And as mentioned earlier, a 1996 study by the National Opinion Research Center of the University of Chicago reported that 46 percent of Americans believed that "God promised the land to the Jews."[2]

There were many reasons for this. Many devout Christians have read their Bibles through and through—sometimes daily—and they surely have encountered the stories of Abraham and Joshua. Members of many churches have heard sermons based on the story of Abraham.[3] And members of many fundamentalist churches were well aware of the prophesied return of the Jews to their land in the End Times. Among the more interesting influences have been the Sunday schools of Britain and the United States, to which we turn first.

The Sunday School Movement

There is a specific reason for focusing on Sunday schools. Professor James W. Fowler of Emory University, author of a number of works on faith development, concludes that what children learn in Sunday school has considerable impact later in life. He argues that children "acquire images and associated emotions" from stories that they learn from people that they love and admire, up to age five and even more so between ages five and ten. These become "bedrock in their minds and may guide selection and actions later in life, even if not consciously."[4] This tends to confirm the intuitive belief of parents and teachers that what they teach young children has considerable influence on their behavior in later life.[5] Sunday schools, of course, focus a great deal of time on children between the ages of five and ten.

Sunday schools originated in late eighteenth-century England as spontaneous local attempts to simply educate working-class children to read and write, frequently using the Bible as a text. They took hold in part due to promotion of the concept by Robert Raikes, editor of the *Gloucester Journal*, whose crusade commenced after his chance discovery in 1780 that many ragged children filled the streets of working-class neighborhoods on Sundays—when they were not employed in local factories.[6] His resulting promotion of Sunday schools through his newspaper had significant impact and earned him the reputation (perhaps unwarranted) of being the originator of popular education. Philip Cliff, the author of the definitive work on the English Sunday school movement, concludes, "Once launched, the Movement quickly became popular with the factory owners because it did not require people to have time off; with parents because it enabled children to 'get on'; with the general public because it took children off the streets on the Sabbath; and with the churches because it provided opportunity to spread knowledge of the Scriptures."[7]

The early schools were quite informal, and teachers were not well trained. With the original focus on reading and writing, students (or "scholars," as they were called) were often dismissed as soon as they demonstrated the ability to read portions of the Bible. Sponsors of these early schools were sometimes individuals, sometimes town assemblies, and sometimes individual churches. As time went on, regional Sunday school unions began to coordinate and improve the quality of teaching. By midcentury, these regional unions had coalesced into a parent group serving Nonconformist churches and a separate Sunday school institute for the Church of England.[8] What had begun as a movement to teach reading and writing gradually took on a religious dimension, in part because government grants were made only to those schools sponsored by one or another denomination. It will be recalled that—unlike the United States—England has its Established Church, and the government considered religious education essential to the national character.[9]

Nonconformist teachers were offered conferences, a magazine, a centralized list of lessons, and a series of course notes. The Anglican Church published its own lesson material, with special emphasis on church doctrine and the Book of Common Prayer.[10] By 1851, 13 percent of the entire population of England, Scotland, and Wales were enrolled in Sunday schools—one-third of those in Church of England schools.[11]

The focus of the Sunday schools changed abruptly from reading and writing to strictly biblical lessons after passage by Parliament in 1870 of an Education Act intended to provide basic education for the masses. There were now two kinds of schools, Sunday schools and the new public day schools, but the Bible continued to be incorporated into the curricula of the public schools well into the twentieth century. Again, this was the influence of the Established Church.[12]

There were sporadic attempts to create American Sunday schools in the eighteenth century, and there was a certain amount of copying from England— especially in the port cities of New York, Boston, and Philadelphia, whose merchants had considerable overseas contact. A number of local "unions" supported and encouraged the idea in the early nineteenth century, including the Female Union for the Promotion of Sabbath Schools in New York City, formed in 1816 with a constitution "lifted from the Bristol Sunday School Union with 'very few alterations.'" As in England, the original schools focused on teaching children of the poorer classes to read and write, but with encouragement from evangelical preachers such as Lyman Beecher, the thrust moved quickly to study of the Bible only. As one commentator put it, "What had begun as charity was converted into a prep school for the whole of evangelical America."[13]

The movement expanded significantly after the War of 1812. One of the early institutions was the Philadelphia Sunday and Adult School Union, formed in 1817. In 1821 the Philadelphia Union employed a missionary who went on to organize over sixty schools in six states.[14] In 1820 the New York Sunday School Union issued a call for an umbrella organization for the whole United States, and one was formed in 1824 as the American Sunday School Union. A rudimentary system of selected uniform lessons was inaugurated in 1826, and the organization began to prepare teaching materials and promote the establishment of more schools. National conventions were held in 1832, 1833, and 1859, but the trend was interrupted by the Civil War.[15]

The movement had a rebirth after the war, and a fourth convention was held in Newark, New Jersey, in 1869, with delegates from twenty-eight states, one territory, Canada, England, Ireland, Scotland, Egypt, and South Africa. It was at the fifth convention in April 1872 at the Second Presbyterian Church of Indianapolis, Indiana, that a decision was made to promote the teaching of the same lesson on the same Sunday in every part of the English-speaking world. A committee for this purpose was formed of clergy and laymen from the Methodist, Presbyterian, Baptist, Protestant Episcopal, and Congregational churches. The plan called for embracing a "course of Bible study for a series of years . . . alternating between Old and New Testaments semi-annually or quarterly . . . and to publish a list of such lessons" for adoption by the Sunday-schools of the whole country.[16] The London Sunday School Union was consulted from 1874 onward and was listed as a corresponding member of the committee shortly thereafter. From a constituency of about 3 million in 1873, the International Lessons expanded by 1905 to provide guidance for more than 17 million teachers and pupils worldwide.[17]

The launching of this system coincided almost exactly with the discontinuation of secular subjects to focus exclusively on the Bible and religious subjects in England after Parliament passed the Education Act of 1870. Commencing in 1871, the British National Sunday School Union (later the National Christian Education Council) instituted annual scripture examinations, initially for teachers and later opened up to scholars of all kinds and ages. And the Church of England Sunday School Institute did the same thing.[18] Themes for the early scripture exams of the Sunday School Union included "The Life of Abraham" (in 1871) and "Joshua and the Entry into Canaan" (1873).[19] The *Notes on the Scripture Lessons (New Series)* published in February 1873 by the Sunday School Union included a lesson in February dealing with "Joshua's Last Appeal," based on Joshua 24:1–28. That includes Joshua quoting God as saying to the Hebrew people, "I gave you [the] land."[20]

During the latter part of the nineteenth century and into the twentieth century, the Sunday School Union published a weekly *Sunday School Chronicle* with both a "morning" and an "afternoon" lesson. The "afternoon" lesson was for the larger Sunday school classes, and it followed the international curriculum.[21] The "morning" lesson was prepared by educators in England for children who only attended on Sunday morning. In general the Old Testament stories were used to teach a moral lesson, but in the case of Abraham and Joshua they also clearly identified Palestine as the ancestral home of the Jews. The morning lesson for July 7, 1878, was on Joshua 1:1–11, and it used Joshua's occupation of the land to teach the lesson that "God has His plan for every man" and gives him "rules to help him."[22] The afternoon lesson for January 30, 1887, was on Genesis 12:1–9 and Abraham's obedience to God's commands, with suggestions that the teacher draw a map to illustrate Abraham's journey to the Promised Land.[23] The morning lesson for January 12, 1890, was also on Genesis 12:1–9, with emphasis on Abraham coming to know that "the land in which he sojourns will be the inheritance of his descendants."[24]

The Church of England covered many of the same subjects but in shorter form to make room for material regarding beliefs of the church itself. The Church of England syllabus for 1906 and 1907 for the "Examination for Acting Teachers" of the Church of England indicates that knowledge of Joshua would be required.[25] Clearly, many in England who would come of age during the first half of the twentieth century would have been exposed in their formative years to stories about Abraham and Joshua in the Sunday schools of both the Nonconformist and Anglican churches.

It is obviously impossible to estimate with precision the number of children in England who heard stories of Abraham and Joshua between 1870 and 1910, but the number appears to have been significant. Total enrollments in British Sunday schools grew from 3.5 million in 1870 to just over 6 million by 1906, when the movement peaked. At that point, 16 percent of the population of England, Scotland, and Wales were reported to be enrolled—of which almost two-thirds were in Nonconformist schools, with the rest in Church of England schools.[26] Incidentally, contrary to a widely held assumption, more people in England, Scotland, and Wales belonged to the "Nonconformist" Presbyterian, Methodist, Congregationalist, and Baptist churches combined than belonged to the Established Church of England in this period.[27] And the Nonconformist churches tended to place more emphasis on the whole Bible, including the Old Testament, than did the Church of England.

Since we have no British public opinion polls on the subject of Palestine at the turn of the century, it is also difficult to estimate with precision the degree to which the idea of the Promised Land or the historical connection between the Jews and Palestine had permeated British thought. There is evidence, however, that the connection between the Jews and the Holy Land was widely known. The *Baptist Times and Freeman* of December 14, 1917, commented that the Balfour Declaration promising the Jews a "national home" and the capture of Jerusalem by General Allenby together brought "the return of the Jews to their own land . . . within the realm of practical politics." The editorial went on to "welcome with enthusiasm the proposal to restore the land to its ancient inhabitants." And a resolution approved by a synod of the Presbyterian Church of England on May 8, 1918, expressed its "gratitude to Almighty God" for the "good prospect of the restoration of Palestine to the children of Abraham, Isaac, and Jacob."[28] Whatever the source, whether Sunday schools or Bible reading, the idea that Palestine had historically been the domain of the Jewish people was clearly imbedded in British Protestant thought.

. . .

That was Britain in the first half of the twentieth century. In America in the second half of the twentieth century, the idea of Palestine being the rightful home of the Jews was even stronger, and the influence of Sunday school teaching was even more apparent. By the end of World War II, the original American Sunday School Union had undergone several reorganizations and name changes, and in 1951 it became one of thirteen agencies that came together to form the National Council of Churches of Christ in the USA.[29] The International Uniform Series of recommended topics continued to be published,[30] but denominations increasingly either developed their own lessons based on it or departed from the guidelines to develop their own series.[31] At the same time, enrollment in the Sunday schools of mainline churches declined steadily while enrollment in more evangelical and independent churches increased.[32] In short, there was a change in structure of the Sunday school movement, but it continued as an integral part of American culture.

Any attempt to examine the content of post–World War II Sunday school lessons for all of the 164 Christian denominations listed in the 1998 National Council of Churches of Christ yearbook proved unrealistic. Instead, an attempt was made to examine the content of lessons for the sixteen American denominations that reported memberships of more than 2 million in 1998.[33] These accounted for 84 percent of all church membership and appeared to constitute a reasonable sample. The churches surveyed include those listed in table 2.1.

In the fifteen denominations for which copies of post–World War II Sunday school lessons could be obtained, each contained stories about Abraham or Joshua or both.[34] It is important, however, to understand the manner in which those stories were presented. In every case, they were used to teach a moral lesson to the children—such as the importance of obedience to what God wants us to do (Abraham's obedience to God's commanding him to move) and recognition that God can sustain and help us (God's support for Joshua's conquest of Canaan). None of the lessons in any way suggested that God's promise of the land justified the Jewish claim to Israel today. They did, however, speak of the Promised Land and clearly identified it as being in the same geographical area as contemporary Palestine, through maps showing where Abraham traveled,

Table 2.1. Membership in American Churches, 1998

Denomination	Membership (millions)
Roman Catholic Church	61.2
Southern Baptist Convention	15.7
United Methodist Church	8.5
National Baptist Convention, USA, Inc.	8.2
Church of God in Christ	5.5
Evangelical Lutheran Church in America	5.2
Church of Jesus Christ of Latter-day Saints	4.8
Presbyterian Church (USA)	3.6
African Methodist Episcopal Church	3.5
National Baptist Convention of America, Inc.	3.5
Lutheran Church–Missouri Synod	2.6
Episcopal Church	2.5
National Missionary Baptist Convention	2.5
Progressive National Baptist Convention	2.5
Assemblies of God	2.5
Churches of Christ	2.2

Source: Yearbook of American and Canadian Churches (New York: National Council of Churches of Christ in the United States of America, 1998), 6–7.

mention of towns (such as Hebron) in that area, and in at least one case asking a question of where "the Promised Land" is today, with the correct answer being "Israel." There is obviously no way to determine exactly what children would have taken away from those stories, but if Professor Fowler is correct, the historic homeland of the Jewish people would have been remembered as Palestine and possibly remembered as "promised to them" by God.

While not a Sunday school program, the educational material for children in Catholic parochial schools on weekdays is well worth noting if for no other reason than the size of that denomination. Catholic schools were free to choose among several series by independent publishers, so long as the content was approved by the Ad Hoc Committee to Oversee the Use of the Catechism of the National Conference of Catholic Bishops. Two of the approved series were published by the Silver Burdett Ginn Company and William H. Sadlier, Inc. Silver Burdett's *This Is Our Faith* included lessons based on Genesis 12:1–7 and passages from Joshua, a definition of the Promised Land as "the land where the People of Israel were to build a just and fair society," and a suggestion that students make a relief map of the Promised Land.[35] Sadlier's *Coming to God's Word* included lessons on "Seeking the Promised Land" (Abraham) and "Settling the Promised Land" (Joshua), plus a matching test in which the correct match for "the Promised Land" was the land "known today as Israel."[36]

Sunday school lessons for the second largest American denomination—the Southern Baptist Convention—also included stories of Abraham and Joshua, and the same material was used by the National Missionary Baptist Convention.[37] In this case, the *Bible Searchers* teacher guides for grades 5 and 6 for 1986 and 1987 specifically called on the teacher to teach the biblical texts in Genesis 12:1–8 and Joshua 1:1–6, which include God's promise of the land to the descendants of Abraham.[38] As stated earlier, the moral drawn from the stories was that God would take care of us if we obeyed Him. They did not suggest that the stories validated a Jewish claim to the land today, but they did clearly identify in the minds of the children that the ancient Jewish home was located in Palestine.

One of the most widely used Sunday school lesson series was that of the David C. Cook Church Ministries of Colorado Springs, Colorado, with offices in Canada and England. Its Bible-in-Life curriculum reportedly reached 750,000 children each week,[39] and it was the preferred curriculum in the Church of God in Christ, the National Baptist Convention of America, and the Progressive National Baptist Convention.[40] It did not follow the guidelines of the International Uniform Series, but it did include stories of both Abraham and Joshua in its preschool, early elementary, and elementary teachers' guides.[41] Its teacher's commentary for grades 4–5 for November 1998 included a map of Palestine showing the Dead Sea, Jericho, and Hebron, and the children's material for that date included a statement that "after Moses' death, God chose Joshua as Israel's new leader to prepare to enter the promised land." The message taught in that lesson was "living by faith," but the story clearly connected the Israelites with Palestine.[42]

The Methodist Church, the third largest American denomination, used material published by Cokesbury that contained stories of Abraham and Joshua in lessons for grades 1–6, with clear references to the Promised Land and suggestions that children draw maps locating it.[43] The National Baptist Convention, USA, the fourth largest American denomination, followed the International Uniform Series lesson sequence, which continually included the stories of Abraham and Joshua.[44]

In 1978 the United Presbyterian Church in the USA (Northern) and Presbyterian Church in the United States (Southern) joined with a number of smaller denominations in creating a new curriculum called Christian Education: Shared Approaches, with three series entitled *Knowing the Word, Interpreting the Word,* and *Living the Word.*[45] A *Living the Word* lesson for grades 5–6 in the fall of 1978 was based on Genesis 12:1–4 and stated that "God promised

Abraham land," with a map of Israel showing where the land was located.[46] In 1988, after the Northern and Southern churches combined to form the Presbyterian Church (USA), two new series were developed entitled *Bible Discovery* and *Celebrate*. One of the *Bible Discovery* lessons for September 1988 was based on Genesis 12:1–9, and stated that "God called Abraham to leave Haran for the 'Promised Land.'"[47]

The Lutherans were also consistent in their coverage of Abraham and Joshua. The Witness Sunday School Curriculum of the Augsburg Press of the Evangelical Lutheran Church in America (ECLA) in its lesson on Joshua 1:1–9 for grades 5 and 6 included the explanation that the theme of the book is "God's fulfillment of the covenant first given to Abraham" and when "God chose Joshua as Moses' successor, the promise was affirmed as Joshua led the people of Israel into the promised land."[48] The Lutheran Church–Missouri Synod used lessons prepared by the Concordia Publishing House, and its material for kindergarten through grade 4 also covered Abraham and Joshua.[49] A lesson for October 1998 was titled "God Leads His People into the Promised Land." As with the other material, none of these lessons suggest that this gives the Jews the right to contemporary Palestine. The stories were used to make the moral point of our need to obey God's commands and the fact that we should trust Him. But they clearly identified Palestine as the ancient home of the Jewish people and mentioned the Promised Land.

The Episcopal material developed by the Virginia Theological Seminary in Alexandria included a lesson for primary grades based on Joshua 1:1–2 containing the story of how Joshua led the "chosen people . . . across the Jordan River into the promised land."[50] The African Methodist Episcopal Church Sunday School Union in Nashville consistently based its lessons on the "International Bible Lessons for Christian Teaching" of the National Council of Churches of Christ, which included stories of Abraham and Joshua.[51] The Assemblies of God did not follow the International Lesson series, but since 1975 it has used the same rotating sequence of topics for primary, middle, and junior grades.[52] Its *Primary Teacher Guide: March–May 1998* was even subtitled *God's People Enter the Promised Land*.[53] And, finally, the material for the primary grades of the Church of Jesus Christ of Latter-day Saints included lessons based on the by now familiar Genesis 12:1–10 (Abraham) and Joshua 1:1–3 and 5–11.[54]

Despite the fact that some of the referenced material comes from more recent years, there is substantial evidence that stories of Abraham, Joshua, and the Promised Land had a prominent place in the Sunday school lessons for children of the major American Christian denominations after World War II. Exactly how many children attended those classes and how many remembered the lessons is another question. But the high percentage of Americans reported to believe that "God promised the land to the Jews" suggests that the Sunday schools had a significant impact.

Armageddon Theology

While Sunday school lessons, Bible reading, and fundamentalist sermons may have influenced the beliefs of a large number of Anglo-American Christians, dispensational premillennialism, or Armageddon theology, appears to have impacted a smaller but more activist group—especially in the United States. Since the English Puritan Revolution of 1642, there had been interest among some in returning the Jews to their biblical homeland.[55] That interest had become more focused during the evangelical revival in England in the early nineteenth century, but among a limited number of people. We have already noted the formation in 1808 of the London Society for the Promotion of Christianity Among the Jews to hasten the Second Coming, and there was the work of John Darby and the Plymouth Brethren from 1831 onward. In addition, there was also the flurry of activity generated by Ashley (later Lord Shaftsbury) in the 1830s. But there is no indication that the full vision of Armageddon theology as espoused by Darby was embraced by large numbers in Britain in the nineteenth century. It was in America in the late twentieth century that it really flourished.

Two institutions have been especially influential in disseminating the doctrine within the United States: the Moody Bible Institute and the Dallas Theological Seminary. Both could be considered clear descendants of Darby's version of dispensational premillennialism, both have trained thousands of preachers in that doctrine, and many of their students have gone on to write widely popular books on the subject. Other smaller Bible institutes and Bible colleges have contributed, but none quite so significantly as those two institutions.

Moody is basically an educational institution, but it considers its mission to be bringing the Word of God to as much of the world as possible. Its twenty-three-acre campus in Chicago normally has 1,500 undergraduate and 350 graduate students from fifty denominations each year, and nearly 80 percent of its 30,000 graduates go on to some type of evangelical career from pastor to missionary. The *Moody Magazine* is published six times a year and reaches more than 290,000 readers. Moody Press releases approximately sixty new titles each year and distributes nearly 3 million Bibles and Christian books each year. The Moody Broadcasting Network owns and operates 28 noncommercial educational radio stations in thirteen states, and provides satellite-fed programming to nearly 400 other stations and cable outlets across North America.[56]

The overall content of Moody's message is evangelical Christianity, and that obviously covers a wide range of topics, but that its theology is dispensational premillennialist is attested to by its doctrinal statement that "The church is an elect company of believers ... [which] ... will be caught up to meet the Lord in the air ere He appears to set up His kingdom."[57] And a 1991 book, *Arabs, Oil, and Armageddon,* by a Moody faculty member, Edgar James, interpreted post–World War II events interwoven with biblical references as predicting the coming of Armageddon.[58] (James, incidentally, was a graduate of Wheaton College and Dallas Theological Seminary.) It is impossible to determine how many Moody graduates or how many of its radio listeners subscribe to the Moody view of the End Times, but it is highly likely that most of them have been at least exposed to it as a matter of course.

And there is one more connection. Jerry B. Jenkins, former vice president for publishing of the Moody Institute, teamed with retired evangelical minister Tim LaHaye to produce the wildly popular series of apocalyptic novels published by Tyndale House Publishing of Wheaton, Illinois. As of this writing there were twelve novels in the series: *Left Behind: A Novel of the Earth's Last Days* (1995), *Tribulation Force: The Continuing Drama of Those Left Behind* (1996), *Nicolae: The Rise of Antichrist* (1997), *Soul Harvest: The World Takes Sides* (1998), *Apollyon: The Destroyer Is Unleashed* (1999), *Assassins: Assignment: Jerusalem, Target: Antichrist* (1999), *The Indwelling: The Beast Takes Possession* (2000), *The Mark: The Beast Rules the World* (2000), *Desecration: Antichrist Takes the Throne* (2001), *The Remnant: On the Brink of Armageddon* (2002), *Armageddon: The Cosmic Battle of the Ages* (2003), and *Glorious Appearing: The End of Days* (2004). Altogether the novels had sold more than 62 million copies through 2004.[59] The subtitles indicate the thrust of the series, and LaHaye is quite clear that the core of the novels is directly in the premillennial tradition. In a June 2000 interview for the *New York Times,* LaHaye affirmed his conviction that the book of Revelation predicts that 144,000 Jews will be converted to Christianity after the Rapture and before the Second Coming.[60] One of the novels, *The Indwelling,* topped the *New York Times* best-seller list in June 2000.[61]

While readers of the novels may not all subscribe to the End Times vision that the novels contain, their popularity suggests that additional millions have become aware of that vision.

The other, and perhaps more influential, institution has been the Dallas Theological Seminary. Founded in 1924, the seminary included in its doctrinal statement a firm conviction in the inerrancy of the Bible and a solid belief in dispensational premillennialism. Its influence has been significant. As of 1999, there were 8,400 living alumni in the United States and 770 in forty other countries. It distributed audiocassettes of faculty and other speakers, and published a magazine and a quarterly theological journal, *Bibliotheca Sacra*. The journal covered a wide range of subjects, but its orientation was clear from a series of articles scheduled for 1999: "Satan's Deceptive Miracles in the Tribulation," "The Wound of the Beast in the Tribulation," "The Second Coming of Christ," and "The Defeat of Antichrist."[62]

A number of Dallas alumni went on to highly influential careers. A 1937 graduate, J. Vernon McGee, had a radio program, "Thru the Bible," that was carried by 600 stations in North America. A 1940 graduate, Jim Rayburn, was the founder of Young Life, a program that had some 90,000 junior and senior high school students meeting weekly in 1,712 Young Life Clubs in the United States. And a 1970 graduate, Joseph Stowell, became president of the Moody Bible Institute in Chicago.[63]

Of special interest has been the career of Dr. John F. Walvoord, with degrees from Dallas Theological Seminary, Wheaton College, Texas Christian University, and Liberty Baptist Seminary. Dr. Walvoord served as professor of systematic theology and president of Dallas Theological Seminary from 1952 until 1986, when he became chancellor. He was the author of numerous books on premillennialism, including *Israel in Prophecy*, which concluded that "the return of Israel to their ancient land and the establishment of the state of Israel is the first step in a sequence of events which will culminate in Christ's millennial kingdom on earth."[64] His 1990 book, *Armageddon, Oil, and the Middle East: What the Bible Says about the Future of the Middle East and the End of Western Civilization*, was clearly in the premillennialist tradition, and it went to a printing of over 1 million copies.[65]

Perhaps the most influential Dallas alumni, however, has been Hal Lindsey. His first book, *The Late Great Planet Earth*, published in 1970, was named by the *New York Times* as the best-selling book of that decade.[66] Since then, he has published at least nineteen more in the same vein,[67] and by 1999 his works had collectively sold 35 million copies.[68] The books were written in a lively, gripping style, and the thesis was a direct descendant of the dispensational premillennialism of John Darby and Cyrus Scofield—brought up to date by melding it with post–World War II events to predict the imminent end of the world. The Rev. Dr. Stephen R. Sizer of Surrey, England, made a careful analysis of the contents of Lindsey's work and concluded that a number of the subsequent books were actually rewrites of earlier works with new titles. In addition, he has found that Lindsey gradually modified his predictions as events unfolded differently than he had originally projected.[69] Nonetheless, Lindsey's work had wide dissemination and undoubtedly added to the belief by many that we were living in the End Times. And, germane to our subject, *The Late Great Planet Earth* quoted from the book of Ezekiel to argue that the return of the Jews to Palestine foretells the imminence of the Second Coming.[70] Why should one not support the State of Israel if its reestablishment was part of God's plan?

Direct Supporters of Israel

What has been discussed thus far has been the media through which knowledge of Palestine as the ancestral home of the Jews, of the promise of that land to them by God, and of their return to Palestine as a prelude to the Second Coming, has been disseminated within the British and to a much greater extent the American electorate. Sunday school lessons have focused on the moral lessons to be drawn from Old Testament stories, but they have included the fact that the Jewish ancestral home was in Palestine and—in many cases—have referred to it as the Promised Land. Perhaps more powerful has been the dissemination of dispensational premillennialism, or Armageddon theology, through fundamentalist seminaries and Bible colleges—most notably Dallas Theological Seminary and the Moody Bible Institute—and a host of novels, books, and radio programs dealing with the End Times. Again, the thrust of these has been a call to accept Christ as one's Lord and Savior in order to be among those saved from the terrible ordeal of the Tribulation. But included in these messages has been a clear indication of the role to be played by the Jews in the End Times—first because their ingathering would be a prelude to the final events, and second because of the role they were to play when 144,000 would be converted and work toward the realization of Christ's kingdom. For the most part this message has been passive, simply providing knowledge to be stored away without a call to action in support of Israel.

On the other hand, there have been a number of organizations and individuals that have translated all of this into a call for action in direct support of Israel. One such organization deserves special mention, not because of its influence in the United States, which has been minimal, but because of the attention that it has received in Israel. This is the International Christian Embassy Jerusalem (ICEJ), located in Jerusalem but with offices all over the world, including the United States. It was founded by Christian supporters of Israel in 1980 when almost all countries moved their embassies and consulates from Jerusalem to Tel Aviv in protest of a Knesset law declaring the whole city of Jerusalem to be the capital of the State of Israel. The driving force behind the ICEJ has been Dutch minister Jan Willem van der Hoeven, and its orientation is solidly premillennial and supportive of Israel. Its goals include being "part of God's purpose in bringing Jews back to Israel," and it provides assistance for immigrants from the former Soviet Union, social welfare aid administered through Jewish agencies, a periodic International Christian Zionist Conference, and an annual Feast of Tabernacles Celebration at the time of the Jewish festival of Succoth for several thousand Christians from all over the world.[71] Speakers at the feast have included Teddy Kollek, mayor of Jerusalem, and Prime Minister Yitzhak Rabin. Professor Yaakov Ariel studied the institution carefully and concluded that most of ICEJ's external support came from European evangelical premillennialists and that many officials in the Israeli government were under the mistaken impression that it spoke for a large number Christians throughout the world—which it did not.[72]

Within the United States, there have been a significant number of small organizations created to support the return of Jews to Israel—often in terms of humanitarian aid as well as educational programs. The nonprofit International Fellowship of Christians and Jews (IFCJ), founded by Rabbi Yechiel Eckstein in Chicago in 1983, worked to "foster better relations and understanding between Christians and Jews [and to] build greater support for Israel."[73] Among other things, the IFCJ supported the return of Jews from the former Soviet Union and Ethiopia through its "Wings of Eagles" program, and provided aid to elderly impoverished Jews in the former Soviet Union through its "Isaiah 58" program. The bulk of its funding came from evangelical Christians.[74]

A unique organization was the Christian Friends of Israeli Communities (CFIC) organized in 1995 by Ted Beckett, a commercial real estate developer in Colorado Springs, to provide comfort and aid to Jewish settlements in "Judea, Samaria, and . . . Gaza by linking them with evangelical congregations in the United States." Each congregation was "taught how to 'link' with its assigned community" through pen pals, e-mail, fund-raising, and sending supplies.[75]

The CFIC believed that "those settlers who choose to live there are fulfilling prophecy and are pointing the way for the rest of the Jewish people back to their roots." As of 1999, participating churches had adopted some forty settlements.[76]

There was also Bridges for Peace (BFP), a charitable organization founded in 1978 by Douglas Young, former president of Trinity Evangelical Divinity School.[77] Based in Jerusalem and Tulsa, Oklahoma, BFP derived its mission more from God's promise of the land to the Jews in Genesis 12:7 and 13:15 than on Armageddon theology, and it focused on providing food, blankets, school kits, and home repair for the elderly in Israel. It published two newsletters, a *Bridges for Peace Israel Teaching Letter* and *Dispatch from Jerusalem*, to publicize its work.[78] Its director, Clarence H. Wagner Jr., authored a book, *Lessons from the Land of the Bible: Revealing More of God's Word*, which promoted the BFP vision.[79]

The three organizations described thus far were essentially designed for humanitarian aid for Jews returning to Israel, based either on God's promise of the land to them or on their expected role in the End Times, or both. Another fairly significant organization has taken quite a different tact. The Friends of Israel Gospel Ministry (FIGM), based in Bellmawr, New Jersey, was founded in 1938, largely in response to Hitler's persecution of the Jews, for the purpose of providing comfort to the Jews and "proclaiming the need for personal salvation, through faith in the Lord Jesus Christ, to the Jew and also to the Gentile." Its doctrinal statement accepted "the Scriptures in their entirety as being inerrant (in the original writings) and infallible," and it believed in "the premillennial and pretribulational return of Jesus Christ."[80] The Friends of Israel had active missionaries to the Jews in the United States, Israel, Canada, Russia, France, England, and Argentina.[81] Its catalog of publications included twenty books on biblical interpretation, including commentaries on the books of Daniel and Revelation, and seven by its executive director, Elwood McQuaid. McQuaid, incidentally, was editor of the organization's bimonthly magazine, *Israel My Glory*, and served as a Bible teacher for the Moody Bible Institute and as editor-at-large of the *Moody* magazine. In his book *There Is Hope*, McQuaid stated that "the Jewish people possess a great wealth of promises from God . . . a land, a kingdom, and a divine destiny . . . [and] . . . Israel will come to a day of reconciliation with their long-estranged Messiah."[82] It is impossible to determine just how far-flung has been the influence of the Friends of Israel, but it was clearly one more in a network of organizations and institutions that have impacted some segment of the American population.

Then, of course, there are the widely known evangelical ministers such as Pat Robertson, Jerry Falwell, and Billy Graham, who have adhered to dispensational premillennialism in varying degrees. In 1986 Pat Robertson's daily "700 Club" radio talk show was reported to reach 16 million "television households," and his Christian Broadcasting Network (CBN) owned three television stations, a CBN cable channel, a worldwide charity system, a university, and a lobbying group.[83] The theology espoused by Robertson was ardently dispensational premillennialism, and he set forth his understanding of the End Times in a 1991 best-seller, *The New World Order*.[84] Jerry Falwell, former leader of the Moral Majority, had been quoted as saying that "the people of Israel have not only a theological but also a historic and legal right to the land … [including] … that area promised to Abraham in Genesis 15:18 … and only when the Messiah Himself rules will Israel dwell in peace."[85] In 1986 Falwell's weekly radio program, "The Old Time Gospel Hour," was reported to reach 5.6 million households.[86] (Falwell's role in support of Israel will be discussed in chapter 5.) Billy Graham is reputed to have preached the Gospel to more people than anyone else in history. A graduate of Wheaton College, Graham's sermons and writing consistently emphasized the Second Coming, even though the dispensational aspects of that had been muted in later years. And while he was not the ardent political supporter of Israel that Falwell was, his worldview has clearly influenced many in terms of the relevance of biblical prophecy.[87]

This discussion of proponents of Armageddon theology by no means exhausts the list of influences that have contributed to a belief by many in the American electorate that the Jewish people are the rightful heirs to the land of Palestine. It does, however, suggest that the influences have been manifold.

Summation

In retrospect, there appear to have been several levels of understanding of the relationship between the Jewish people and the land of Palestine. There has been a generalized knowledge that Palestine was the historic home of the Jews in biblical times. This may not have caused many to take action in support of a restoration, but neither has it caused them to oppose actions taken by others. Then there has been the idea that God really promised the land to the Jewish people. Some fundamentalist individuals and groups have taken this to be a divine decree that should not be questioned. In a few cases, this belief by itself has led to active support of the restoration. And then there has been the belief that we are living in the End Times and the ingathering of the Jews to Palestine is a prelude to the Second Coming. Some people of this persuasion have been extremely active in support of that return.

Widespread knowledge by the general population that Palestine had been the historic home of the Jews appears to have begun with the Protestant Reformation and its emphasis on the Bible as opposed to the Catholic Church as the source of truth, coupled with the printing and distribution of the Bible in English. At the same time there was a general move away from the Augustinian interpretation of the Bible as allegory to one in which it was taken quite literally. All of this came to a head during the Puritan Revolution in England, when talk of restoring the Jewish people to their homeland began to be taken seriously. By the nineteenth century, general Bible reading and the development of the Sunday school movement in England led to further dissemination of the idea that Palestine was the ancient home of the Jews. And by the second half of the twentieth century, that idea had become widespread in American Sunday schools.

The idea that God had actually promised the land to the Jews became increasingly powerful with the fundamentalist revolt against the historical/critical approach to biblical interpretation that came out of Germany. The revolt was originally led by the Presbyterians of Princeton Theological Seminary, but it became imbedded in the teaching of institutions such as the Moody Bible Institute and Dallas Theological Seminary. The Presbyterians have since moved to a more liberal position, but the doctrine of the Bible as the inerrant and infallible Word of God is fairly widespread among more fundamentalist denominations. And research has shown that those denominations tend to be the most supportive of Israel.

Most dramatic, however, was the widespread dissemination of Armageddon theology in the last half of the twentieth century. The original formulation of that theology as we know it originated with John Darby in England early in the nineteenth century, but it was carried forward by many people, including Dwight Moody, William Blackstone, and Cyrus Scofield—especially Scofield and the Scofield Reference Bible. The doctrine received immense attention during the cold war when fear of a nuclear holocaust and the creation of the State of Israel were seen as foretelling the coming Battle of Armageddon. Hal Lindsey's apocalyptic *Late Great Planet Earth* was perhaps the best known of the those predictions, but the doctrine has been deeply imbedded in the theology of a number of institutions, including the Moody Bible Institute and Dallas Theological Seminary, and their graduates.

While it is difficult, if not impossible, to establish the exact impact of any one or all of these influences on the attitudes of the general public, there is substantial evidence that, working together these influences have created a predisposition on the part of a substantial portion of the British and American people, including some key leaders, to support the Zionist cause and the State of Israel. In the case of Britain there is only anecdotal data from the time of the Balfour Declaration (to be discussed in chapter 3) to support this statement. But in the case of the United States, there are a number of polls that bear this out:

· A Gallup poll in 1998 reported that 79 percent of Americans said they had received religious training as a child. The percentage was slightly higher among Catholics than among Protestants.[88]

· A Gallup poll in 1996 found that 93 percent of Americans said they had a Bible or other scripture in their house. And among that group, 47 percent said that they read the Bible at least once a week.[89]

· A Gallup poll in 1999 found that 33 percent of Americans believed that "the Bible is the actual word of God and is to be taken literally, word for word."[90]

· A 1996 study by the National Opinion Research Center of the University of Chicago found that 46 percent of Americans believed that "God promised the land to the Jews."[91]

· A survey completed by the ICR Survey Research Group for the Associated Press in 1997 found 66 percent of Americans believed that "Jesus Christ will return to earth at some time in the future," and 36 percent believed that He would return within their lifetime.[92]

· And a special Gallup poll of 1,071 Americans in 1999 found that 45 percent were more sympathetic with the Israelis than with the Palestinian Arabs. Only 13 percent were more sympathetic with the Palestinian Arabs. The remainder said "both," "neither," or "don't know/refused."[93] (Polls on the subject varied significantly in the 1980s, reflecting events in the Middle East from 1980 onward, but the figures here serve as a reasonable benchmark.)[94]

Of course, polling is not an exact science, and many other factors may be at work, but all of this appears to support the argument that Christian teaching has tended to create support for the Israeli cause among a sizable number of people. In subsequent chapters, we will see how this has played out in four instances: the Balfour Declaration, the British Mandate, Truman's decision to recognize Israel, and congressional support for Israel in the latter part of the twentieth century.

II

British and American Policy

3

The Balfour Declaration and the Palestine Mandate

On November 2, 1917, in the midst of World War I, Arthur James Balfour (later Lord Balfour), the British foreign secretary, sent a letter to Lord Rothschild, a prominent British Jew, declaring British support for the Jewish Zionist movement. It read:

> I have much pleasure in conveying to you, on behalf of His Majesty's Government, the following declaration of sympathy with Jewish Zionist aspirations which has been submitted to and approved by the Cabinet:

> His Majesty's Government view with favour the establishment in Palestine of a national home for the Jewish people, and will use their best endeavours to facilitate the achievement of this object, it being clearly understood that nothing shall be done which may prejudice the civil and religious rights of existing non-Jewish communities in Palestine, or the rights and political status enjoyed by Jews in any other country. I shall be grateful if you would bring this declaration to the knowledge of the Zionist Federation.[1]

This was the famous Balfour Declaration, a major milestone in the long process that culminated in the founding of the State of Israel. Although its origin was fairly complex, it was seen by most people as a wartime "measure designed to attract to the Allied cause the moral and material resources of the Jewish communities of the world."[2] But its intent was written into the Palestine Mandate, which the League of Nations gave to Britain in 1923, and it became the ambiguous cornerstone of British policy until the Mandate was finally surrendered in 1947. The intervening years saw intense rioting—most notably in 1929 and 1936—as Arabs fought against displacement by the Jews. The British government wavered back and forth as it tried to reconcile the irreconcilable demands of both parties. finally, with resources bled dry by World War II, it gave up.

A tremendous amount has been written about all of this, much of it emphasizing both Zionist influence and the perceived national interest of the British in World War I and afterwards. And the British Labour Party has been identified as a staunch supporter of the Zionist cause.[3] This study does not disagree with any of that. It simply highlights the underlying influence of Christian teaching about the Promised Land in the minds of many of the participants on both sides of the Atlantic. It especially notes the influence of British Methodism within the Labour Party.

The Methodist Movement and Labour

Before examining the process by which the Balfour Declaration came into being, and recounting the anguish of the Mandate period, it would be helpful to go back and explore the connection between Methodism and the Labour Party.

To put it succinctly, the Methodist movement and the British Labour Party both grew out of the working-class environment that existed in Britain during the industrial revolution.[4] A number of Labour leaders honed their organizational and speaking skills in early Methodist Church work. In the early twentieth century, the party even gained the reputation of being "more Methodist than Marxist."[5] This was by no means the only reason that Labour supported the Zionist cause, but the strong Christian orientation of leaders such as Arthur Henderson and Philip Snowden appears to have been a contributing factor. Jewish representation within the party itself and the socialist orientation of both Labour and the early Jewish immigrants in Israel were major influences, but the grounding in the Bible of a number of Labour leaders through their Methodist background created a clear predisposition for the return of the Jews to their ancient homeland. This is in addition to the influence of biblical stories among the population at large.

The Methodist movement was exactly that—a movement originally within the Established Church of England that evolved into a separate denomination and spread to many parts of the world. Its inspiration came from John Wesley (1703–1791), an Anglican clergyman at Oxford who underwent an intense conversion experience in 1738 and went on to become a powerful preacher and organizer of small religious groups, or "chapels," throughout Britain. Wesley's almost reluctant decision in 1744 to ordain ministers for administering the sacraments outside of the Established Church eventually led to separation of the movement from that body. Many of these chapels had lay leaders, and these were gradually organized into "circuits" with an eventual annual "convention" for oversight.[6] The movement had strong appeal among the working classes, and it was the experience of organizing and leading within this movement that gave some of the early Labour leaders their training and confidence to lead in political matters.

Wesley was not theologically doctrinaire, and his message was based on conversion, the assurance of salvation through faith in Christ and the leading of a highly moral life. (His difference with Calvinism was a belief that Christ came to atone for the sins of all mankind, not just the elect, as in Calvinism.) In his preaching, Wesley emphasized the need for thrift and hard work, and his view that "poverty was caused either by indolence . . . or by the selfishness and greed of the rich infused his economic teaching with a stern morality."[7] He urged his followers to accumulate only what wealth they actually needed and to give away the rest to the needy. He also believed that "all great spiritual movements surged from the poor."[8] It is not difficult to see how those doctrines would appeal to many in the working classes and lead to early interest in a kind of non-Marxist Christian socialism.[9]

In the nineteenth century, the British Methodist movement split into several branches, including the Wesleyan Methodists, the Methodist New Connexion, the United Methodist Free Churches, the Bible Churches, and the Primitive Methodists, based in part on differences over the degrees of freedom or fervor of evangelism desired—not on doctrine. All of these British Methodist groups recombined in 1932 as the "Methodist Church." The earliest records of membership date from 1767, when there were 23,110 Methodists in England, Wales, and Scotland. By 1900, this number had grown to 770,406 for all Methodist groups combined in England, Wales, and Scotland.[10] It was a sizable movement, with many active lay leaders and a strong social conscience.

In addition to Methodists, there were a number of other Nonconformist Christians in the early Labour movement, but the personification of the staunch Methodist labor unionist and labor leader was Arthur Henderson (1863–1935). Born in Glasgow in 1863, the son of a cotton spinner, he was apprenticed at age twelve as an iron-molder and became a lifelong member of the Friendly Society of Iron Founders. He was brought up in a Congregationalist Bible-reading home, but at age sixteen he underwent an intense conversion experience, testified "how Jesus Christ had transformed his life," and joined a

Wesleyan Methodist Mission chapel. For the rest of his life he was active in the church as a lay preacher, participant in national conferences, and member of organizations to alleviate social problems. In politics, he rose to mayor of Newcastle and was elected to Parliament as a Labour member in 1903. He chaired the Labour Party in 1906, presided over the Iron Founders union in 1911, and served as a minister in two coalition governments from 1915 through 1917. He served thereafter in various capacities until his death in 1935, but most notably as foreign secretary in the second Labour government at the time of the 1929 riots in Palestine. Later in this chapter, we shall hear more about the pivotal role he played in the British reaction to those events.[11]

The Labour Party was a latecomer to the British political scene. Several abortive attempts to secure trade union representation in Parliament had been made in the late nineteenth century, but the party itself did not really come into being until 1900. In that year, Keir Hardie's small Independent Labour Party, founded in 1893, persuaded the Trades Union Congress and several other small groups to form the Labour Representation Committee in a joint effort to gain a foothold in Parliament.[12] It only won two seats in the election of 1902, but through by-elections this soon grew to three. In 1906, with its name changed to the Labour Party, it won twenty-nine seats. This was quite small in comparison with the Conservatives' 166 and the Liberals' 399 seats that year. But it was a start. In 1910, the last election before the war, Labour won 42 seats.[13] However, its influence exceeded its numbers during World War I, because of the interest of two prime ministers in gaining Labour support for the war effort. Arthur Henderson joined several other Labour representatives in the government as the war progressed. (Henderson himself resigned from the government in 1917 because of a disagreement with Lloyd George.)[14] However, for this study, our primary interest in the Labour Party during the war falls outside the government, in the party's early support of the Zionist movement.

Interest had developed during the war for some kind of joint declaration of war aims by members of the Socialist Second International, of which the British Labour Party was a member. When Henderson withdrew from the government, he turned his attention to become the driving force behind this idea. Together with Ramsay MacDonald and Sidney Webb (later Lord Passfield), he created a draft document[15] and presented it to a joint meeting of the Labour Executive Committee and the Labour Parliamentary Party in August 1917, three months before the Balfour Declaration. From there, this "War Aims Memorandum" went to a Special Conference of the Labour Party and British Trades Union

Congress in December 1917 and on to an Inter-Allied Labour and Socialist Conference in London in February 1918.[16] The document contained a long list of both practical and idealistic proposals—establishment of a league of nations with an international court and legislature, Belgian independence, realignment of disputed borders based on self-determination, and many others.[17] Most important for our purposes was a section dealing with the Jews and Palestine. It read:

> "The Conference demands for the Jews in all countries the same elementary rights of freedom of religion, education, residence and trade and equal citizenship that ought to be extended to all the inhabitants of every nation. It further expresses the opinion that Palestine should be set free from the harsh and oppressive government of the Turk, in order that this country may form a Free State, under international guarantee, to which such of the Jewish people as desire to do so may return and may work out their own salvation free from interference by those of alien race or religion."[18]

It is impossible to know precisely why Henderson, MacDonald, and Webb chose to include the Zionist cause in these War Aims, but there are several possible reasons. For one thing, Labour leaders had been the object of a fair amount of Zionist lobbying—especially from the World Alliance of Poalei Zion (Zionist-socialist parties in the Diaspora). And the Labour press had been supportive of the Zionist cause, notably the Fabian socialist *New Statesman,* the editorial board of which Sidney and Beatrice Webb were cochairs during this period. Ramsay MacDonald later revealed surprisingly strong feelings about his religious upbringing and the spiritual ties between the Jewish people and Palestine in a little book, *A Socialist in Palestine,* describing a visit there in 1921.[19] And finally there was Arthur Henderson, solidly grounded in his Methodist biblical faith. The truth may lie in some combination of Zionist lobbying, socialist orientation that sympathized with the Jewish socialist experiment in Palestine, and biblical upbringing.

The Balfour Declaration

The events leading up to the Balfour Declaration have been so thoroughly analyzed by scholars over the years that it is not necessary to enter into a detailed discussion.[20] It will suffice to review the sequence and highlight the thread of

Christian influence that ran throughout. This will make it clear that perceived national interest (in this case, British war aims), a Zionist lobby, and a biblically derived predisposition on the part of key individuals to support the return of the Jews all pointed in the same direction. That will not be the case in all of the episodes to be described later.

The idea of a return of the Jews to Palestine had a long though muted history. Their dispersal throughout much of Europe and North Africa actually began in ancient times as periodic warfare resulted in Jews being captured and carried to other lands as slaves. It expanded in Roman times through the travels of merchants and traders, and then the two disastrous Jewish revolts against Roman rule in 70 C.E. and 135 C.E. decimated and radically reduced the remnants of Jews still living in Palestine. The idea of a return began to take form in the sixteenth and seventeenth centuries through the teaching of several self-proclaimed Messiahs, but their following was minuscule. The idea really began to be taken seriously late in the nineteenth century as a result of increasing persecution, particularly in Eastern Europe and among the Germans living in Austria. The first wave of Jewish immigrants began in the 1880s, but it was the Austrian journalist Theodor Herzl (1860–1904), aroused by the anti-Semitic Dreyfus affair in France, who really founded the political Zionist movement. In 1896 he published a pamphlet, "Der Judenstaat" ("The Jewish State"), calling for a safe haven for Jews in one territory. In 1897 he organized the first in a series of Zionist congresses in Basel, Switzerland, and received the most support from the Jews of Eastern Europe. Many West European Jews initially opposed the movement, since they had ardently chosen to assimilate in their home countries. The movement initially was centered in Vienna, but Herzl found considerable sympathy among the English, who had long espoused the idea of a return, and he established the financial instruments of the movement in London.[21] He died quite suddenly in 1904, but the Zionist movement had been launched.

After Herzl's death, the movement lapsed into a spirit of pessimism, and its focus moved to supporting low-level immigration to Palestine rather than seeking governmental support for its program. When war broke out in 1914, and particularly when the Ottoman Empire joined the side of Germany, the Zionists took heart that an opportunity had arisen to achieve their aims. The Zionist organization set up a bureau in the neutral city of Copenhagen, and semi-independent groups formed in England and the United States. In America the leadership fell to Louis Brandeis (1856–1941), who in August 1914 was chosen to chair the Provisional Executive Committee for General Zionist Affairs, and who in 1916 was nominated to the Supreme Court by President Woodrow Wilson. Brandeis resigned as chair of the Provisional Executive Committee when he ascended to the Supreme Court, but he remained active in Zionist affairs as a close contact with President Wilson.

In England the unquestioned leader was the indefatigable Dr. Chaim Weizmann (1874–1952), a Russian chemist on the staff of Manchester University, who created a formula for acetone for the British War Office and who became the self-appointed advocate for the Zionist cause to the British government. Weizmann was supported by a number of others, including Nahum Sokolov, Lord Rothschild, and C. P. Scott, the non-Jewish editor of the *Manchester Guardian*. But it was Weizmann who conducted most of the negotiations with the British government.[22]

Weizmann's efforts were successful in large part because the British had other compelling reasons to support the Zionist cause. Foremost of these was an interest in ending the war with a strong position in the eastern Mediterranean in order to protect its hold on Egypt, the Suez Canal, and its seaborne communications with India. This included keeping the French out of Palestine, and it found expression in the secret Sykes-Picot agreement of May 1916 dividing claims in the old Ottoman Empire after the war between Britain, France, and Russia. Britain was to receive the ports of Haifa and Acre in the north of Palestine and a "sphere of influence" over the territory as far east as Iran, while the French were to receive a coastal strip of Syria (today's Lebanon) and a "sphere of influence" extending into the Syrian hinterland.[23] (This, of course, was in conflict with a prior commitment of October 1915 by Sir Henry McMahon, British high commissioner in Egypt, to Sherif Husein of Mecca that the British would support Arab independence in much of the same area in return for Husein's support of the British cause, a conflict that caused considerable embarrassment after the war.)[24]

All of this had been thoroughly discussed within the upper echelons of the British government long before Weizmann made his concerted effort in 1917 to obtain a British statement. And it had already occurred to a number of key individuals that some sort of British protectorate over a Jewish entity in Palestine would serve British interests well.[25] Then, in 1917, the Russian Empire collapsed into revolution, and a rumor circulated that the Germans were about to declare in favor of the Zionist goals in Palestine. The motives were strong for the British to shore up their cause before the Germans stole their thunder.

The year 1917 was particularly propitious for a convergence of Zionist lobbying and British war aims for yet another reason. Both David Lloyd George,
the British prime minister, and A. J. Balfour, the secretary of state for foreign
affairs in that year, came from strong biblical backgrounds that made them
thoroughly conversant with Palestine as the ancient home of the Jewish people
and the prophesies foretelling their return. Lloyd George (1863–1945) grew up
under the tutelage of his uncle, a part-time Baptist preacher,[26] and was quoted
in later life as saying, "I was taught far more about the history of the Jews than
about the history of my own people."[27] Balfour (1848–1930) came from a well-
educated aristocratic Scottish background, and in the long Victorian battle
between science and religion, he stood on the side of religion, as evidenced by
a book he published on that subject in 1879.[28] In Blanche Dugdale's biography
of her uncle, she is clear that "Balfour's interest in the Jews and their history was
lifelong. It originated in the Old Testament training of his mother, and in his
Scottish upbringing."[29] And in a House of Lords debate in 1922 over British
acceptance of the Palestine Mandate, Balfour argued that acceptance of the
Mandate was

> "in order that we may send a message to every land where the Jewish race
> has been scattered, a message that will tell them that Christendom . . . is
> not unmindful of the service that they have rendered to the great religions
> of the world, and most of all to the religion that the majority of Your
> Lordships' house profess, and that we desire to the best of our ability to
> give them that opportunity of developing, in peace and quietness under
> British rule, those great gifts which hitherto they have been compelled to
> bring to fruition in countries that know not their language and belong
> not to their race."[30]

None of this meant that a biblical background was the primary reason for
Lloyd George and Balfour's support of the Zionist cause. It is clear that war aims
and Zionist lobbying were directly influential, but the biblical background of
both men created a mind-set that made it easier for those arguments to prevail.
Weizmann met Balfour in 1906 and convinced him that, "in the eyes of the
Jews themselves, Palestine offered the only satisfactory solution of their problem." In 1916 Weizmann gave to the British government his process of making
acetone, which was critical to the manufacture of high explosives. At that point
Lloyd George was minister of munitions and Balfour was first lord of the Admiralty in the coalition government of Prime Minister H. H. Asquith. Weiz-

mann's action therefore brought him to the attention of Lloyd George and created a position for him as a chemist in Lord Balfour's Admiralty. When Lloyd George acceded to the position of prime minister in late 1916 and Balfour moved from Admiralty to the Foreign Office, Weizmann was well placed to overture the British government.[31] Other British Zionists worked on others in the British government, but it was probably Weizmann's efforts that were most critical.

Early in 1917 Sir Mark Sykes (head of British Intelligence for the Near East) was appointed to conduct official talks with the Zionist leaders, and in February he met with a number of them, including Weizmann, Lord Rothschild (then considered the lay head of English Jewry), Nahum Sokolov (representing the International Zionist Movement), Harry Sacher, and Herbert Samuel (later the British high commissioner in the British Mandate). In March, Weizmann had a meeting with Balfour, the new foreign secretary, to discuss the issue. Then, during a visit to the United States in April and May, Balfour had several meetings with Brandeis, who assured him that President Wilson favored the Zionist cause.[32] The network of contacts had become quite small.

In June, Lord Rothschild and Dr. Weizmann met with Balfour and suggested that the time had arrived for a public declaration in favor of the Zionist cause. Balfour asked that a draft be prepared, and when a much reworked draft[33] was finally presented to the War Cabinet on September 3, an intense debate ensued.[34] There were various issues, but the most critical were the objections raised by Edwin Montagu (1879–1924), secretary of state for India and a prominent spokesman for assimilated Jews in England. He feared that focus on advocacy of a "national home for the Jewish people" would work to the disadvantage of Jews who, like himself, wanted to be considered full members of English society. He also argued that support of the Zionist cause would cause problems with the Muslims of India.[35] (It should be remembered that the Muslim states of Pakistan and Bangladesh were then part of British India.) For separate reasons, neither Lloyd George nor Balfour was present at this meeting, and it concluded with a decision that President Wilson should be consulted.

Recent scholarship has made it clear that Wilson was predisposed to support the Zionist cause all along, only withholding [clear] endorsement until a clear request was made to him by the British government.[36] Wilson (1856–1924) was the son of a Presbyterian minister and president of Princeton Theological Seminary from 1902 until 1910, at the time of the fundamentalist debate involving that institution. While Wilson took a more liberal stance than the fundamentalists, he was deeply steeped in the Bible and reportedly read it daily. Professor Richard Lebow has singled out Wilson's biblical orientation as the principal reason that he ultimately supported the Declaration.[37]

Brandeis learned of William Blackstone's earlier memorial to President Harrison, sought him out, and encouraged him to prepare a second memorial, this time addressed to Wilson, in support of a Jewish return to Palestine. Blackstone did so and wrote a cover letter to Wilson, indicating that he had obtained "the endorsement of the Presbyterian General Assembly, the Ministers' Meetings of the Methodists and Baptists and many representative individuals and officials." The letter went on to say that the time had arrived "for benign action in behalf of the Jews, similar to that exhibited by Cyrus of Persia" and urged Wilson to "seize the opportunity of securing to yourself and our nation the blessing promised by God to Abraham and his seed, by showing loving kindness to Israel." At Brandeis's instigation, the letter and memorial were shown unofficially to Wilson by Stephen Wise on June 30, 1917.[38] Wilson thus had not only his personal orientation but evidence that his views were shared by significant segments of the American population. And all of this was *before* formal British overtures regarding a possible declaration.

On September 30, a British query to President Wilson was cabled to Colonel Edward House, who served as an influential personal advisor to the president, completely bypassing Secretary of State Robert Lansing. (Brandeis also relied heavily on his contacts with House, who he believed favored the Zionist cause. House, however, had a Machiavellian streak and let Brandeis believe that he was a supporter while at the same time advising the president against a positive reply.) The cable only asked whether Wilson favored a declaration of sympathy for the Zionist cause; it was not specific as to what form it should take. House discussed the matter with Wilson and cabled London that the president thought "the time not opportune for any definite statement." This was interpreted in London to be a veto of the project, and when Weizmann learned of this, he went to work on an intense campaign to have the matter reopened, including an appeal to Brandeis to use his influence on the president. Balfour also cabled Brandeis urging him to bring pressure to bear on Wilson. Brandeis then contacted House and obtained a slightly more favorable impression of Wilson's attitude. Shortly thereafter the British War Cabinet again discussed the matter and sought Wilson's opinion. On October 6, Balfour cabled House with a draft of the proposed text and concern that Germany was about to declare for the Zionist cause. It is unclear what discussions then took place, but on October

13 Wilson told House to cable his concurrence with the draft—provided that there would be no public announcement of his support at that time. (This presumably was to avoid a problem with Turkey, with which the United States was not then at war.) On October 31, both Lloyd George and Balfour were in attendance at another meeting of the War Cabinet, and Balfour made it quite clear that he wanted a statement on the issue post haste. The War Cabinet agreed, and two days later Lord Balfour delivered the famous letter to Rothschild.[39]

Arthur Henderson had withdrawn from the Cabinet early in 1917, and his efforts to obtain agreement for Labour's War Aims were in progress in exact parallel with the events just described. The War Aims, of course, included support for a Jewish homeland in Palestine, and this would have added public support for the actions of the government. In addition, Sir Edmund Allenby had assumed command of the British Egyptian Expeditionary Force in June, and had received orders to strike hard at the Turks in Palestine. (While this was not the stated objective, this would have the effect of creating "facts on the ground" by British occupation of Palestine at the end of the war.) Allenby launched an attack in October, and by the end of the month had reached as far as Beersheba. Jerusalem was taken on December 8. This success drew the attention of the British public to that part of the world and probably contributed to the generally favorable press comment that the Declaration received.[40]

The Nonconformist churches were quite pleased with the developments. The multidenominational *Christian World* editorialized on November 15 that "side by side with the splendid success of General Allenby's forces in Palestine comes the announcement, made in a letter of Mr. Balfour to Lord Rothschild, that the British Government view with favor the establishment in Palestine of a national home for the Jewish people." It added, "In the days of Cromwell, and ever since, the vision of the restoration of Palestine to the Jews has been continuously before British eyes."[41] The *Baptist Times and Freeman* said that Allenby's success in Palestine combined with "Mr. Balfour's letter to Lord Rothschild" brought "the return of the Jews to their own land . . . within the realm of practical politics." It ventured that all of the Great Powers would "welcome with enthusiasm the proposal to restore [Palestine] to its ancient and rightful inhabitants."[42] The *Methodist Recorder* said, "It will be best to wait until events mature the possibilities, but the possibilities have at last appeared above the horizon, and . . . they have moved many pious souls."[43] The Church of England, with its long-established presence in Jerusalem, was a bit more reserved. Its *Church*

Times of November 16, 1917, noted that "Palestine may mean much to the Jew, as the land whence he has been driven; but it means infinitely more to the Christian, as the Holy Land, the setting of that Life in which he reposes all his hopes." And it added, "It must be an absolute condition that the Holy Places be in Christian hands."[44] The Presbyterians took a different tack. The following year, the Synod of the Presbyterian Church in England adopted a resolution saying, "The Synod desires to express its gratitude to Almighty God . . . for the occupation of Jerusalem by the British Army; and for the good prospect of the restoration of Palestine to the children of Abraham, Isaac, and Jacob."[45]

On the other side of the Atlantic, it appears that Wilson would have been correct in assuming that the American people would generally support the Declaration that he approved. In the summer of 1922, the House of Representatives and Senate approved a Joint Resolution, stating "that the United States of America favors the establishment in Palestine of a national home for the Jewish people, it being clearly understood that nothing shall be done which may prejudice the civil and religious rights of Christian and all other non-Jewish communities in Palestine, and that the holy places and religious buildings and sites in Palestine be adequately protected."[46]

The record of the debate over the Resolution suggests that one of the motivating factors was a desire to respond favorably to overtures by American Zionists.[47] But some of the justifications presented in discussion of the Resolution are revealing. When Hamilton fish, a member of the House Committee on Foreign Affairs, introduced the Resolution on the floor of the House, he said that it was "an expression of our sympathetic and favorable attitude in establishing in Palestine a refuge for the persecuted Jews of the world . . . in the ancient land of their fathers, given by Jehovah to Abraham and consecrated in the hearts of the Jewish people as the birthplace of their traditions."[48]

The "extended remarks" included in the *Congressional Record* by a number of congressmen are replete with references to the Bible. Representative Clyde Kelly of Pennsylvania noted, "It was 40 centuries ago that Jehovah promised Palestine to the children of Abraham" and "Twenty million Sunday school students now study weekly the history of the House of Israel."[49] Representative Simeon Fess of Ohio argued that "the lessons taught us in the years of our childhood sink the deepest and abide with us the longest. Those of us who in those early days heard in the Sunday School or church the recital of the famous Bible stories vividly remember the tragedy of the 'chosen people' driven from their homeland, and the promise that in time these people would return to occupy the land of their ancestors."[50] Clearly, the idea of the Promised Land had become imbedded in the American consciousness. It will be recalled that this was a period when fundamentalism and biblical literalism were becoming quite strong in the United States. The Dallas Theological Seminary was founded in 1924, and the Scopes trial took place in 1925. The congressmen were either directly influenced by their own biblical backgrounds, or they were convinced that their constituents would appreciate that line of reasoning, or both.

Nothing that has gone before should be taken to minimize the influence of national interest and the Zionist lobby on the issuance and approval of the Balfour Declaration. Those two factors were clearly the driving forces. The emphasis here on the Christian background of key participants—Lloyd George, Lord Balfour, Arthur Henderson, and Woodrow Wilson—and the quotations cited simply bring to the forefront the predispositions that made it easier for the Zionist lobby to be effective.

The Palestine Mandate

Implementation of the Balfour Declaration in the form of a British Mandate for Palestine got off to a rocky start. In July 1920, the British appointed Herbert Samuel to be responsible for affairs on the ground in Palestine. He attempted to deal evenhandedly with both Arabs and Jews, but the Arabs were intransigent. When the Muslim and Christian Palestinian Arabs realized that they would not be included in an independent Arab nation based in Damascus, and then that Palestine itself would not become an independent country, they met in Haifa in December 1920 as a Palestinian Arab Congress and demanded recognition for their cause. They refused every scheme Samuel proposed for joint representation of Arabs and Jews in some type of advisory council and continued to demand that the Balfour Declaration be rescinded and Jewish immigration be halted. Then, in May 1921, bloody rioting broke out in Jaffa, Tel Aviv, and elsewhere, with numerous Jewish casualties.[51]

The British sent out a mission of inquiry that ultimately reported back to the new colonial secretary, Winston Churchill. Considering the issues, Churchill in July 1922 issued a "White Paper" defining British policy. He tried to compromise by asserting that His Majesty's government did not "contemplate that Palestine as a whole should be converted into a Jewish National Home, but that such a home should be founded *in Palestine* . . . in order that it may become a center in which the Jewish people as a whole may take, on grounds of religion and race, an interest and a pride."[52] Not wishing to offend their benefactor, the Zionists acquiesced, but the Arabs continued in adamant opposition. There was considerable argument over the White Paper in the British Parliament, but Churchill prevailed, and it became the official position.[53] The League of Nations approved a British Mandate for Palestine in the same month, with most of the text of the Balfour Declaration incorporated into its Preamble, and the stage was set for a quarter century of bitter conflict.

In his 1942 study of British policy in Palestine, Paul Hanna concluded, "Fearful of breaking its openly pledged word to the Zionists and thereby incurring the enmity of world Jewry, but equally afraid of losing the friendship of the Arab peoples of the Near East and of displeasing the Moslem world, the British government struggled to harmonize two irreconcilable interests."[54]

· · ·

There was a fair amount of shifting of strength between the Conservative and Labour Parties in the 1920s, with the Conservatives heading the government from 1922 to 1924, Labour briefly in 1924, and then the Conservatives again from 1924 until 1929. Labour came back into power as a result of a general election in May 1929, with a minority government headed by Ramsay MacDonald as prime minister and Arthur Henderson as foreign secretary, Philip Snowden as chancellor of the exchequer, and Lord Passfield (Sidney Webb) as colonial secretary. Responsibility for Palestine affairs were vested with the Colonial Office, which gave some idea of how the British viewed the Mandate. There had been no change in Labour's support of the Zionist movement, and British policy continued to be governed by the terms of the Churchill White Paper. As far as the government was concerned, Palestine affairs appeared to be at least under control. The British garrison there was significantly reduced in order to cut expenses. In retrospect, this was a grave mistake.

The situation on the ground in Palestine was growing increasingly tense. An underlying cause was Arab resentment of continuing Jewish immigration and land purchases, but an immediate cause of friction was Jewish access to the "Wailing Wall," remnants of the Second Temple that had been incorporated in the outer wall of the Temple Mount (the Haram al-Sharif or "Noble Sanctuary" to the Arabs). This was in an area owned by Muslims, but Orthodox Jews had for centuries used a narrow passageway through Arab property to reach the Wall and to pray. Starting with disagreements in 1928 over Jewish access to the Wall, arguments grew increasingly acrimonious until they finally erupted in massive violence in August 1929. Arab attacks on Jews started in Jerusalem, but expanded to bloody massacres in Hebron and Safad. The British called in troops from Egypt, and by the time the situation was under control 133 Jews and a reported 116 Arabs had been killed.[55]

In England there was strong reaction in all quarters to the bloodshed, and the religious press showed a special concern. The Presbyterian Church of England along with the Church of Scotland had supported a Jewish Mission there since the 1880s, with a small college for Arabs and Jews in Safad and a hospital in Tiberias.[56] And the Church of England had a long-standing presence in Jerusalem. These and similar connections with the Holy Land added to traditional Christian concern over events in the area. The *Methodist Recorder* argued that "it must be made clear to the Arab majority that further rioting will not only bring economic loss, but . . . might curtail the privileges which they presently enjoy."[57] The *Baptist Times* was a bit more balanced, observing that when "young Zionist arrogance and Moslem fanaticism clash upon the same narrow ground, holy to both, the danger demands precautions from the Government responsible for keeping the peace between them."[58] The *Church Times,* presumably reflecting the Church of England's close ties with the British government, editorialized that the "acceptance of the Mandate . . . following the Balfour Declaration, has pledged this country to a policy which implies, not only the sanction, but the encouragement of Jewish immigration. This immigration brings inhabitants and capital to a sparsely populated and underdeveloped country, and must obviously, in the long run, be of advantage to the Arab population."[59] This later viewpoint, incidentally, was widely expressed in subsequent debates in the House of Commons over Palestine policy.

The government sent out a commission, headed by Sir Walter Shaw, retired chief justice of the Straits Settlements, to "enquire into the immediate causes" of the riots and to "make recommendations as to the necessary steps to avoid a recurrence."[60] The Commission, influenced in part by the outlook of the British administrators in Palestine, expanded the terms of their study and moved into an examination of overall government policy. It acknowledged Arab responsibility for the riots themselves, but saw the underlying cause as Arab resentment of continuing immigration and displacement of Arab fellahin through land purchases. It recommended curtailing immigration, forbidding the Jewish Agency for Palestine to participate in matters of government, commissioning another study to determine agricultural policies that would improve the lot of the fellahin, and issuing a new statement defining policy toward "the second part of the Balfour Declaration . . . providing for the safeguarding of the rights of non-Jewish communities in Palestine."[61] Another commission was sent out under the leadership of Sir John Hope Simpson to study the related questions of immigration, land settlement, and development. Among other things, his report back to the government in August 1930 recommended curtailment of Jewish purchase of cultivable land and criticized "the policies of the Jewish National Fund, which forever removed from the market land purchased in its name and required lessees to employ only Jewish labor."[62]

With these reports before it, the Colonial Office under Lord Passfield drafted a White Paper that was released on October 21, 1930. It reaffirmed the commitments to both parties, but went on to deny the Jewish Agency for Palestine any role in governance, announce plans for agricultural development to benefit Arab fellahin, assert the need for more stringent control of immigration, and describe plans for increased military and police presence. It was rather tactlessly worded and was taken by the Jewish community as curtailment of development of their "national home."[63] The reaction was immediate and intense.

Weizmann announced his intention of resigning as president of the World Zionist Organization and the Jewish Agency. The English Zionist Federation supported Weizmann's protest, and American Jews began to organize to exert pressure on the British government to reconsider this policy. The Conservative leadership, Stanley Baldwin, Austen Chamberlain, and Leopold Amery, published an open letter accusing the Labour government of violating the intent of the Balfour Declaration, the terms of the Mandate, and the stated policy of every preceding British government.[64] Even the Anglican press joined in. The *Church Times* said that "it was surely possible for the administration, the incompetence of which is apparent in Sir John Hope Simpson's Report, to have cooperated with the Jewish Agency, so that capital should be invested in the most profitable manner, new land should be cultivated, and the rights of the Arabs safeguarded, while the promise to the Jews faithfully kept. . . . Lord Passfield has blundered badly, and the prompt repudiation of his policy by Mr. Baldwin, Sir Austen Chamberlain and Mr. Amery is evidence, among other things, of the belief that the Jewish vote will go against Labour at the General Election."[65]

An intense debate took place in the House of Commons on November 17.[66] Ramsay MacDonald and Dr. Drummond Shiels, colonial undersecretary of state, attempted to defend the White Paper, saying that it was not *really* a change of policy. David Lloyd George took strong exception, arguing that it "is almost universally regarded as a revocation of the Mandate," and that it had been issued without consulting the League of Nations, the Allies, or the Dominions.[67] Former colonial secretary Leopold Amery said, "Jewish feeling all over the world has been mobilized against this country. Is that not a disaster which a little prudence and forethought, a little psychology and a little tact, might have averted?"[68] Sir Herbert Samuel, reflecting his long-standing conviction that it was possible to reconcile Jewish and Arab interests, made a more moderate statement, arguing that "with proper agricultural and industrial development Palestine could, in the very near future, support a population of 2,000,000" or more in a generation.[69] Even a prominent Labour member of the House, Harry Shiel, took exception—especially to the proposed restriction on immigration. He argued that "a carefully selected and well trained Jewish immigrant...brings with him energy, creative ability, and some knowledge of modern processes," and he is "able to create a great deal more wealth than the Arab generally believes."[70] In general, criticism of the White Paper appears to have been focused on its perceived repudiation of long-standing policy and concern over Jewish reaction, with arguments presented to justify a return to the more balanced approach of the Churchill White Paper.

What happened next is best described in the study by Joseph Gorny of the relationship between Labour and Zionism. He concludes that the general uproar and continuing Zionist pressure persuaded MacDonald to appoint a Cabinet Committee, headed by Foreign Secretary Arthur Henderson, to develop a response to the criticism. Henderson, a longtime supporter of the Zionist movement, had been out of the country when the Passfield Paper had been discussed by the Cabinet, and he moved promptly to rectify the damage. Henderson set up a meeting involving both government officials and representatives of the Jewish Agency, including Weizmann. Lord Passfield attended but was cut short by Henderson on several occasions. The meeting collectively hammered out language to be included in a letter from MacDonald that "explained" the White Paper in such a way that it, in effect, nullified the offending document. MacDonald issued the letter on February 13, 1931, and British policy returned to the basic posture on the Churchill White Paper.[71]

In the context of this study it is important to note that Arthur Henderson, the lifelong Methodist lay preacher and active participant in Methodist affairs, was the key individual in returning British policy to one more supportive of the Zionist cause. Although he appears to have favored a slow rather than a rapid growth of a Jewish homeland, his views on the justice of a Jewish return were certainly consistent with his thorough knowledge of the Bible. Taken together with the views expressed in Parliament by David Lloyd George, the other key individual with a biblical background, there appears to have been as least an undertone of Christian orientation in the support offered the Zionist cause in 1930 and 1931. In his November parliamentary attack on the White Paper, Lloyd George had argued that "the dominant idea [of the Mandate] was that there should be a national home for the Jews in Palestine, a recognition of the special position of the Jewish people in the country whose name they have made immortal. . . . It was an opportunity for recreating a Hebrew culture which has already rendered such eternal service to mankind."[72] While they obviously had political positions to consider as well, both Henderson and Lloyd George took positions that were consistent with their biblical orientation.

· · ·

The issues and arguments that surfaced between 1929 and 1931 continued unabated throughout the rest of the decade. The Labour government fell out of power in August 1931, and Arthur Henderson died in October 1935. Labour continued to be supportive of the Zionist movement, but with a bit less enthusiasm and with some division within its ranks. Jewish immigration—both legal and illegal—increased significantly, in part because of rising anti-Semitism in Germany and Eastern Europe. Arab bitterness over Jewish immigration and land purchases grew more intense,[73] resulting in more bloodshed. Through a series of investigative commissions and White Papers, the British government continued to struggle unsuccessfully to reconcile the conflicting demands of the Zionist movement and Arab leadership. And the British churches took a more balanced position, generally hoping that the problems could be solved somehow rather than expressing strong support for one side or the other. There is much less evidence of direct Christian influence on British policy in the latter part of the 1930s than had been evident in development of the Balfour Declaration and the reaffirmation of the Balfour policy in 1931.

Arab concerns were exacerbated by the immigration issue. Before World War I, the Jewish population of what became Palestine was estimated at about 80,000, or 11 percent of the total. By 1936, as a result of immigration it had grown to 370,483, or 28 percent of the total. Friction was intense. After much internal dissension, Arab leadership finally coalesced around an Arab Higher Committee, headed by the British-appointed Mufti of Jerusalem, Haj Amin al-Husaini, and on April 20, 1936, it called for a general strike. The Higher Committee demanded an end to Jewish immigration, the prohibition of land transfers, and a national government responsible to a representative legislative council—none of which the British were prepared to grant. Civil disorder grew intense, and terrorist bands including recruits from surrounding Arab lands were increasingly active. Military reinforcements, curfews, deportation of undesirables, collective fines on villages, and demolition of the homes of those who had committed a crime failed to restore order.[74] Some of the principal agitators were detained by the British, and Haj Amin al-Husaini fled to Iraq to avoid arrest.

In July 1936, the new colonial secretary, William Ormsby-Gore, a longtime supporter of a Jewish national home, appointed a nonpartisan Royal Commission headed by Lord Peel to investigate and make recommendations. To the surprise of many, the commission concluded that, in spite of the requirements of the Mandate to promote a Jewish national home in Palestine, the interests of Arabs and Jews were simply irreconcilable, and the only solution was partition. It suggested a partition that would give the Jews a sovereign state in the north of Palestine and along the coast and would give the Arabs a sovereign state encompassing Trans-Jordan and most of the rest of Palestine, with Jerusalem and a strip leading to Jaffa near present-day Tel Aviv and the coast under permanent British control.[75] Simultaneously with publication of the Peel Commission report in July 1937, the government issued a White Paper adopting its recommendation of partition in principle. This initially met with opposition of varying intensity from the Arab Higher Committee, the Zionist Executive, the Jewish Agency, the governments of Iraq, Trans-Jordan, and Saudi Arabia, the Labour Party, and the Permanent Mandates Commission of the League of Nations. Weizmann, as a tactical move, later persuaded the Twentieth Zionist Conference in Zurich to accept partition in principle, contingent on further discussion with the British government on the details of a Jewish state. The Arabs, however, were adamant against any surrender of Arab territory to the Jews.[76]

In January 1938, when it became apparent that no Arab representative would come forward to discuss partition, the British government appointed *another* commission, under Sir John Woodhead, to work out possible boundaries for the proposed new states. By this time, events in Europe were becoming tense over the issue of Czechoslovakia, and the British were increasingly aware of the strategic importance of Arab and Muslim friendship in the event of war. In November, the Woodhead Commission reported that no plan of partition could be devised that offered any hope of success, and the idea was abandoned. The new British colonial secretary, Malcolm MacDonald, then called for a conference of delegates from Egypt, Iraq, Saudi Arabia, the Yemen, Trans-Jordan, and Palestine to meet with delegates from the Jewish Agency, with assistance from both Zionists and non-Zionists from Britain, the United States, and Palestine to address the problem. Conferees met in London in February and March 1939, but the conference was handicapped by the fact that the Arabs would not sit with Jews, and two factions within the Palestinian delegation would not sit with one another either. It came as no surprise that a solution was not forthcoming.[77]

Evidence in 1939 that war with Germany was imminent hardened the position of the British government into announcing its own solution. In a White Paper of May 1939, Colonial Secretary Malcolm MacDonald announced an intent to eventually create an independent state "in which the two peoples of Palestine, Arabs and Jews, share authority in such a way that the essential interests of each are secured."[78] The plan was to establish within ten years an independent state in alliance with Great Britain, with Palestinians replacing British in all departments of government and the creation of a legislature if at all possible within the first five years. A constitution would have to be prepared that recognized the special position of a Jewish national home. The plan would permit the immigration of 75,000 persons within the first five years, in addition to the regular 10,000 per year and an extra 25,000 at the discretion of the High Commissioner, and allow the High Commissioner to curtail land purchases.[79] This received a storm of protest in Parliament and was rejected by the Permanent Mandates Commission as not in compliance with the terms of the Mandate. But Hitler invaded Poland in September, and the legal status of the White Paper was left unclear as everything else was put aside for prosecution of the war.

. . .

The Arab uprising in 1936, and the statements of policy attempting to deal with it, prompted periodic parliamentary debates on the subject. Many of the arguments were the same as before, but biblical references almost disappeared and questions of imperial security began to become prominent. In the House in June 1936, David Lloyd George pointed out, "We have a most important line of communication between us and the East which is very dependent on Palestine, and more dependent on Palestine than when we had complete control over Egypt."[80] Commander Locker-Lampson argued, "We . . . want some absolutely secure centre which will guarantee that you can fly from England to the East and be certain of landing on territory that is safeguarded and secure." He added, "By conquering Palestine [Allenby also] guaranteed security to the Canal."[81] Even some of those more sympathetic to the Arab cause raised questions of security, but from a different perspective. Colonel Clifton Brown agreed that Palestine "is the most important communication point of the British Empire. It is vital to the British Empire that in Palestine, surrounded as it is by Arab countries, and with Arab countries all round the shores of the Mediterranean, any action [we take] should carry with it the good will of the Arab races."[82] The strategic importance of the Arab world to Imperial security had become a factor in the calculus of decision making.

The voices of the churches during this period became more neutral. In May 1936, the *Baptist Times* was concerned that "whatever objections the Arabs may have to the Government of the country, there is no excuse for rioting and dishonesty."[83] But by October it had concluded that "co-operation between Jew and Arab seems impossible, and the Arab dread of being swamped by Jewish immigrants strains the relationships between the two races."[84] In January 1937 it noted that "Moslems and Jews are struggling for what both regard as their holy land."[85] The General Assembly of the Church of Scotland regularly voted to approve Deliverances (Resolutions), hoping that "wise counsels may prevail and a satisfactory settlement be found, which will secure the termination of strife in Palestine."[86] True to their beliefs, the Society of Friends (Quakers) worked throughout the period for reconciliation between Jews and Arabs. The 1937 report of its Palestine Watching Committee was concerned that "strenuous efforts to bring moderate Arabs and Jews together in Palestine have unfortunately proved unavailing," and the discussion of the report included the comment that "the difficult situation between Arab and Jew . . . has resulted from the British policy inaugurated by the Balfour Declaration."[87]

The *Methodist Reporter* reported on events throughout 1936 and 1937, and after the Peel Commission report had been made public, it commented, "While the proposal to divide Palestine among Jews and Arabs has been generally well received in this country as the only eligible solution to a very difficult problem, it has not found such hospitality among the peoples most directly involved." And it noted "a fairly significant passage in the report which points out that, though ultimately the mandate became unworkable because of the two conflicting nationalisms in Palestine, it was the very fact of Jewish immigration into Palestine which gave birth to the Arab nationalist spirit. It is equally true that the Balfour Declaration created Jewish nationalism."[88] Many of the church governing bodies understood the situation and hoped, almost wistfully, for a peaceful resolution. The Church of Scotland, Presbyterians, Quakers, and

Church of England all had presences on the ground in Palestine, and this gave them a bit more perspective on the Arab point of view.

Summation

It has long been understood that the Balfour Declaration originated with a convergence of the Zionist movement and British national interests, both in winning the war and in creating a protective buffer for communications with the empire in the East. It has also long been recognized that the Labour Party, in the 1920s and 1930s, had been a faithful supporter of the Zionist enterprise, because of its socialist orientation and the inclusion of a significant number of Jews in its ranks. What has been added here is emphasis on a third factor, which has been given only scattered recognition. That is an underlying predisposition on the part of the Methodist-influenced Labour Party and key British and American leaders to favor a return of the Jews to their ancient homeland. This was especially true in 1917 when the Balfour Declaration was formulated and in 1931 when its promise was reaffirmed.

In retrospect, it is clear that the attempt to create a Jewish homeland in an area already populated by Arabs was doomed from the beginning. Lloyd George appears to have conceived of the "homeland" as a cultural haven, while the Zionists, perhaps from the beginning but certainly as time went on, were striving for an independent Jewish state. And the Arabs strongly objected to the intrusion. The Methodists had it right. It was the very fact of Jewish immigration into Palestine that gave birth to an already germinating Arab nationalism,[89] and it was the Balfour Declaration and the events that followed it that intensified Jewish nationalism. And the British, with their belief in the efficacy of compromise, legislative processes, protection of minority rights, and the rule of law, continually strove to find a solution agreeable to all sides. Unfortunately, those beliefs are not shared by every culture in the world, and in this case it proved impossible to reconcile the irreconcilable. In addition, the government of the neighboring Arab states of Egypt, Saudi Arabia, Trans-Jordan, and Iraq were beginning to take an interest in the fate of their co-religionists in Palestine. The seeds were planted for the events that followed World War II, including the surrender of the Mandate and the passing of the baton to the United States.

4

Truman, the Bible, Israel, Oil, and the Soviet Union

The decision by Harry Truman to recognize the State of Israel immediately after its creation in 1948 has been so well researched by historians that it would appear almost redundant to bring it up again.[1] For the purpose of this study, however, it is well to review the salient facts and to cover what is well known from a slightly different perspective, focusing on the interaction between the national interest as perceived by the Departments of State and Defense (opposing prompt recognition), a combination of the Zionist lobby and Truman's closest advisors (favoring prompt recognition), and the underlying influence of Christian teaching about the Jews and the Holy Land. The context within which a decision had to be made included the withdrawal of Britain from empire, the onset of the cold war, the growing importance of Arab-controlled oil, American awakening to the horror of the Holocaust, and the upcoming presidential elections. The Zionist lobby and Truman's advisors won out over State and Defense, but it appears that Truman's biblical background at least predisposed him to favor prompt recognition. Also at work was a growing climate of opinion among Christian clergymen and political leaders in favor of creating a Jewish state in Palestine. This outlook had been carefully nurtured by Jewish American Zionists, and Truman had been supportive of this movement in the early 1940s. As will be seen in the next chapter, the same three forces, in somewhat different form, were very much alive fifty years later. The decision would consistently come down on the side of Israel, much to the distress of many in the Arab world.

The Climate of Opinion in the 1940s

During World War II, there was growing awareness of the plight of the Jews in Europe and steadily increasing support for the idea of a homeland in Palestine. The effort was influenced only in part by knowledge of the Bible—which was widespread but not yet as activated in support of Israel as it was to become later. The Sunday school movement was in full swing, and many Americans knew the stories of the Bible, but fundamentalists had not yet turned the full force of their preaching toward the restoration movement. There was, on the other hand, a concerted drive on the part of American Zionists to enlist clergy and political leaders in support of their cause. And it was quite effective.

The earliest instance of Jewish influence in organizing Christians was the formation in 1930 of a small Pro-Palestine Federation of "ministers of the Gospel, college professors, professional men, and . . . statesmen . . . embodying the finest Christian principles . . . in defense of the Jewish national home cause as defined in the Mandate for Palestine." The Federation was a somewhat spontaneous organization of Christian leaders in Chicago, but it was actually run by Aaron Elias, the only Jewish member, and it received limited financial support from American Zionists.[2] The Federation was never very large, growing to only 300 members by 1937, but it continued to be active mainly in organizing conferences and issuing statements calling for "restoration of the Land of Israel to the children of Israel . . . [as a] . . . natural place of refuge" from the barbarism under way in Europe.[3]

Ultimately of more significance was the American Palestine Committee (APC), organized in January 1932 at the instigation of Emanuel Neumann, an active American Zionist, in reaction to the British Passfield White Paper of 1930.[4] It is noteworthy that, in a preparatory meeting prior to formation of the committee, Neumann had been advised by William Hopkins, former city manager of Cleveland, that "we are most likely to gain supporters among . . . Christians who have been brought up on the Scriptures, and who have a sentimental and emotional attitude toward the Holy Land, which makes them pre-disposed to favor the Zionist cause."[5]

Neumann never forgot this advice, but in contrast to the heavily religious membership of the Pro-Palestine Federation, the APC was composed mainly of public figures, including Vice President Charles Curtis, Supreme Court Justice Harlan Stone, House Majority Leader Henry Rainey, and Senator Robert Wagner of New York.[6] Its "Statement of Aims and Principles" was in the Blackstone tradition: "The fulfillment of the millennial hope for the reunion of the Jewish people with the land of its ancient inheritance, a hope that accords with the spirit of biblical prophecy, has always commanded the sympathy of the liberal Christian world."[7]

The APC was heavily Republican in composition, and with the election of

Franklin D. Roosevelt in 1932, the Zionists transferred their attention to the Democratic Party. Neumann was sent to London and then to Palestine by the World Zionist Organization, and the APC lapsed into quiescence.

The onset of World War II changed all of that. Growing concern in 1939 over the need for action led American Zionists to form an Emergency Committee for Zionist Affairs, later renamed the American Zionist Emergency Council (AZEC). Neumann was called back to the United States and placed in charge of its Department of Public Affairs and Political Action. There he became an ally of Rabbi Abba Hillel Silver of Cleveland, who had begun to fight for broad-based grassroots political action rather than quiet influence in the upper echelons of government advocated by the highly respected Rabbi Steven Wise of the Zionist Organization of America.

One of Neumann's first tasks in his new role was to reactivate the American Palestine Committee. The APC broke into public view with a major dinner at the Shoreham Hotel in Washington on April 30, 1941, and it became a prime mover in the drive for American support of the Zionist cause. Its aim, as with the original committee, was advocacy for the "reunion of the Jewish people with the land of its ancient inheritance."[8] The chairman was Senator Robert Wagner of New York, and its executive committee included Dr. Daniel Marsh, president of Boston University, Senators Claude Pepper and Arthur Vandenberg, House Majority Leader John McCormack, Eric Johnston, president of the U.S. Chamber of Commerce, William Green, president of the AFL, Philip Murray, president of the CIO, Daniel Poling, editor of the *Christian Herald,* Professor William Albright of Johns Hopkins University, and Professor Carl Friedrich of Harvard. With the help of AZEC, the APC undertook an intensive organizing campaign, and by mid-1942 it reportedly had a membership of 725, including 67 senators, 143 congressmen, 22 governors, and numerous jurists, educators, clergymen, publishers, editors, writers, and civic leaders. Behind-the-scenes funding for the effort was provided by AZEC, amounting to $72,000 per year in the first years and raised to $150,000 annually by 1947–48.

The American Palestine Committee was largely composed of public officials, and Neumann's second task was mobilization of Christian clergy and academics. In this he found an especially valuable ally—Reinhold Niebuhr (1893–1971), professor of Christian ethics at Union Theological Seminary in New York and a widely respected writer on theological and political issues. Niebuhr had a long-standing and intense concern over the plight of Jews in Europe, and unlike many other liberal theologians in the 1930s he had not joined the ranks of the pacifist movement. He urged strong measures against Hitler and the Nazis. Nor had he joined forces with biblical literalists in claiming Palestine as a "Promised Land" to which the Jews were historically entitled. He also understood the concerns of the Arabs should a homeland be created. With all of this in mind, he argued that Christians had a strong moral responsibility to support the creation of a refuge for the Jews of Europe—preferably in Palestine, but not necessarily there. Neumann had no difficulty persuading Niebuhr to express these views in a two-part article in the *Nation* in February 1942. The article was reprinted and given wide distribution by AZEC and the APC during the war.

In December 1942, Neumann encouraged a small group of Christian supporters of Zionism who had been meeting since 1938–39 to organize into a Christian Council on Palestine (CCP) to concentrate on winning clergymen and leaders of Christian opinion to the cause of establishing "a Jewish Commonwealth in Palestine . . . in the postwar era."[9] Its executive committee included Niebuhr, theologian Paul Tillich, William Albright, Carl Friedrich, and Daniel Poling. The CCP was responsible for numerous pamphlets and books, public meetings, letters to the editor, and full-page advertisements in the *New York Times*. By 1946 it had a membership of some 3,000 prominent clergymen and lay Christian leaders. The APC and the CCP were eventually incorporated as subgroups of an umbrella American Christian Palestine Committee, with continuing support from AZEC.

A major turning point in the efforts of American Zionists occurred at a conference held at the Biltmore Hotel in New York in May 1942. Originally organized as a moderate affirmation of the "national home" concept, the conference ended by unanimously adopting a declaration that demanded that "Palestine be established as a Jewish Commonwealth integrated into the structure of the new democratic world."[10] The term *commonwealth* was used rather than *sovereign state* in order to make it sound less threatening, but there was no doubt as to the intent. This became the so-called Biltmore Program, but it was not yet adopted by all of American Jewry. That occurred at a tumultuous American Jewish Conference meeting of some sixty-five Jewish organizations in 1943. The conference was originally dominated by moderate Zionists such as Steven Wise, but it was taken over by the fiery oratory of Hillel Silver, and it ended with an overwhelming endorsement of the Biltmore goal of a Jewish commonwealth. Zionist advocacy now accelerated.[11]

The American Palestine Committee had not waited for full endorsement of the Biltmore Program by the whole of American Jewry. On November 2, 1942, the twenty-fifth anniversary of the Balfour Declaration, it sent its own Declaration to the president of the United States, signed by 68 senators and 193 House members, affirming support for a Jewish Homeland and Commonwealth in Palestine. It said, in part:

> The [Balfour] Declaration was published to the world with the approval of the other powers allied with Great Britain in the World War, and with the encouragement and support of the Government of the United States. ... A few years later, the House of Representatives and the Senate of the United States adopted a Resolution favoring the establishment of a Jewish National Home.... [It has] become the declared and traditional policy of the United States to favor the restoration of the Jewish National Home ... and to pave the way for the establishment of a Jewish Commonwealth. ... Faced as we are by the fact that the Nazi government is attempting to exterminate a whole people, we declare that, when the war is over, it shall be the common purpose of civilized mankind to right this cruel wrong ... [and] ... to enable large numbers of survivors to reconstruct their lives in Palestine.[12]

While the American Palestine Committee had been sponsored and financially supported by AZEC, American lawmakers had been clearly influenced by what was becoming known of the plight of the Jews in Nazi Germany.

The combined efforts of the American Zionist Emergency Council, the American Palestine Committee, and the Christian Council on Palestine resulted in considerable grassroots pressure on Congress and the administration. In 1944 over 3,000 non-Jewish organizations—churches, labor unions, Rotary clubs, and farm granges—passed pro-Zionist resolutions and sent telegrams to Congress.[13] In February 1944, Senators Wagner of New York (with a large Jewish constituency) and Robert Taft of Ohio (one of whose supporters was Rabbi Silver) introduced a joint resolution to the Senate (with an identical one introduced in the House) urging the United States to "use its good offices and take appropriate measures to the end that the doors of Palestine be opened for free entry of Jews into that country . . . so that the Jewish people may ultimately reconstitute Palestine as a free and democratic Jewish commonwealth."[14]

The resolutions, and several similar ones, were referred to the respective foreign affairs committees of both houses, but action was deferred in response to a letter from Secretary of War Henry Stimson asserting that it was "the considered judgment of the War Department that . . . further action on them would be prejudicial to the successful prosecution of the war."[15] However, as a result of growing support for the Zionist cause, both the Democratic and Republican platforms in 1944 included planks in favor of a Jewish commonwealth in Palestine. The Republican platform, adopted at its convention in June, stated: "In order to give refuge to millions of distressed Jewish men, women and children driven from their homes by tyranny, we call for the opening of Palestine to their unrestricted immigration and land ownership, so that . . . Palestine may be constituted as a free and democratic Commonwealth."[16]

The Democratic platform, adopted in July, was similar: "We favor the opening of Palestine to unrestricted Jewish immigration and colonization, and such a policy as to result in the establishment there of a free and democratic Jewish Commonwealth."[17]

While the platforms undoubtedly reflected genuine concern over the plight of Jews in Nazi-controlled Europe, and while most biblically knowledgeable Americans would have seen Palestine as a logical place of refuge, there is little question but that the efforts of the Zionist lobby had begun to bear political fruit. The continuing use of the term *commonwealth* attests to that.

Just prior to the election of 1944, Stimson changed his mind. On October 10, 1944, he wrote to Senator Taft that although "there is still strong feeling on the part of many officers in my Department that the passage of such . . . [resolutions] . . . would interfere with our military effort, . . . political considerations now outweigh the military, and the issue should be determined upon the political rather than the military basis."[18] However, the issue did not come up again until the next year. In response to a special appeal by the Zionist lobby and its affiliates in September 1945, two-thirds of the Senate was contacted by constituents in one day, and twenty-seven senators gave speeches on the floor of the Senate shortly thereafter.[19] The result was passage by both Houses in December 1945 of a Concurrent Resolution calling for "free entry of Jews" into Palestine "so that they may freely proceed with the upbuilding of Palestine as the Jewish national home and . . . establish Palestine as a democratic commonwealth in which all men, regardless of race or creed, shall have equal rights."[20]

Support for the resolution was strong, but the debate on the Resolution in the Senate suggests that lawmakers were becoming acutely aware that Arab residents of Palestine had strenuous objections to a Jewish state on their land.[21]

After the war, the general public became increasingly knowledgeable of the issue. A series of polls taken by the Gallup Organization and the National Opinion Research Center in 1946, 1947, and 1948 revealed strong support for admitting Jewish refugees into Palestine and support for a Jewish state but opposition to committing American troops to keep order or to funding the project with taxpayers' money. Most polls started by asking whether the respondent had followed the discussion about the issue, and the results reflected the opinions of those who said they had (usually about half). A Gallup poll in December 1945 found that 76 percent of these respondents favored permitting Jews to settle in Palestine, while only 7 percent opposed it. Another Gallup poll in May 1946 asked whether "you approve or disapprove of our sending troops to Palestine to help England keep order there." In this case, only 21 percent approved while 74 percent disapproved. A Gallup poll in September 1946 found that 63 percent of the respondents believed the Arabs would "go to war to prevent the Jews from making Palestine a Jewish nation." When asked by Gallup in May 1947 whether they approved of the United States financing a major development program for the Arabs in return for their acceptance of a Jewish state, 30 percent agreed whereas 52 percent did not. But in March 1948 a National Opinion Research Center poll found that 53 percent favored "dividing Palestine into two countries (one for the Jews and one for the Arabs)" while 27 percent disapproved.[22] While not as strong as the Resolutions passed by Congress, the general public was also tending to support the idea of a Jewish state, provided it did not involve American troops or American money.

To recapitulate, at the end of World War II there was substantial support among the general public for creating a Jewish state in Palestine as a safe haven for the remnant of persecuted Jews of Europe. There was even stronger support in Congress, orchestrated by the Zionist lobby. That lobby had appealed to American revulsion over what had happened to the Jews under Nazi rule, a desire to provide the survivors with a place of refuge, and a biblically derived understanding of Palestine as the historical home of the Jewish people. This support was not in response to fundamentalist teachings about a prophesied role of the Jews in the End Times. That came later. However, in 1948 it was clear that there would be no political opposition of any consequence to recognition of the newly formed State of Israel. In fact, it would have been politically expedient for Truman to do so, given the upcoming presidential elections and the importance of the Jewish vote—especially in New York. There were, however, serious reasons not to act hastily from the viewpoint of national security.

National Security, Oil, the Arabs, and Soviet Expansion

In the new millennium it is difficult to remember that prior to World War II the United States was a net *exporter* of petroleum to the rest of the world. A premonition that the United States might become a net *importer* occurred as early as 1941, when Secretary of the Interior Harold Ickes called to Roosevelt's attention the fact that increasing domestic demand over the past ten years was causing a steady decline in the ratio of proven domestic reserves to annual production, suggesting that thought be given to "the future of the United States with respect to oil."[23] An internal study that he forwarded to Roosevelt in October 1941 argued that "the United States must have extra-territorial reserves to guard against the day when our steadily increasing demand can no longer be met by our domestic supply."[24] Throughout wartime discussions of America's strategic position there was increasing worry over future access to petroleum resources. The actual shift from net exporter to net importer did not occur until 1948,[25] but it was foreseen long before that, and this was a matter of grave concern to military planners as tension with the Soviet Union coalesced into the cold war.[26]

By mid-1943 the problem of future supply had begun to percolate into the upper echelons of the American government, and at the same time Saudi Arabia came to the attention of senior officials as a potential source. A United States Navy estimate prepared in May 1943 suggested that Middle East reserves were more than double those of the United States—approximately 56.4 billion gallons, compared with 20 billion gallons in the United States. And Saudi Arabia accounted for some 22.2 billion gallons of that Middle East total.[27] These numbers were ridiculously small by comparison with today's figures, but they were enough to focus considerable attention on Saudi Arabia. And it became known that an American company, the Arabian American Oil Company (Aramco), a joint subsidiary of Standard Oil of California (Socal) and Texaco, held a concession there that had great promise. The concession dated back to 1933, but oil had not been struck until 1938, and production had just begun when war caused operations to be suspended. The geologists, however, were clear as to its potential.

•   •   •

Saudi Arabia was (and is) a unique country, and its ruler, 'Abd al-'Aziz ibn 'Abd al-Rahman Al Faisal Al Sa'ud, was a unique individual. ('Abd al-'Aziz is the currently preferred name, though Ibn Sa'ud was more common in American records of the time.)[28] He was a powerfully built man of great personal courage, insight, and knowledge of Bedouin ways. The kingdom was his personal creation, forged through thirty years of desert warfare, completed only in 1930. He and his warriors were strict adherents to the extremely conservative Wahhabi sect of Sunni Islam, and he bound his volatile tribesmen into a coherent whole by astute use of religion, money, and marriage. Wahhabism gave them common cause, and financial subsidies from the king kept the tribes from their old pattern of raiding one another. But ʿAbd al-ʿAziz also took advantage of the Islamic permission for four wives and easy divorce. Over the years he created kinship ties by marrying the daughters of numerous tribal leaders, fathering children, divorcing those wives (setting them up comfortably), and marrying others. By this process he had thirty-two sons, the basis of the present royal family of Saudi Arabia.[29]

Several aspects of ʿAbd al-ʿAziz's nuanced thinking are still in evidence in Saudi concerns today. One was the king's continuing need for money in the 1930s to subsidize his tribesmen. Saudis continue to need funds to sustain their infrastructure and social programs. And in the 1940s there was an astute use of subtle threats to cancel Aramco's concession as a way of extracting more funds, but the king never actually did so because he was well aware of the value of the concession to him. In more recent times, the Saudi government has pushed for as much revenue as possible, but has been careful not to let the price of oil go so high as to encourage serious development of alternative sources of energy. And as custodian of the Islamic holy cities of Mecca and Medina, ʿAbd al-ʿAziz was well aware of his responsibilities to the Islamic world, and he expressed much concern over Zionist moves to create an enclave in Palestine. The present Saudi government retains this attitude but attempts to balance Islamic concerns over Israel's treatment of the Palestinians against a need to maintain good relations with the United States.

Saudi ties with the United States began during World War II partly as a result of the Aramco concession and partly as a result of an American desire to build an airfield at Dhahran as a stopover point for flights to the Soviet Union and India.[30] It matured during a meeting between ʿAbd al-ʿAziz and Roosevelt aboard the USS *Quincy* as Roosevelt was returning home from the Yalta Conference in March 1945. Shortly thereafter, ʿAbd al-ʿAziz addressed a long letter to Roosevelt setting out his concerns over Zionist intentions in Palestine. After giving a long history of Arab occupation of that land, he wrote:

> The solution of the problem of persecuted Jews in the world differs from the fictitious problem of Zionism. For to provide homes for the scattered

Jews is something in which the whole world can cooperate, and here Palestine has borne more than its full share. But to bring these scattered people, put them in countries already occupied, and do away with the original occupants is an act unparalleled in human history. . . . [T]he formation of a Jewish state in Palestine will be a deadly blow to the Arabs and a constant threat to peace, for disturbed conditions are bound to prevail between the Jews and the Arabs, and if the patience of the latter is one day exhausted and they will despair of their future then they will be obliged to defend themselves and future generations against this aggression. . . . [This] is an uneasy situation which threatens the peace of the Middle East. . . . All that we ask is that the Allies should fully realize the rights of the Arabs and for the present prevent the Jews from going ahead in any new matter which may be considered a threat to the Arabs . . . in order that they . . . may be assured of justice and equity in their lands.[31]

Roosevelt replied to ʿAbd al-ʿAziz on April 5, recalling their "memorable conversation" in which he had gained a "vivid" understanding of the king's viewpoint.

[It is] our desire that no decision be taken with respect to the basic situation in that country without full consultation with both Arabs and Jews . . . [and I will] take no action, in my capacity as Chief of the executive branch of the Government, which might prove hostile to the Arab people.[32]

Seven days later, on April 12, Roosevelt was dead and Harry Truman became president of the United States.

· · ·

The mantle that descended upon Harry Truman was not an easy one. Germany capitulated in May 1945, and Japan surrendered in August, but the specter of Soviet expansion soon replaced war as the central concern among American diplomatic and military planners.[33] The first real issue was in the Middle East. Under the terms of a British-Soviet-Iranian treaty of 1942, Soviet troops had been stationed in northern Iran for the duration of the war, with a promise to withdraw within six months after the end of hostilities. That deadline fell on March 2, 1946, and the Soviets not only refused to withdraw but fomented a separatist movement that would have brought northern Iran within the Soviet sphere of control. Western pressure plus adroit maneuvering by the Iranian government ultimately caused the Soviets to withdraw, but the alarm bell had been sounded. That issue plus Soviet intransigence in Eastern Europe was the background for Winston Churchill's famous pronouncement at Fulton, Missouri, on March 5, 1946, that an "iron curtain" had fallen, dividing Europe into East and West.

Churchill's speech caught the public's attention, but it was an incisive analysis of Soviet motivation by George Kennan, then a brilliant young foreign service officer in Moscow, that coalesced thinking within the Departments of State, War, and Navy. (In 1947, War, Navy, and Air Force were combined as the Department of Defense.) In February 1946, Kennan sent back a long, detailed telegram describing Soviet monolithic internal control, its paranoid view of the rest of the world, and its respect for nothing but countervailing power. The telegram was given wide circulation within the government, and its central argument was repeated in his famous article (under the pseudonym "X") on "The Sources of Soviet Conduct" in the journal *Foreign Affairs* in July 1947. Kennan's rationale became the basis for America's containment policy in the early years of the cold war.

George C. Marshall assumed the office of secretary of state in January 1947, and shortly thereafter the government was confronted with another crisis. A Communist insurrection was under way in Greece, and considerable Soviet pressure was being exerted in Turkey, both recipients of financial assistance from Britain. But British resources had been exhausted by World War II, and in February 1947 the British notified the American government that it could no longer support those two countries. The move really signified the beginning of the end of the British Empire, and it now became clear that the United States might have to replace Britain as the bulwark against Soviet expansion in the eastern Mediterranean and Middle East. The decision was to do just that, and on March 12 Truman called on Congress to approve significant aid for Greece and Turkey. In the course of his speech, he argued "that it must be the policy of the United States to support free peoples who are resisting attempted subversion by armed minorities or by outside pressures."[34] That single sentence was what became known as the "Truman Doctrine," and the thinking behind it affected American policy for a long time thereafter. An immediate consequence was a staff study initiated by Undersecretary of State Dean Acheson on how many other countries would need aid and how much. The outcome of *that* study was the European Recovery Program, better known as the Marshall Plan, also initiated in 1947. The early stages of the cold war were well under way.

Military planners, however, had not waited for the president and the State

Department to begin their own postwar work. It is standard military procedure to undertake staff studies based on the most likely opponent (or opponents) in a possible conflict and to draw up plans to deal with that contingency. Such studies provide the basis for determining force requirements and planning in the areas of organization and military procurement. With this in mind, the Joint Chiefs of Staff had determined that the obvious opponent in any possible future war would be the Soviet Union, which now controlled the most powerful military establishment left in the world outside of the United States and the only significant one left with possible hostile intent toward this country. As a consequence, the Joint Chiefs of Staff had begun contingency planning in December 1945, beginning with studies under the code name "PINCER," and by June 1946 a tentative strategic concept had been developed for war with the Soviet Union.[35] It envisioned the main offense in Western Eurasia combined with active defense in eastern Asia, holding key lines of communication (including the Mediterranean), and strategic bombardment of vital areas in the western Soviet Union.[36]

It soon became clear that the U.S. Navy was the service most concerned about logistics for a long war and the one most worried about oil and defense of the Persian Gulf area.[37] But there was a problem. In early 1948 it was estimated that it would take at least *six divisions* to defend the area, and under overall war plans the only available American force left was *one reinforced Marine battalion* to be sent from Guam to Bahrain to assist in evacuation and denial operations. The picture was so bleak that in April 1948 the Joint Chiefs of Staff and the National Security Council had begun to work out a detailed plan (NSC-26) for denial of the Saudi oil fields to the Soviets in the event of war through destruction of aboveground facilities and plugging of oil wells.[38] There is no indication that this plan was ever approved or that it was ever discussed with 'Abd al-'Aziz, but its consideration in 1948 was indicative of the scarcity of resources to defend the area.

This lack of defense capability was at total variance with the importance placed on Middle Eastern oil in concurrent planning for logistic support of an extended war. A Joint Logistics Committee study in early 1947 concluded that in "a major future war of five years duration . . . the total United States military and civilian consumption requirements . . . [could not] . . . be met after M+3 years by all of the current production in the United States and United States controlled foreign sources, including that in the . . . Middle East, even with the . . . drilling, new refinery, and synthetic plant building programs proposed." The study strongly recommended development of American plants to produce "synthetic petroleum from . . . domestic reserves of natural gas, coal and shales." But in the meantime it called for conservation of domestic and U.S. controlled reserves—other than those in the Middle East—by "maximum importation . . . of crude petroleum from the . . . Middle East." It also noted that Saudi Arabia was especially valuable to the United States because of the American concession there.[39] Military planners considered it critical that the United States draw on Saudi and other Middle Eastern reserves as much as possible during peacetime in order to conserve other resources for the eventuality of war. The Department of State held similar views. In addition to strategic considerations, State was worried about supplies for Western Europe, which was undergoing terrible weather in the winter of 1947–48 and in critical need of petroleum from the Middle East to sustain itself. A major State position paper in late 1947 argued that it was essential that the development of Saudi oil "be allowed to continue and that the United States and other friendly nations have access to it. [And] for this to occur, it [would] be necessary to keep the goodwill of the King and other important Saudi Arabs."[40] Threats to that goodwill would seriously threaten America's ability to sustain Western Europe and to resist Soviet expansion.

For these reasons, by 1948 the Departments of Defense and State had reached a firm consensus that it was in the American national interest to maintain good relations with Saudi Arabia and ʿAbd al-ʿAziz. Access to Saudi and Middle Eastern oil was vital to America's ability to protect Western Europe and to contain—and possibly win a war against—the Soviet Union. It was apparent that overt American support for the Zionist cause would seriously strain that relationship. This was the position that State and Defense brought to the debate over whether (and how soon) to recognize the State of Israel when the British withdrew and Israel was proclaimed in May 1948. That position was diametrically opposed to the political support for Israel that had been fostered by the American Zionist lobby. It was Harry Truman who would have to decide between the two viewpoints.

Harry Truman and the Bible

Harry S. Truman (1884–1972) was a staunch, lifelong student of the Bible.[41] His family had been Baptist when they lived on a farm near Grandview, Missouri (on the outskirts of Kansas City), but they attended the First Presbyterian Church in Independence, Missouri, when they lived there between 1896 and

1903. He attended Sunday school regularly in the Presbyterian Church in Independence when the Sunday school movement was in full swing in the United States and the debate over biblical literalism was raging throughout that denomination. He also claimed to have read the Bible through twice before the age of twelve. When he was eighteen, he joined the Baptist church back in Grandview and maintained his membership there for the rest of his life, because he believed that the Baptist Church gave "the common man the shortest and most direct approach to God."[42] He came away from all this with "an almost fundamentalist respect for the Bible"[43] and a thorough knowledge of its stories, including those about the Promised Land. Throughout his life, he was fond of quoting what he considered relevant verses. Clark Clifford recalled that from Truman's reading of the Old Testament "he felt the Jews derived a legitimate historical right to Palestine ... [sometimes citing] ... Deuteronomy 1:8, 'Behold, I have given up the land before you; go and take possession of the land which the Lord hath sworn unto your fathers, to Abraham, to Isaac, and to Jacob.'"[44] Further evidence of Truman's underlying support of the Jewish right of return was his membership in the American Palestine Committee in the early 1940s and his inclusion in weekly meetings that Justice Brandeis held in his home during that same period.

Truman also considered himself a student of history, especially the role of great men in history. He wrote in his diary that since the age of seventeen he had spent a great deal of time reading about great men, and in a 1934 memorandum he wrote:

> In reading the lives of great men, I found that the first victory they won was over themselves and their carnal urges. Self-discipline with all of them came first. . . . I admired Cincinnatus, Hannibal, Cyrus the Great, Gustavus Adolphus of Sweden, Washington and Lee, Stonewall Jackson and J.E.B. Stuart. . . . They fought for what they thought was right and for their countries. They were patriotic and unselfish.[45]

In addition, Paul Merkley has argued that "Truman was thoroughly convinced of the Divine directing of his life and everybody else's." He pondered "the extraordinary circumstances that brought him where he was. He studied soberly his own strengths and weaknesses—fully at peace with his own humble origins." And he became convinced that someone—perhaps himself—would someday be called upon to emulate Cyrus, the Persian ruler who returned the Jews from exile in Babylon back to their homeland in 538 B.C.E.[46] This may appear naive in today's more cynical and jaundiced world, but Truman was a simple man with a simple and steadfast faith, and such an assessment should not be discounted.

To recapitulate, Truman brought to the argument between the Zionist lobby and the Departments of State and Defense a biblically derived predisposition to favor early recognition of the State of Israel. This does not mean that this predisposition was the ultimate deciding factor, but the historical record strongly suggests that it played a part in it. The actual decision-making process was a complex and confusing one, and historians have differed on the real reasons influencing Truman's decision to recognize Israel when that country declared itself a state on May 14, 1948.

Britain's Labour Party and Palestine

A bit of background would be helpful at this point. The Labour Party came into power in Britain in July 1945, with Clement Attlee as prime minister and Ernest Bevin as foreign secretary. It was therefore the Labour Party that had to deal with postwar issues, the decline of empire, the Soviet threat, and the Palestine problem.[47] Labour had a long history of support of the Zionist movement, and there were holdouts for that policy in the new cabinet—notably the colonial secretary, Arthur Creech Jones (a Methodist in the Arthur Henderson tradition). But the diminishment of British power was a reality that had to be faced, and the debate within the British government was intense. It was clear that Britain could not maintain the peace in Palestine if the increasing conflict between Arabs and Jews were to escalate into full-scale warfare. And British public opinion was becoming alienated by Zionist terrorist attacks on British troops—especially after twenty British soldiers were killed in an attack on the Jerusalem officers' club and two British sergeants were hung and their bodies booby-trapped in retaliation for the execution of Zionist terrorists.[48]

The Foreign Office warned that Russia's "primary objective . . . was to undermine Britain's position in the Arab countries and to replace it with Russian influence." It argued that any settlement in Palestine unfavorable to the Arabs "would give Russia the conditions to further its plans," probably starting with Iraq and spreading to the Levant. Diminished British influence in Iraq and Iran could mean possible loss of oil supplies, which "would be particularly serious in the light of growing dependence of Britain and the Empire on Middle Eastern oil supplies both in peace and war." The Imperial General Staff was concerned about Britain's ability to fight a war from the Middle East and wanted to maintain some sort of foothold in Palestine "as a screen for the defence of Egypt."

Furthermore, "if one of the communities had to be antagonized, it was prefer-
able that a solution be found which did not involve the continuing hostility of
the Arabs."[49] The issue was how to devise a settlement that recognized the remnant of Britain's obligation under the Balfour Declaration and the Mandate,
dealt with the problem of Jewish refugees from Europe, and did not lead to
"continuing hostility of the Arabs."

The British task was not made easier by pressure from the United States.
Immediately after the end of the war, Truman had sent Earl Harrison, a former
commissioner of immigration and naturalization, to Europe to assess the
situation facing displaced persons there. Harrison reported back in August
1945, and his findings profoundly impressed Truman with their dismal plight
—especially that of the Jewish displaced persons. This concern, along with
continuing pressure from the Zionist lobby, led him to consistently press the
British to admit 100,000 Jews into Palestine. The British suggested a joint
Anglo-American committee of inquiry to study the issue, and Truman readily
agreed. When the committee reported back on April 20, 1946, it unanimously
endorsed Truman's recommendation, creating consternation within His Majesty's government.[50] Truman further angered the British with a speech on
October 4, 1946 (in time for midterm congressional elections), suggesting "a
solution along the lines proposed by the Jewish Agency."[51] Agreeing to this, in
the British view, would defeat all hope of maintaining sound relations with the
Arab world.

Amidst the cabinet debate, Arthur Creech Jones continued to favor partition—if a solution could be found agreeable to both Jews and Arabs. With the
blessing of the cabinet, he set out to discover whether such a plan could be
devised. A conference was convened in London in late January 1947 with delegates from a number of Middle Eastern countries. The Jewish Agency declined
to take part, but Creech Jones arranged with David Ben-Gurion for members
of the executive to be in London for informal discussions.

Initial meetings of British officials with the Arabs on the one hand and the
Zionists on the other hand revealed the intransigence of the protagonists. Jamal
Husseini of the Palestine Arabs was adamant against partition, because "the
Arabs wanted self-determination." Dr. F. Jamali of Iraq complained that "the
Arab peoples were the only ones who seemed called upon to pay for what Hitler
had done to the Jews." Faris Bey Khouri of Syria argued that the Jews "had to be
persuaded to abandon the idea of a state based on religious and racial principles." C. Bey Chamoun of Lebanon implored the British to consider what the
reaction would be "if a third power were to impose upon her an alien element

whose presence was of a nature to disrupt her national life and her political and territorial unity." Ben-Gurion, while admitting that the word *state* had not been included in the Mandate, argued that "the future of the Arab peoples and culture did not depend on" Palestine as it did for the Jews. The Zionists needed Palestine "for the unborn generations of the Jewish people." With a display of impatience, Bevin noted that "it was a dreadful thing that Jews should be killing British soldiers who had fought their battles for them against Germany." The conference broke up with the foreign and colonial secretaries concluding that there was no prospect of a solution acceptable to both parties.[52]

A further intense debate ensued when Bevin and Creech Jones reported back to the cabinet. In frustration, the cabinet concluded that no solution could be found that protected British interests, and the best approach would be to submit the problem to the United Nations without any British recommendation. (This was the same period, January 1947, when the cabinet was taking the agonizing decision to phase out British control of India and to turn over responsibility for Greece and Turkey to the United States.) After consultation with the other members of the Security Council, the British representative to the United Nations, Sir Alexander Cadogan, requested a special session of the General Assembly, which met in New York on April 28.

Cadogan told the General Assembly that Britain "would welcome any acceptable solution, but should not have sole responsibility for enforcing one not accepted by both parties."[53] The upshot was appointment of a United Nations Special Committee on Palestine (UNSCOP) made up of eleven neutral states, not including any of the Great Powers or an Arab state. Worldwide sympathy for the Jews and anti-British outbursts were created when the British turned back the refugee ship *Exodus-1947,* with 4,500 Jewish displaced persons aboard, from Palestine during the time that UNSCOP was considering what to recommend. How much that episode influenced the Committee is not known, but when UNSCOP reported back on August 31, the majority suggested partition into an Arab state, a Jewish state, and an internationally administered city of Jerusalem.[54] The issue was now in the hands of the United Nations, of which the United States was an active member.

The United Nations and the United States

When the question of whether or not to adopt the recommendations of the Special Committee on Palestine came up in the General Assembly, the United States took a position generally supportive of partition but was not initially active in lobbying other members for approval.⁵⁵ The Arab delegations were unalterably opposed to partition and preferred some sort of international control of an undivided Palestine, with a long-range hope of full Arab sovereignty over the whole of that land. Some Zionist extremists, such as Menachem Begin, leader of the Jewish underground army, the Irgun, adamantly called for gaining the whole of Eretz Israel (the Land of Israel).⁵⁶ But there were moderates such as Chaim Weizmann, the grand old man of the Zionist movement, who had argued as far back as the British consideration of partition in 1937 that "it was possible to take two bites of the cherry" and that one could "look toward future expansion by some means or other."⁵⁷ The Zionists agreed among themselves to strive for partition as at least the final realization of a state of their own, and they furiously began to work through whatever channels they could to reach the home governments of wavering delegates to gain their votes.⁵⁸

At one point in the debate, the question came up as to whether or not the Negev should be included in the area to be assigned to the Jews, and here the Zionists believed that they needed the direct support of President Truman. But they had a problem. On the one hand, Chaim Weizmann, while president of the World Zionist Organization, had met with Truman in August 1945, and the two had acquired a high degree of mutual respect. But in 1946 the firebrand Rabbi Abba Hillel Silver had replaced the moderate Weizmann in the leadership of the WZO, and Silver had made the mistake of pounding on Truman's desk in a meeting in July. As a result of that incident, and other continuing pressures, Truman had decreed that Silver or any other spokesman for the WZO would be forever barred from his office. But the issue of the Negev was too important, and WZO leaders swallowed their pride in 1947 and asked Weizmann, who at that point had no official position in the WZO, to intervene.⁵⁹

Weizmann had returned from England to be on hand during the critical debate, and after several weeks he gained an audience with the president at 1:00 p.m. on November 19.⁶⁰ The timing of that meeting could not have been more fortuitous. Hoping to diminish Arab resistance to partition, the State Department had informed the American representative at the United Nations, Herschel Johnson, that the United States would agree to adding the Negev to the proposed Arab state, and Johnson was meeting with representatives of the Jewish Agency at 3:00 p.m. to inform them of the decision. Weizmann waxed eloquent in discussing the history and geography of the Negev, and he told Truman that the Jews could make the desert "bloom as the rose." Truman had not followed the details of the debate, but he liked the elderly gentleman, and he agreed that the area could stay within the proposed Jewish state. To ensure that his decision was carried out, Truman telephoned Johnson at the UN, just as Johnson was starting to tell the Jewish delegation that the United States would support deletion of the Negev from the Jewish state. After being called to the telephone just as the meeting was getting under way, Johnson returned and told the delegation the exact opposite—the Negev would remain in the Jewish area. A close call. And a premonition of a highly embarrassing case of mixed signals between the president and the State Department six months later.

Weizmann continued to appeal by mail to Truman for American support of partition, and he made one more highly effective move while he was in New York. He was granted permission to address the UN General Assembly, and he used the occasion to appeal directly to Christian statesmen through the use of biblical language. He quoted from Isaiah 11:11–12: "[T]he Lord shall set his hand again the second time to recover the remnant of his people.... And he shall set up an ensign for the nations, and shall assemble the outcasts of Israel, and gather together the dispersed of Judah from the four corners of the earth."

Many of those present believed that Weizmann's appeal made the decisive difference. Whatever the reason, on November 29 the General Assembly approved partition by a vote of 33 to 13. *All eleven Muslim states voted against partition.* Britain abstained.[61] The issue now was implementation.

The plan called for creation of a UN commission (with representatives from Czechoslovakia, Bolivia, Denmark, the Philippines, and Panama plus a sizable staff) to carry out a fairly detailed sequence of events.[62] The commission was to arrive in Palestine in late December and progressively take over administrative responsibility from the British, starting at the Egyptian border and working northward. The Mandate would be formally terminated no later than August 1, 1948, and during an interim period the committee was to work with the Jewish Agency and the Arab Higher Committee to create provisional governments in both areas with a joint economic council. The British were also supposed to make available a port to allow for substantial Jewish immigration.

Almost at once the plan proved unworkable.[63] The British announced that they would complete withdrawal and terminate the Mandate by May 15, 1948, and for administrative and security reasons they would not permit the commission to enter Palestine until two weeks prior to that. No port would be made available for Jewish immigration. Presumably to placate the Arabs, they simply chose not to facilitate partition. The commission itself did not get organized until January, and it set up operations in New York, not Palestine. The Arabs, for their part, were vehemently opposed and refused to cooperate with the commission. King Farouk of Egypt and King Abdullah of Trans-Jordan both warned that they might resist partition by force of arms, and Arab irregulars—including contingents from Syria and Iraq—entered Palestine to fight alongside Palestinian guerrillas. Begin's Irgun launched its first operation against the Arabs at Haifa on December 11. By the spring of 1948 it became clear that the partition plan was impossible to implement without a major commitment of armed forces by Britain or the United States. And no one in either country wanted to go down that path.

On February 16, the Palestine Commission reported that it would require an international police force to implement partition, and the United States began to waver. The commission's assessment was shared by the CIA and the National Security Council, and support for creation of a Jewish state was now opposed by the secretary of defense (James Forrestal), the secretary of state (George Marshall), the undersecretary of state (Robert Lovett), the assistant secretary of state for the United Nations (Dean Rusk), the director of the State Department's Near Eastern desk (Loy Henderson), and most of those assigned to the UN. As a result, Truman authorized preparation of a contingency plan—not to be broached without his concurrence—for withdrawal of the partition plan and substitution of a Trusteeship to replace the Mandate once the British withdrew. On February 24, Warren Austin, the U.S. representative on the Security Council, recommended that the five permanent members collectively decide what to do under the prevailing circumstances. Their delegates met but were unable to reach a consensus.

The Zionists were seriously worried. Jewish groups in the United States launched an intensive campaign to shore up American support. In one week in February, some 22,000 communications regarding Palestine were received in the Department of State; the United Jewish Appeal raised $35 million in two weeks; and clandestine smuggling of arms from America to Palestine continued unabated. In March, the Jewish Agency announced that it was making preparations to set up a provisional government in Palestine as soon as the British left regardless of what the international community might decide. Support from the United States would be highly desirable, and that called for an appeal directly to President Truman. Weizmann had gone back to England, but since he was the only person who might be able to make that appeal directly, he was asked to return.

Weizmann sailed for the United States, and on February 10 he requested an appointment at the White House. But by this time Truman was so irritated by continuous Zionist pressure that he declined to meet. He said that he had heard all of the arguments and did not need to hear more. At this juncture, Zionist leaders *really* swallowed their pride and appealed to Eddie Jacobson, Truman's old wartime friend and haberdashery store partner in Kansas City, to try to open the door. Jacobson and Truman had a warm personal relationship, and Jacobson had entrée to the White House whenever he wanted it. Jacobson was not a committed Zionist, but he agreed to come to Washington. He had never asked Truman for personal favors, but this time he did. After an emotional entreaty, Truman, in his colorful language, is reported to have said, "You win, you baldheaded son-of-a-bitch. I will see him."[64] Weizmann would have his day in court.

Weizmann met secretly with Truman on March 18. There are no minutes for that off-the-record meeting, but both men's memoirs report that Truman assured Weizmann that he personally favored and would support partition. It appears that, from the very first, Truman had supported the idea of a Jewish sanctuary in Palestine—in part for humanitarian reasons, in part because of his biblically derived knowledge of Palestine as the ancestral home of the Hebrew people. His wavering from time to time appears to have been hesitance to take action counter to the advice of his military and diplomatic advisors, especially that of the wartime hero George Marshall. In this case, he made a personal commitment to Weizmann, a man whom he admired greatly.

Unfortunately, Truman neglected to inform the State Department of his meeting with Weizmann, and the State Department neglected to inform Truman that, on the very next day, March 19, Ambassador Warren Austin would release to the United Nations the contingency statement suggesting a temporary trusteeship. Truman awoke the next morning to bitter newspaper headlines critical of the administration for its reversal in policy. He was furious, and there was a mad scramble to cover over the glitch by claiming that the American *long-range* commitment remained unchanged; it would simply require more time to be implemented peacefully. Truman, for his part, sent word to Weizmann to assure him that his personal commitment had not changed. Weizmann was quietly reassured. He had a gentleman's word.

The Decision to Recognize Israel

By this time the question of what the United Nations would or would not do was rapidly becoming moot. The British would complete their withdrawal by May 14, the Jews would declare the establishment of a new state with or without international sanction, and the surrounding Arab countries would attack. Looming in the background was increasing concern over Soviet intentions. Czechoslovakia had succumbed to Communist control in February, and in early March General Lucius Clay, commanding officer of U.S. forces in Germany, had warned of threatening Soviet moves against the encircled enclave of Berlin. (This was a precursor of the Berlin Blockade, which reached full force in June.) And there were indications that the Soviets might recognize a new Jewish state in a move to preempt U.S. influence. On the domestic front, it was clear that the general public and influential newspaper editorialists favored the Jews, and a presidential election was coming up in which the New York Jewish vote would be a factor. The question was what posture the United States should take regarding the new Jewish state. Recognition would be politically expedient, but Truman's military and diplomatic advisors were adamantly opposed to any actions that might jeopardize America's strategic position in the Arab world. In the final analysis, it was Harry Truman who would have to decide. As he had so frequently proclaimed, the buck stopped in the president's office.

Into this picture stepped Clark Clifford, counsel to the president, and David Niles, the president's advisor on minority affairs, who had strong connections with the Jewish community. Clifford was a brilliant Missourian, legally trained, with keen political instincts and excellent command of the written word. While Niles was absent on medical leave in February and March, his duties were temporarily assumed by another aide, Max Lowenthal, a kindred political spirit. With advice from Lowenthal and Niles, Clifford undertook to respond to Truman's requests for advice on dealing with the Palestine issue.

In early March, Clifford wrote two long position papers designed to give Truman arguments to use in defending his position on partition during the political debates leading up to the elections of 1948.[65] Somewhat disingenuously, Clifford prefaced his argument by stating, "One's judgment in advising what is best for America must in no sense be influenced by the election this fall. I know only too well that you would not hesitate to follow a course of action that makes certain the defeat of the Democratic Party if you thought such action were best for America. What I say is, therefore, completely uninfluenced by election considerations."[66] This is what Truman would like to hear, and Clifford, the political insider *par excellence,* knew this.

Clifford, who knew next to nothing about the Middle East, went on to argue that "partition is the only course of action with respect to Palestine that will strengthen our position vis-à-vis Russia." Furthermore, "The fact of the matter is that the Arab states must have oil royalties or go broke. . . . Their need of the United States is greater than our need of them." (In this he was later proven to be right—at least in the case of Saudi Arabia.) He said that by pulling back from partition at this point, the United States would be in "the ridiculous role of trembling before the threats of a few nomadic desert tribes." And, he said, we should answer arguments that our policy was adrift by clear and firm support of the United Nations resolution on partition.[67] In a later meeting, Clifford added the argument that "it is important for the long-range security of our country . . . that a nation committed to the democratic system be established there, one on which we can rely."[68] (This point is still being made fifty years later.) In short, Clifford provided arguments in the vocabulary of national security rather than political expediency to make a case for what was politically expedient. But they did shore up Truman's resolve to adhere to the course of action upon which he had already decided.

The issue between Truman's military and diplomatic advisors and his White House staff came to a head in the president's office on May 12—two days before the Jews were determined to declare statehood in Palestine. This meeting has been analyzed in minute detail by many historians.[69] While the issue before the house was whether or not to grant American recognition of the new Jewish state, the real issue was how to reconcile Truman's strong desire to grant recognition with his equally strong desire to avoid a break with General Marshall, a man for whom he had tremendous personal respect and a man who added considerable political credibility to the Truman administration. With this in mind, Truman assigned Clifford the task of convincing Marshall. Prior to the meeting, he told Clifford, "I want you to get ready for this as if you were presenting a case to the Supreme Court. You will be addressing all of us present, of course, but the person I really want you to convince is Marshall."[70]

The meeting assembled in Truman's office at 4:00 p.m. Wednesday, March 12. Besides Clifford and Marshall, it included David Niles, Undersecretary of State Robert Lovett, and several aides. Truman indicated that the purpose of the meeting was to discuss what, if any, actions should be taken in view of the imminent declaration of a Jewish state. Lovett opened with a long statement on reasons why premature recognition would be counter to American national interests—the strategic issues that by this point were well known to all parties. Clifford then took the floor (literally; he stood, as though addressing a court) and went into his well rehearsed reasons for quick action. The reality was that the Jewish state was going to be declared. Immediate recognition—before the

Soviet Union acted—would gain maximum political and diplomatic advantage. He offered a draft statement that the president could make at a news conference the next day, announcing his intent to recognize both the Jewish state and an Arab state, if and when they were declared.

Marshall was furious. In a memo that he dictated immediately after the meeting, Marshall recorded that he had said this was a transparent attempt "to win a few votes. . . . The counsel offered by Mr. Clifford was based on domestic political considerations, while the problem which confronted us was international." He asked why, when this was a matter of foreign policy rather than domestic politics, Clifford was even in the meeting, to which Truman replied quietly that he was here "at my personal request." The meeting went from bad to worse. In an attempt to lighten the mood, Truman said, "Well, General, it sounds to me as if even you might vote against me in November if I go ahead and recognize." Perhaps in jest, or perhaps in all seriousness, Marshall replied, "Yes, Mr. President, if I were to vote at all, I might do just that." A dead silence fell over the assembled group. This portended a split of the kind Truman wanted desperately to avoid. Seeing that nothing more could be accomplished at this point, Truman terminated the meeting without a decision but leaving the impression that Marshall had prevailed.[71]

What followed next was a classic case of behind-the-scenes bureaucratic efforts to salvage a situation. Recollections differ on which one initiated the contacts, but Lovett, the sophisticated Washington insider, and Clifford, the intimate to the president, met to work out a compromise that would permit recognition without resulting in Marshall's resignation. The upshot was success by Lovett in obtaining an agreement from Marshall not to publicly oppose Truman's decision if he chose prompt recognition *once a state had been declared*. Marshall was a soldier, through and through. He respected Truman as commander in chief, and he would not act counter to a decision once it was made. When Marshall's intent was conveyed back to Truman via Clifford, recognition was in sight.

The actual process of recognition resembled comic opera more closely than high diplomacy. The time when a Jewish state would come into being was to be one minute after midnight Palestine time (6:01 p.m. Washington time) on Friday, May 14. After consultation as to the proper procedure for granting recognition, Clifford and Loy Henderson both telephoned Eliahu Epstein, the Washington representative of the Jewish Agency, to work out the mechanics of recognition. They told Epstein that diplomatic practice was to respond to a request from the provisional government. Epstein had no authority from Tel Aviv to submit such a request, but he did so anyway. With suggestions from Clifford as to the content, he drafted a note and sent copies to both the State Department and the White House. The boundaries of the state were to be those in the November 29 UN resolution, but he did not yet know its name, so he simply typed in "Jewish state." While the taxi was en route he heard over the radio that the name was to be "Israel," and he sent a messenger who caught the taxi at the White House gate and corrected the name in ink. Clifford drafted a news release for the president to authorize, but held it until Lovett reached Truman to officially confirm Marshall's position. That came at 4:00 p.m., but to avoid a premature leak, Truman wanted to wait until the last minute to make the announcement. At 5:40, Truman finally authorized release, and it was read to the press at 6:11 p.m., ten minutes after the new state had come into being.

Understandably, there was wild jubilation among Jewish Zionists in the United States and in Palestine and total dismay in the Arab world. It was the American delegation at the United Nations that was most caught by surprise. The day before, on May 13, the delegation had been authorized to withdraw the trusteeship proposal and substitute one calling for a UN mediator to work for a truce and resolution of the problem. An American delegate was actually addressing the General Assembly on the issue when word of the president's action reached them. Most of the delegation came close to resigning over the position in which they had been put, but Marshall and Rusk prevailed, and this did not happen.

The press release that generated all of this reaction was quite simple: "Statement by the President. This government has been informed that a Jewish State had been proclaimed in Palestine, and recognition has been requested by the provisional government thereof. . . . The United States recognizes the provisional government as the de facto authority of the new State of Israel."[72]

General Marshall confirmed de facto recognition by formal letter two days later, and the Soviet Union conferred de jure recognition on May 17. The United States did not confer de jure recognition until a year later.

Harbingers of Things to Come

While the swift act of recognition was largely symbolic, and significant American material aid did not come until much later, the act was a clear indication that the role of chief Western supporter of a Jewish enclave in the Arab world had been transferred from Britain to the United States. And most of the issues that dominated policy debates for the next fifty years were already apparent in embryonic form. The original refugee crisis was created by a combination of the fear spread among Arabs by the Irgun massacre of several hundred men, women, and children in the village of Dir Yassin, near Jerusalem, on April 9, and the advice proffered by the armies of Egypt and Trans-Jordan for Arabs to evacuate "temporarily" when they attacked as soon as the British withdrew. But rather than pushing the Jews into the sea, as they so boastfully proclaimed they would do, the Arabs found themselves forced into a stalemate by fierce Israeli resistance in the first of the series of Arab-Israeli wars. What eventually developed on the ground was a form of asymmetrical warfare, pitting Arab terrorists against Israeli armed might.

Within the United States, the issues and forces present in 1948 continued to be present at the turn of the century. American and European dependence on Arab oil was still a concern, albeit more from an economic than a military point of view as it had been in 1948. The argument made by Clark Clifford in 1948, that Israel represented a dependable democratic ally in an unstable region, had grown considerably in prominence as a rationale for American support. And genuine feeling for the suffering of Jews under the Holocaust was combined with growing understanding of the anguish of Palestinian Arabs who had been forced from their ancestral homes as a result of the conflict. There continued to be a strong pro-Israel lobby in the United States, now in the most visible form of the American Israel Public Affairs Committee (AIPAC). Also important, as in 1948, was widespread support for Israel among the American electorate, partly due to familiarity with the Bible, and now partly due to repugnance over Arab terrorist tactics. The U.S. government found itself struggling to satisfy all of these interests through support of, and taking the initiative in, a prolonged and difficult peace process.

Summation

A review of the record confirms that by 1948 a highly effective Zionist lobby had been at work for over a decade and that it had appealed to an American concern for the plight of the Jews in Europe and a biblically derived understanding of Palestine as their historical homeland. As a result, it appeared to be politically expedient to give prompt recognition to the new state. On the other hand, the institutions most directly responsible for defending American interests, the

Departments of Defense and State, were adamant in opposing premature recognition in the belief that it would seriously endanger America's strategic position at the outset of the cold war. The two most articulate proponents of these positions were Presidential Counsel Clark Clifford and Secretary of State George Marshall, and it was Harry Truman who would have to decide.

Historians reviewing the same facts have reached different conclusions as to what was most influential in Truman's final decision. Their conclusions have ranged from simply a concern for the New York Jewish vote to general political expediency considering widespread public and political support for a Jewish state, and from an intense humanitarian concern for the plight of Jewish displaced persons to his own biblically derived belief that God had promised the land to the Hebrew people.

While the other factors were obviously there, Truman's biblical background clearly predisposed him to favor the return of the Jews to Palestine. Thus Truman (a Baptist) stood in the tradition of Lord Salisbury (an evangelical Anglican) and the British Restoration Movement; the millennialist William Blackstone and his memorials to Presidents Harrison and Wilson; David Lloyd George (tutored by a Baptist preacher uncle); Arthur Lord Balfour (schooled in the Old Testament); Woodrow Wilson (a staunch Presbyterian); and Arthur Henderson (the Methodist lay preacher who scotched the Passfield White Paper). This religious influence would become increasingly apparent among the general American population as the twentieth century wore on.

5

Christian Influence and
Congressional Support of Israel

It is well beyond the scope of this study to review the entire involvement of the United States in the Middle East over the last half of the twentieth century. This has been meticulously dissected by scores of authors of many persuasions. Instead, it is the intent here to examine the circumstances surrounding the 1995 congressional vote to move the American embassy from Tel Aviv to Jerusalem. The bill contained a clause permitting the president to defer the action if he deemed deferment to be in the national interest. He so deemed it, and the move did not take place. The vote was therefore of purely symbolic value, but the reaction in the Arab world was highly negative. It was seen there to clearly indicate a bias toward Israel on the part of the United States, or at least on the part of Congress. That reaction was not surprising. As it later became quite apparent, the issue of Jerusalem was a highly volatile one among Muslims in the Arab world. With all of this in mind, it appears that the climate of opinion in the United States and its possible influence on Congress at the time of the vote are well worth examining.

Much had occurred between 1948 and 1995. A great deal had changed, but the underlying issues between Jews and Arabs remained very much the same. The cold war had ended, replacing the threat of global confrontation with a focus on regional conflicts. The Iranian Revolution of 1979 had transformed a military ally of the United States into a hostile power, viewing America as "the Great Satan," calling for the return of Jerusalem to Islamic control, and support-ing anti-Israel forces such as Hizbullah in Lebanon. Iraq had been transformed by Saddam Hussein from at least a neutral position vis-à-vis the United States into a serious regional threat, provoking the Gulf War of 1990–91 and ending up the subject of UN sanctions and American air surveillance both north and south. Israel had fought four wars with its neighbors, in 1948–49, 1956, 1967, and 1973, and expanded its control to all of Jerusalem, the West Bank, and the Gaza Strip. It had achieved peace with both Egypt and Jordan and had come to an uneasy truce with Syria, but the neighborhood was still a dangerous one, requiring Israel to maintain a strong military as a deterrent against attack.

Displacement of Arabs from their homeland in 1948 and 1967 had led to the emergence of the Palestine Liberation Organization, led by Yasir Arafat, as the umbrella for a number of anti-Israeli groups. Hamas, a smaller but more virulent organization with an Islamic core, had emerged adamantly opposed to any compromise with Israel. And Israel had scattered settlements throughout the West Bank and Gaza as part of Israeli hard-liners' attempt to create "facts on the ground" for control of Eretz Israel (the Land of Israel). On the other side of the ledger, the United States had intervened to sponsor the Camp David accords of 1978, laying the groundwork for an agonizingly slow peace process for the next seventeen years. The difficulty of achieving peace was made excruciatingly clear by the Palestinian Arab uprising, the *intifada*, begun by frustrated youth and taken over by the PLO in 1988. By 1995 the situation had cooled a bit, but the region was still tense, and it was in this context that Congress chose to act.

The Bible and American Political Culture

The human brain is a fascinating phenomenon, especially in the way in which it attempts to deal with complex events in a fast-moving world. Faced with unclear or ambiguous information, it tends to organize incoming data around old beliefs about what is true or important based on things heard, seen, or read long ago. As one scholar has noted, "Confronted with the need to draw conclusions and make policy on the basis of ambiguous evidence, people tend to fit data into a preexisting framework of beliefs."[1] Christians are no exception. Having grown up hearing Bible stories of Abraham, Joshua, and the Promised Land, or having read about or listened to accounts of the End Times and the ingathering of Jews to Palestine as a prelude to the Second Coming, it is not surprising that many, though certainly not all, Americans simply assume that it is right and proper for Jews to return to Palestine and create their own state there.

As we have seen in chapter 2, a great number of Americans had been exposed to those stories, sermons, and books in the twentieth century. The Sunday school movement was in full swing when many Americans alive in 1995 had been children. And Armageddon theology was a frequent theme of fundamentalist preaching and popular novels. As noted earlier, these influences had become deeply imbedded in American culture. Various polls have reported that 79 percent of Americans said they had received religious instruction as a child; 93 percent said they had a Bible or other scripture in their home; 33 percent believed that the Bible was the inerrant word of God; 46 percent believed that God promised the land to the Jews; 66 percent believed that Christ would return to earth at some time, and 36 percent believed that it would be in their lifetime. Finally, a 1999 poll found that 45 percent of Americans were more sympathetic to the Jews and only 13 percent were more sympathetic to the Palestinian Arabs. Attitudes varied significantly in the 1990s, depending on events in that part of the world, but that distribution appears to be a reasonably accurate reflection of American attitudes toward the Arab/Israeli conflict.

That last statistic is significant: approximately 13 percent of Americans were reported to be more sympathetic to the Arabs. It bears out the fact that, biblical conditioning notwithstanding, not all Americans were unqualified supporters of Israel. And this is consistent with an analysis of the relationship between religious orientation and support for Israel reported by a team of five analysts in 1996: "Evangelical Protestants are more favorable to the State of Israel than mainline Protestants, who in turn are more supportive than Catholics or secular citizens. Even within the evangelical tradition, some stark differences were noted, with Pentecostals and fundamentalist groups friendliest toward Israel. And within each Christian tradition, [belief in] an eschatological doctrine—dispensational premillennialism—predicts positive assessments of Israel."[2]

This, in turn, is roughly consistent with an examination of the positions taken by leadership groups in the major American denominations. Rank-and-file members frequently do not agree with their leaders, but it is significant that the strongest calls for a balanced "land for peace" settlement of the Arab/Israeli conflict have come from mainline Presbyterian, Episcopal, and Evangelical Lutheran churches, with Catholics, Methodists, and Mormons not far behind. Most of the leadership in mainline denominations tend to be more liberal in their understanding of scripture.

Among the sixteen largest American Christian denominations, nine have not taken a position, and only the Assemblies of God have come out strongly in support of Israel. The nine who have not taken a position tend to be more literal in their reading of the Bible, and it could be assumed many of their members fall within the group generally supportive of Israel.[3] A case in point is the Southern Baptist Convention with its 15.7 million members. In 1948, the SBC voted not to take any position on the subject of Israel because it did not want to become involved in a political issue. Then, in June 2000, an increasingly conservative leadership persuaded the SBC to adopt a new statement on "Baptist Faith and Mission" that included belief in the Bible as "written by men divinely inspired ... [and] ... without any mixture of error" so that "all Scripture is totally true and trustworthy."[4] Not all members of the Southern Baptist Convention are happy with that statement, but presumably a significant number are in agreement, and therein lies another group potentially supportive of Israel.

It would be well to interject a comment on the terms *evangelical* and *fundamentalist* as they are used here. As defined by the *Random House Dictionary*, *evangelical* refers to churches that emphasize the authority of scripture and stress "that salvation is achieved by personal conversion to faith in the atonement of Christ." *Fundamentalism* goes one step further. It "stresses the inerrancy of the Bible not only in matters of faith and morals but also as a literal historical record." Not all evangelicals are fundamentalists, but virtually all fundamentalists are evangelical. As used in this study, *fundamentalism* refers to those who adhere to the literal/prophetic interpretation of scripture as opposed to the more liberal historical/critical approach. There are gradations of belief within most denominations; the best one can say is that a particular denomination *tends* to lean one way or the other.

Voices Crying in the Wilderness

There appear to be at least two reasons why several mainline Protestant churches tend to be strong advocates of a balanced "land for peace" approach. The leadership of the Presbyterian Church (USA), Episcopal Church, and Evangelical Lutheran Church in America all *tend* to emphasize social justice over literal interpretation of scripture, and all three have long-standing ties with that part of the world. Presbyterian missionaries arrived in Beirut as early as 1820, and in 1866 they created the Syrian Protestant College, which later became the American University of Beirut.[5] The Anglican Church established a presence in Jerusalem in the middle of the nineteenth century, and American Episcopalians continue to support the work of St. George's College, the Anglican Center in the Diocese of Jerusalem.[6] Lutheran involvement also began in the nineteenth century, when the Evangelical Church in Prussia established a bishopric, hospital, orphanage, and school for girls in Jerusalem. Service to the

Palestinian people was continued after World War II by the Lutheran World Federation, and since the early 1980s the Evangelical Lutherans in America have been active in Middle East advocacy.[7] This involvement has made the leadership of those three churches acutely aware of and sensitive to the plight of the Palestinian people, especially since the 1967 war and Israel's occupation of the West Bank and Gaza.[8]

The General Assembly of the Presbyterian Church approved Overtures expressing support for a balanced resolution of the conflict in 1969, 1974, 1976, 1977, 1984, 1986, and 1995. These generally recognized the right of Israel to exist within secure borders, but called on that country to cease its systematic violation of the human rights in occupied territories, terminate its settlement policies, and end its occupation of the West Bank and Gaza.[9] As early as 1974 it also called for negotiation of "a shared common authority for a unified Jerusalem that will . . . protect the legitimate religious interests of Jewish, Christian, and Muslim groups, including free access to all holy places."[10]

Like the Presbyterians, the General Convention of the Episcopal Church has affirmed the right of Israel to live within secure borders, but it has also affirmed the right of Palestinians to self-determination.[11] It has gone on record that it considers "Israeli settlements in the Gaza Strip, West Bank, and East Jerusalem [to be] illegal and an obstacle to peace."[12] And as early as 1985 it expressed "opposition to the movement of the United States Embassy from Tel Aviv to Jerusalem, except within the context of a broad resolution of Middle East problems."[13]

The Evangelical Lutheran Church in America has taken similar positions. In 1989 it affirmed the right of Israel to exist within secure borders and the right of Palestinians to self-determination, "including the possibility for an independent state," and it called on the U.S. government to "assist both sides in developing conditions for negotiation."[14] It has also called upon the international community "to respect and protect the unique historic nature of the Holy City of Jerusalem . . . as being sacred to Jews, Christians, and Muslims."[15]

It might be noted that the total combined membership of these three churches in 1998 was only 11.4 million,[16] and regardless of the positions taken by their leadership, they do not form a politically active voting bloc.

The Catholic Church, or at least the National Conference of Catholic Bishops, has taken a position similar to those three, but not quite so adamant. In a lengthy and carefully written statement issued in November 1989, the bishops said that they had "a deep and abiding relationship of respect for the Jewish people and support for ... Israel." But they also felt "with new urgency the pain and hopes of the Palestinian people." They quoted from a statement by the pope in 1987 that "Catholics recognize ... that Jews have a religious attachment to the land, which finds its roots in biblical tradition" and that "they have a right to a homeland." But this "right to a homeland also applies to the Palestinian people, so many of whom remain homeless and refugees." They called for a negotiated settlement that would result in two sovereign states and security for Israel. They also called for "an appropriate juridical safeguard" for the "special religious status" of Jerusalem. Again, it is difficult to say the degree to which American Catholics follow the lead of their bishops in matters such as this.[17]

The United Methodist Church has taken no formal stand in the Arab/Israeli conflict,[18] but one of its official periodicals, *World Outlook*, has carried a number of informative articles on the subject with a generally balanced view of the issues.[19] It did, however, carry a piece in 1948 by the president of the American University in Beirut, who observed, "Rightly or wrongly, our strong support of political Zionism, our original pressure on behalf of the partition of Palestine, and our recent frantic haste to extend de facto recognition to Israel, have led [our friends in the Middle East] to believe that the principle of the self-determination of people ... is just a phrase to which America pays lip service only." The same article echoed the concern over American dependence on Arab oil that had been voiced by the Departments of State and Defense in 1948.[20] Despite not having taken a formal position on the issues, several divisions of the United Methodist Church have joined in appeals for a balanced resolution made by Churches for Middle East Peace, a coalition to be discussed in a moment.

The Church of Jesus Christ of Latter-day Saints (Mormon) has also taken no formal position on the Arab/Israeli issue,[21] but its beliefs are unique. From their earliest days, Mormons have felt a special affinity with the Jewish people and their hopes of restoration to the land of their ancestors, "an affinity forged by a comparable quest for a territorial patrimony, and autonomous state, and a unique culture."[22] In recent times, this affinity has been joined by an equal concern for the Arab peoples, as explained in an article by two professors from Brigham Young University in a 1993 issue of the Mormon periodical, the *Ensign*. They noted, "The land that in recent centuries has been called Palestine and Israel was promised in ancient times to the descendants of Abraham ... based on obedience to the laws of God." But in the Mormon view, Jews and Arabs are *both* descendants of Abraham (the Arabs through Ishmael), and "both the tribes of Israel and the Palestinians have a divine commission to come to terms acceptable to each other" and "as a church we do not take sides."[23] While benign, this position does not lead to political activism on the subject.

In addition to individual church advocacy, there was a coalition of like-minded churches and agencies, the Churches for Middle East Peace, which attempted to provide a united voice for a negotiated "land for peace" settlement. Participants in that organization included not only agencies of the Presbyterian, Episcopal, Evangelical Lutheran, and Methodist churches but ten others: the American Friends Service Committee, the Christian Church (Disciples of Christ), the Church of the Brethren, Friends Committee on National Legislation, Maryknoll Missioners, Mennonite Central Committee, National Council of Churches, Reformed Church in America, Unitarian Universalist Association of Congregations, and the United Church of Christ. In an open letter to President Clinton in October 1998, the organization recognized both Israel's need for secure borders and the Palestinians' right of self-determination, but it went on to call for compliance with UN Resolution 242 and an end to "Israel's demolition of homes, destruction of olive groves, confiscation of land, and expansion of settlements." And it expressed the conviction that "a resolution of the question of Jerusalem is essential for peace and cooperation among the three Abrahamic faiths."[24]

Two things are especially apparent in all of this. One is the perceived importance of working out the issue of Jerusalem within the context of a negotiated final settlement. The other is the fact that appeals for a more balanced position have had little noticeable effect on Congress.

Evangelicals, Fundamentalists, and Support for Israel

Americans in general are the most religious people in the developed world, and from a sociological viewpoint there are a number of probable reasons for this. Many of the original settlers were religious migrants, seeking freedom to practice deeply held beliefs. The absence of a state church tied to a traditional regime plus constitutional guarantees separating church and state left people free to adhere to and practice a wide variety of religious beliefs. And as people moved west, churches became the social groups around which people could cluster. Furthermore, in troubled times, religion in general and fundamentalism in particular provide an explanation of the world, a sense of purpose, a guide to action, and the satisfaction of being part of a social group of like mind. The prophetic view especially provides reassurance that God is, indeed, in charge. He has a plan, and we can be a part of that plan.[25] This is powerful stuff.

How strong are the evangelical and fundamentalist movements in the United States? A great deal of work has been done on this question, and much of it has been reported in *The Diminishing Divide*, a collective work by Andrew Kohut, John C. Green, Scott Keeter, and Robert C. Toth. It is difficult to summarize their overall results, but several conclusions are especially relevant. They found that white evangelical Protestants (both strong and less strong believers) represented 24.1 percent of the American population. As a subset of that number, the 16 percent of Americans *strongly* committed to traditional beliefs were predominantly female (57 percent); residents of the South (52 percent), Midwest (25 percent), West (13 percent), and Northeast (10 percent); and residents of small towns or rural areas (69 percent) or large cities or suburbs (30 percent). The distribution was similar among less strongly committed white evangelicals. (African Americans comprised 10 percent of the total American population, but African American Protestants were not broken down between evangelical and mainline in the summary.)[26] In general terms, it can therefore be concluded that evangelical beliefs are strongest among women, and people holding those beliefs are concentrated in the South and Midwest and in small towns and rural areas. These, of course, are generalizations, but they do give some idea of the strength of evangelical and fundamentalist movements in the United States.[27]

In a sense, the rise of the Religious Right is not a new phenomenon in American history. There have been recurring surges of religious intensity ever since the Puritan settlement of New England. There was the First Great Awakening in the mid-eighteenth century, the revival movement in the early nineteenth century, and the Second Great Awakening in the late nineteenth century.[28] However, evangelicals and fundamentalists tended to remove themselves from politics in the mid-twentieth century until the social upheavals of the 1960s and 1970s roused fears that the country was sliding into moral decay. From that time onward, there was booming growth in conservative Protestant churches, and evangelicals and fundamentalists became more politically involved. As one commentator has put it, they became engaged in a "'defensive offensive' . . . against what they perceived as aggressive secular and liberal forces bent on disrupting their enclaves of traditional religion." And they attempted "to shape domestic and foreign policy according to their own . . . theological agendas."[29]

Most of the issues taken up by the Religious Right were domestic concerns

such as school prayer, abortion, and pornography. But strong convictions about
the inerrancy of the Bible also led to positions on foreign policy—primarily
support for return of the Jews to Palestine. A key rationale for this can be found
in a Resolution approved by the Assemblies of God General Council in October
1945. While the Assemblies as an organization are not formally affiliated with
agencies of the Religious Right, and the Resolution predated recent events, its
contents are instructive as to how biblical convictions can lead to support of
Israel in fundamentalist circles. Extracts are worth noting:

> We do not fail to recognize that God had redeemed the children of Israel
> unto Himself to be His people forever . . . (Deut. 7:7, 8; II Sam. 7:23, 24;
> Jer. 31:3) . . . despite all Israel's failures, the Spirit of God tells us they are
> still "beloved for the father's sake" (Rom. 11:28). And the promise is given
> that He who has scattered them will gather them again unto Himself (Jer.
> 29:14; Ezek. 34:12, 13). . . . Every child of God who finds joy in the revealed
> will of our Father delights in the glorious promise of Israel's restoration
> (Ezek. 37:24–28; 39:25–29; Jer. 30:10, 11). . . . It was no small territory that
> God promised Abraham when He said, "Unto thy seed have I given this
> land, from the river of Egypt unto the great river, the river Euphrates"
> (Gen.15:18).[30]

For those who consider the Bible the revealed Word of God and who use
proof-texts such as this, there can be no doubt that Israel must be protected.

The second reason for fundamentalist support of Israel, also based in a
literal/prophetic reading of the Bible, has been the End Times theology discussed in chapter 1. And the ingathering of Jews to Palestine in the twentieth
century has been widely interpreted to mean that the End Times were at hand.
There was some evidence of this in excited fundamentalist reactions to Britain's
wresting Palestine from the Turks as far back as 1918, and even more when the
State of Israel was founded in 1948. These were seen as "signs of the times." But
Israel's initial territory was incomplete because it had not occupied all of Jerusalem. When Israel took the rest of Jerusalem in 1967, it was viewed by some as
proof that the Second Coming was fast approaching.[31]

· · ·

Not all Americans are of a fundamentalist persuasion, of course, but they do
tend to be quite religious. Members of Congress are by no means exempt from
this tendency, whether it is out of genuine personal conviction, out of awareness

that their constituents expect it of them, or some combination of the two. This is most noticeable in the inclusion of religious orientation in the brief bio-graphical sketches included in standard congressional directories. This is in contrast with the practice in Britain, where religious orientation is most fre-quently omitted in such reference works and where that information must be ferreted out in other sources. In American directories it is standard practice to include the religious affiliation of members of the House and Senate. And it can be assumed from an examination of that information that many members of Congress themselves have been exposed to the influences discussed above. In a congressional directory of 1999, 87 percent of the members of the Senate and 91 percent of the members of the House were reported to be affiliated with Christian denominations, as given in table 5.1.

A further question is the degree to which Christian lobbying on the subject of the Arab/Israeli conflict has had an impact on Congress. To probe this ques-tion (and a number of others), the author conducted a series of interviews in the fall of 2000 with staff aides to congressmen and senators representing a geo-graphical cross-section of the United States, most of whom served on the for-eign relations committees of the House or Senate. While the aides reported

Table 5.1. Religious Affiliation of Members of the United States Congress in 1999

Denomination	House	Senate
Catholic	124	23
Baptist	57	10
Methodist	52	13
Presbyterian	41	10
Episcopal	30	10
Lutheran	17	5
Mormon	11	4
Protestant*	24	2
Christian*	14	0
Other Christian**	24 (91%)	10 (87%)
Jewish	24	8
None Listed	17	5
	435	100

Source: Table developed from data in *Congressional Yellow Book: Who's Who in Congress* (New York and Washington: Leadership Directories, Summer 1999).

*Listed only as "Protestant" or "Christian."
**Includes African Methodist Episcopal Church, Assembly of God, Christian Reformed, Christian Science, Congregationalist, Disciples of Christ, Eastern Orthodox, Evangelical, Greek Orthodox, Nazarene, Seventh-day Adventist, Unitarian, and United Church of Christ.

occasional letters and contacts from constituents, there was no awareness of extensive organized lobbying from Christian denominations as such. There were a few reports of contacts from Catholic and Presbyterian representatives, favoring "land for peace," but the nearest thing to a well-organized religious lobby was a combined Jewish-Christian group, the National Unity Coalition for Israel, advocating—as the name implies—strong support for Israel. (The intense lobbying came from the American Israel Public Affairs Committee, with some input from a group known as Americans for a Safe Israel, both of which will be discussed below.)

The National Unity Coalition for Israel was founded in 1990 as Voices United for Israel by Esther Levens, who was Jewish, and Allen Mothersill, who was Christian. They set out to sign on as many organizations as they could, with considerable success. Its letterhead claimed that it spoke for "200 Jewish and Christian organizations representing 40 million members dedicated to a secure Israel," but that appeared to be a rather generous interpretation of the number of affiliates and their membership. Most of the support came from groups such as the Zionist Organization of America and the Hebron Fund on the Jewish side, and Friends of Israel Gospel Ministry, Christian Friends of Israel, Bridges for Peace, and the International Christian Embassy Jerusalem on the Christian side; or from individuals such as Undersecretary of Defense Douglas J. Feith and Congressman Jim Saxton (R-NJ). Its Web site listed its activities as communicating with newspapers, radio stations, television stations, and members of Congress; maintaining a Speakers Bureau; and convening conferences in support of Israel.[32]

On April 8, 1997, Congressman Benjamin Gilman (R-NY), chair of the House Committee on Foreign Relations, entered into the *Congressional Record* the fact that he had addressed a conference convened by the National Unity Coalition at which Israeli Prime Minister Benjamin Netanyahu was the keynote speaker. The April 7 conference had unanimously adopted a resolution of the group's "solidarity with Israel." It said, in part:

> We, the members and friends of the National Unity Coalition for Israel, give unanimous congratulations and commendation to the people of the State of Israel in their tenacious struggle to survive and flourish in their God-given homeland, Eretz Israel. We are firmly committed to Jerusalem as the legitimate, undivided capital of the Jewish state.... We commend the U.S. Congress for passage of the Jerusalem Act of 1995 and urge immediate implementation of the move of the U.S. Embassy from Tel

Aviv to Jerusalem. . . . Israel stands as the single bastion of democracy in the Middle East and therefore remains an invaluable ally to the United States. . . . [N]o people in the history of humanity has a more legitimate right to a place in the ancient land of their fathers. We hold that Israel's biblical, historical and moral right to the land is inviolable, and, as a body representing more than 200 organizations of Zionist Christians and Jews, we stand unanimously with the people of Israel."[33]

The National Unity Coalition held a similar conference in Washington in April 1998, again with Netanyahu as keynote speaker. The audience included a large contingent of evangelical Christians as well as significant political figures—Senators Trent Lott (R-MS) and Sam Brownbach (R-KS) and Representatives Dick Armey (R-TX), Tom DeLay (R-TX), and Dick Gephardt (D-MO).[34] The conferences and the 1997 resolution were clearly reminiscent of work of the American Palestine Committee and the Christian Council on Palestine in the 1940s, although not quite as influential. They did, however, contribute to an image of extensive Christian support of the State of Israel.

Two things were particularly notable in the 1997 resolution. One was continuing mention of Jerusalem as the "legitimate, undivided capital of the Jewish state." This was becoming a touchstone for registering support for Israel. The other was the statement that "Israel stands as the single bastion of democracy in the Middle East and therefore remains an invaluable ally to the United States." This definition of the American national interest ran all through the interviews that the author conducted with congressional aides. Whether or not it was a valid definition of the broad national interest, it apparently became a widely used mantra on the subject.

One of the best known Christian supporters of Israel in the last quarter of the twentieth century was Jerry Falwell. Theologically, Falwell was solidly in the fundamentalist camp, and he gained national attention in the 1980s through his participation in the Moral Majority and his advocacy of conservative causes via an extensive radio network. Before 1967, however, he had steered clear of political involvement in general and the Arab/Israeli issue in particular. It appears to have been Israel's capture of East Jerusalem that impressed him, along with many other dispensational premillennialists, as a "sign of the times." But it was Prime Minister Menachem Begin's deliberate wooing of Falwell that brought him into full support of the Israeli cause. Falwell was invited to visit Israel in 1978 and 1979, shown the royal treatment, and ultimately given a jet aircraft and awarded the Jabolinsky medal for his work on behalf of Israel.[35] His support, however, was not at all inconsistent with his personal faith. Falwell had been quoted as saying that he solidly believed Genesis 12:1–3, wherein God promised the land to the Hebrew people and ordained that he would "bless those that bless thee, and curse those that curse thee." It was therefore for the benefit of America as well as Israel that Israel should be supported absolutely.[36]

Falwell had also suggested that he converted Jesse Helms (R-NC), chairman of the Senate Foreign Relations Committee, to the Israeli cause. It is true that Helms had been adamantly opposed to support for Israel for a long time, especially the use of taxpayers' money for that purpose. During the Reagan administration he suddenly changed course and added his name to a letter to Reagan in which "he portrayed Israel as America's best ally in the Middle East and urged the president to help Israel retain the illegally occupied Arab territories of the West Bank, Gaza, the Golan Heights and Arab East Jerusalem." Grace Halsell has suggested that his conversion was due to a combination of influences. Falwell and Helms were known to be friends, and Helms, a staunch Baptist, saw eye-to-eye with Falwell on conservative domestic issues. Then there was the fact that much of Helms's financial support had come from the Religious Right in his home state, and Israel had become one of their causes. But there was also pressure from the conservative Israeli lobby Americans for a Safe Israel. Whatever the reason, Helms was converted to the cause.[37]

It is difficult to determine exactly how much impact Falwell had on American policy toward Israel. On the one hand, Israeli leaders from Begin through Netanyahu saw him as an important ally. When Begin ordered the bombing of Iraq's nuclear reactor in 1981, the first person he called in the United States for support against a negative reaction was not a Jewish senator or rabbi—it was Jerry Falwell.[38] Shortly thereafter Falwell preached a sermon on his radio network in support of Israel and asked the most influential of the 80,000 ministers associated with the Moral Majority to do likewise.[39] Following Israel's invasion of Lebanon in 1983, Falwell called a meeting of lower-echelon members of the American government in Annapolis, Maryland, to urge support. When Benjamin Netanyahu came to power, he followed in the Begin tradition. During his years as Israel's representative at the United Nations, Netanyahu had regularly spoken at the Christian Right's Prayer Breakfasts for Israel,[40] and when he came to Washington as prime minister he regularly made contact with Falwell.

On the other hand, there is little evidence of extensive direct lobbying of

Congress by Falwell or other prominent members of the Religious Right on the subject of Israel. Interviews of congressional staffs by Ruth Mouly in the 1980s[41] and by this author in 1999 found minimal direct contact from Christian groups on this subject. The best that can be said—and this is undoubtedly true— Falwell and others contributed directly to the *image* of their generating widespread support for Israel and Israel's policies. But whether or not this support is a direct result of actions taken by Falwell and other fundamentalists is beside the point. There is ample evidence that support for Israel is deeply imbedded in the Christian community, and Falwell and others simply reflect the most visible manifestation of that support.

To sum up, biblical influences had created an understanding among much of the American electorate that Palestine was the historical home of the Jews and that it was promised to them by God. There were also a substantial number who saw the ingathering of Jews to Palestine as preceding the return of Christ. When it came to translating biblical understanding into policy, the leadership of mainline churches had generally spoken for a balanced "land for peace" approach, but they had minimal influence. Fundamentalist theology had led a large portion of the population—especially in the South and Midwest—to solid support of Israel. This had been articulated and fostered by a number of small organizations and by leadership of the Religious Right rather than Christian denominations as such.

AIPAC and the Pro-Israel Lobby

In the halls of government, one of the best known American Jewish lobbies on behalf of Israel had been the American Israel Public Affairs Committee (AIPAC).[42] It was viewed by some as the preeminent reason why the American government, and especially Congress, had become a consistently strong supporter of Israel. But the truth was more complicated. It is true that AIPAC had grown into a powerful lobbying organization. And it is true that the lobby became viewed as almost invincible—a force to be reckoned with. AIPAC became highly visible in Washington, but there were a multitude of other Jewish organizations working in behalf of Israel, which was seen by many Jews as a psychological and physical safe haven in a world where Holocausts can happen.[43] Jews might, and did, disagree among themselves as to how much support should be given to particular Israeli governments or policies,[44] but the State of Israel had become a source of real pride for many Jews, fostering strong support for its continuing existence.[45] And, as one commentator has pointed out, the real successes of American Jews has come when "they have powerful allies or face no direct opposition.... Even the community's vaunted success at securing American economic and military assistance for Israel has depended less on the proficiency of its own lobbying efforts than on the pro-Israel sentiments of American Christians, who constitute . . . Israel's secret weapon in the heartland."[46] This is consistent with the detailed study of senatorial voting patterns by Robert Trice in 1977, which concluded that the "pro-Israel sentiments of major, non-Jewish segments of the articulate public are probably at least as important in determining congressional support as the electoral and financial strength of the Jewish community in the United States."[47] AIPAC was a powerful lobby, but it was operating within the context of an electorate generally supportive of the Jewish state.

AIPAC was created by I. L. Kenen and several others in 1954, and for its first two decades it was a rather small operation. Kenen retired in 1974, and his successor, Morris Amitay, expanded the staff to several dozen with an annual budget of $1.2 million. Amitay was followed in 1980 by Tom Dine, and Dine, in his thirteen years as director, expanded the staff to 150, with an annual budget of $15 million and a nationwide membership of more than 55,000. Dine left in 1993, and real control of the organization was reported to have gone to a group of four very wealthy, staunch Republicans—Lawrence Weinberg, Mayer Mitchell, Robert Asher, and Edward Levy Jr.[48]

The attitude of the American government toward Israel had begun to change in the 1970s under the Nixon administration, when Israel began to be seen as a strategic cold war asset. With encouragement from AIPAC, financial aid was channeled toward Israel to shore up a potential ally. But the episode that really brought AIPAC to national attention occurred in 1981, during the eleven-month fight over the sale of five AWACs (airborne warning and command system aircraft) to Saudi Arabia. The campaign against the sale was waged by a broad coalition of Jewish organizations, with AIPAC responsible for the direct lobbying of Congress. AIPAC actually lost the battle; Congress did not vote to cancel the sale, and it was finally approved by President Reagan. But the strength of the lobbying made a profound impression in Washington. J. J. Goldberg has argued that the AWAC battle created the image of AIPAC's power.[49] There was another interesting development. "Given its awesome reputation among lawmakers on Capitol Hill as the political voice of organized Jewry," writes Goldberg, "the lobby could often sell administration policies that the White House itself could not sell. AIPAC was regularly enlisted to line up congressional support for the overall foreign aid package, an unpopular program with little grassroots backing outside the Jewish community." And in 1983, AIPAC's Tom Dine "was the only professional lobbyist named to a blue-ribbon citizens' commission assembled by Secretary of State George Schultz to review the U.S. foreign-aid program."[50] The image of power creates power.

Another of AIPAC's efforts had been an annual policy conference in Washington, climaxed by a congressional dinner with hundreds of members of Congress and dozens of foreign diplomats in attendance. The conference chair always read a lengthy "roll call" naming every senator, representative, and ambassador present. The dinner was followed by receptions hosted by AIPAC regional divisions. Those who would like Jewish campaign support found it beneficial to be included in the roll call and to attend the receptions. The importance of Jewish support had been brought home by knowledge of what had happened when AIPAC and other Jewish organizations campaigned *against* a candidate. One of the best known cases was that of Senator Charles Percy (R-IL), whose defeat in 1984 was due—in part—to massive Jewish opposition.[51]

AIPAC maintained branch offices in Atlanta, Chicago, Dallas, Florida, Houston, Los Angeles, Montana, New York, San Francisco, and Seattle, and through these channels it was able to mount massive grassroots campaigns of telephone calls, letters, and e-mail to members of Congress whenever a critical issue was pending. It did a certain amount of direct lobbying of key representatives and senators by regular visits to their offices to discuss current issues and quietly make its presence known. But its most effective approach was probably the exceptionally well researched material on the Middle East that it distributed to congressmen in the form of a biweekly *Near East Report* and periodic special studies. One of these documents, entitled "Israel: A Fellow Democracy," made its argument quite clear:

> As an alliance between two free and democratic nations, the U.S.–Israel relationship has a strength, resiliency, and longevity not possible in relationships with nondemocratic countries. Our relationship with Arab countries depends on continued control of the current dictator, monarch, or regime. It is in our interest to strengthen relationships with democracies.[52]

The argument that Israel should be supported because it was a reliable democratic ally in the Middle East was heard again and again in this author's interviews with congressional aides in September 2000. People may have brought that idea with them when they came to Washington, but it is clearly one that resonated with members of Congress and their aides, and it had been hammered home by AIPAC. The result of all this led *Fortune* magazine in 1997 to report that AIPAC had become the second most powerful lobby in Washington, second only to the American Association of Retired Persons (AARP).[53]

The other pro-Israel group mentioned by almost all of the congressional aides interviewed was Americans for a Safe Israel (AFSI). Founded in 1971 as a "think tank" for conservative professors and other Middle East experts, AFSI had expanded into a membership organization with essentially the same mission as AIPAC, but on a far smaller scale. It argued that "the existence of a strong Israel is of great importance to the security of the United States and Western interests in the Middle East," and it was "convinced that a peaceful settlement of the Arab-Israeli conflict [would] only occur when the Arabs" realized that Israel could not "be defeated militarily or any other way." Like AIPAC, Americans for a Safe Israel held annual conventions, issued position papers, and published a monthly magazine, *Outpost,* with information and commentary on Israel and the Arab-Israeli conflict.[54] It is difficult to assess the impact of AFSI, but it constituted one more source of data on the Middle East provided to members of Congress.

In general, the most important reason cited by congressional aides for support of Israel was the fact that Israel was a democratic ally "in a dangerous part of the world." But Judeo-Christian cultural ties to the Holy Land were also mentioned. One especially insightful aide observed that "the trips which Jewish groups organize for staffers and members of Congress have an impact which Jews do not understand. They emphasize security and Jewish historical links to the land, but to Christians, seeing the places associated with Christianity (such as Bethlehem) creates a visceral link to the land for them. Seeing potentially unruly Palestinians at those sites makes them want to be sure the sites are protected by Israel." To repeat what has been said earlier, AIPAC and other pro-Israel Jewish organizations constitute a powerful influence on the American Congress, but they are operating in a cultural context generally supportive of Israel. For many congressmen and senators, there is something to be gained through support and nothing to be gained from opposition. And while there are voices in America calling for a more balanced approach, there are no counter lobbies as effective as AIPAC.

Israel as a Strategic Ally

The onset of the cold war, the perceived alignment of Egypt and Syria with the Soviet Union, and the Arab-Israeli wars of 1967 and 1973 caused many in Washington to view Israel as a major strategic ally. Israel was also seen as a source of useful intelligence from inside the Soviet bloc in Eastern Europe. This view was clearly encouraged by the pro-Israel lobby, and it found no serious opposition from other major groups. In 1983 the General Accounting Office was commissioned to do a major study of all aspects of American aid to Israel, and it canvassed numerous agencies for input—including the Departments of State and Defense and selected American and Israeli civilian and military officials. The opening statement of its report presumably reflects a broad consensus of thinking in Washington at that time:

> The United States has a commitment to Israel's continued national existence. This commitment is predicated not only upon *Israel's value as a strategic asset* but upon U.S. friendship with Israel which dates back to when President Truman recognized Israel on May 14, 1948. Additionally it is rooted in shared cultural, religious, and political values. . . .
>
> The United States and Israel are in general agreement concerning the nature and extent of the Soviet threat to the region. However, the Israeli Government is concerned about U.S. efforts to assist various Arab countries to improve their military forces and thus achieve a strategic consensus against Soviet intrusion into the region. . . . On the one hand, the United States has not yielded from its commitment to assist Israel to maintain its economic health and qualitative military superiority.... [But it also recognizes that] certain Arab nations, such as Saudi Arabia, are an important source of oil for the United States, Western Europe, and Japan. Other Arab countries in the Middle East serve to check ... Soviet expansion in the region.[55]

The statement expressed clear support for Israel, but it also noted the need to maintain a relatively balanced position vis-à-vis Israel and its Arab neighbors.

Circumstances changed, but the American position did not. The Soviet Union collapsed, and the cold war ended; Syria lost the backing of the Soviets; and Egypt turned from the Soviet Union to the United States as a source of support. Then, in the Gulf War, Israel deliberately stayed out of the fighting to make possible an American alliance with Saudi Arabia and Syria, making

Israel's value as a military ally problematic. But the rest of the statement remained true. American support continued to be "rooted in shared cultural, religious, and political values." That position was reinforced by a pro-Israel lobby and not opposed by any significant block of voters. And access to oil remained an issue.

In economic terms, America's support of Israel had been tangible and continuing. Succeeding American administrations had recommended and Congress had approved substantial subsidies for both the Israeli economy and its military. Between 1949 and 1995, this amounted to a total of $65 billion. Since 1976 Israel had been the largest single recipient of U.S. foreign assistance, and since 1985 Israel had received over $3 billion annually. The assistance had been broken down into military loans, military grants, economic loans, economic grants, and other special grants and loans (see table 5.2).

In a 1999 report on aid to Israel, the Congressional Research Service noted that "U.S. aid to Israel has some unique aspects, such as loans with repayment waived . . . a pledge to provide Israel with economic assistance equal to the amount Israel owes the United States for previous loans . . . permitting the use of U.S. military assistance for military purchases in Israel [rather than in the United States as required of other countries, and] receiving all of its assistance in the first 30 days of the fiscal year rather than in 3 or 4 installments as other countries do [permitting Israel to earn interest on the money before it was spent]."[56] In financial terms, this was a clear indication of solid American support for Israel.

In the political arena, the argument that Israel should be supported because it was a *strategic* ally continued well past the demise of the Soviet Union. In the election year of 1992 it appeared in both the Democratic and Republican national platforms. The Democratic statement was fairly short, affirming that the "end of the Cold War does not alter America's deep interest in our long-stand-

Table 5.2. U.S. Assistance to Israel, FYs 1949–95 (millions of dollars)

Military loans	$ 11,212.5
Military grants	27,214.9
Economic loans	1,516.5
Economic grants	21,922.4
Other loans and grants	3,164.6
Total	$ 65,030.9

Source: CRS Issue Brief: Israel: U.S. Foreign Assistance (Washington: Congressional Research Service, Library of Congress, October 28, 1999, Order Code IB5066), CRC 13 and 14.

ing special relationship with Israel, based on shared values, a mutual commitment to democracy, and a strategic alliance that benefits both nations."[57] The Republican platform was considerably longer, but it ran along the same lines. It declared that "Israel's demonstrated strategic importance to the United States, as our most reliable and capable ally in this part of the world, is more important than ever. This strategic relationship, with its unique moral dimension, explains the understandable support Israel receives from millions of Americans."[58]

Solid American support for Israel might be thoroughly understandable for other reasons, but Israel's military value in defense of America's other regional interests (such as oil) had become questionable. That fact notwithstanding, political rhetoric emphasizing Israel's strategic importance continued unabated. There was even one curious statement in the Republican platform to the effect that the "strong ties between the U.S. and Israel were demonstrated during the Gulf War when Israel chose not to retaliate against repeated missile attacks, even though they caused severe damage and loss of life."[59] Strong ties, yes, but in that instance, Israel appeared to be a strategic *liability* rather than a strategic *asset*.

Be that as it may, it had become politically expedient to include statements such as these in the national platforms of both parties. As will be seen below, the executive branch strongly preferred to hold back and resolve the status of Jerusalem in final negotiations, but the legislative branch had no such compunctions.

Congress, the American Embassy, and Jerusalem

Although the congressional vote on moving the American embassy from Tel Aviv to Jerusalem did not come until 1995, the issue had a long history, dating back as far as 1949, when the government of Israel began to move the offices of the president, the prime minister, and the Knesset to West Jerusalem. Most countries of the world, including the United States and almost all European countries, kept their embassies in Tel Aviv, but over time fourteen smaller countries—mostly in Latin America—established theirs in Jerusalem.[60] Pressure on the United States to move its embassy to Jerusalem began in 1978, when the Zionist Organization of America was responsible for the submission of over 100,000 letters to the White House, calling for such a move.[61] Then, in 1980, the Israeli Knesset approved a bill declaring Jerusalem to be the undivided capital of the State of Israel. In reaction, the UN General Assembly, by a vote of 99 to 0 with 20 abstentions, called upon all nations with embassies in Jerusalem to move them out, since the final status of Jerusalem had yet to be determined by negotiation. Sixteen nations complied, leaving only two small ones in Jerusalem—Costa Rica and El Salvador.[62] In the United States, the issue began to receive increasing attention.

In September 1983, Senator Daniel Patrick Moynihan (D-NY) offered an amendment to a State Department authorization bill that would have made it law that the "United States . . . maintain no embassy in Israel that is not located in the city of Jerusalem." Senator Charles Percy (R-IL), then chair of the Senate Foreign Relations Committee, prevailed upon Moynihan to withdraw the amendment by promising to hold full hearings on the issue as soon as it could be arranged. As a consequence, independent bills were introduced to have the embassy moved, and extensive hearings were held before the Senate Foreign Relations Committee, commencing in February 1984,[63] and concurrently before a joint meeting of two subcommittees of the House Foreign Affairs Committee, starting in April 1984.[64] The testimony before those committees provides an excellent overview of the arguments on both sides of the issue. (Some of the statements would be eerily predictive of the dynamics of the al-Aqsa intifada, which exploded in Jerusalem sixteen years later.)

There were more than two dozen witnesses before the House committees—almost equally divided between those who supported and those who opposed the legislation. In testimony before the House committees, Alleck Resnick, president of the Zionist Organization of America, argued that Israel was America's "staunchest friend and democratic ally in the Middle East" and withholding the American embassy from the Israeli capital was "an unjustifiable insult to the people of Israel."[65] Tom Dine, executive director of AIPAC, argued that passage of the bill would "bring U.S. policy in line with the 35-year reality that Jerusalem is the capital of the Jewish State" and recognize that "Jerusalem is the embodiment of Jewish history, the heart and soul of the Jewish people. For 3,000 years, Jerusalem has been the focus of their national and religious yearning. . . . No Israeli Government which so much as implied relinquishing Jerusalem as Israel's capital would survive in power for a day. Nor would any duly elected Israeli Government, regardless of its political complexion, countenance an outside party again being given control of the nation's capital."[66]

The Religious Right was supportive of this line of argument, but for different reasons. Jerry Falwell, as president of the Moral Majority, testified that "Tel Aviv is the brainchild of man; Jerusalem is the heartthrob of God. Moving our embassy from exile in Tel Aviv to its rightful home in Jerusalem would tell the world that our commitment to this single democracy in the Middle East is irrevocable; that ... we stand behind Israel's right to exist.... [No] shortage of oil or any other reason will allow us to sacrifice our friend on the altar of expediency." He also noted that "there are hundreds of references to Jerusalem in both the Old and New Testaments," but God "made no reference to Tel Aviv."[67] Richard Hellman, representing the International Christian Embassy, Jerusalem, went further. He argued that "this is an issue of principle which is based on the Holy Scriptures—both the Jewish Scriptures and the New Testament. . . . The Lord has greatly blessed . . . the United States . . . in every way. I believe this is in order that we might bless Israel, for it says in Genesis 12:3, 'I will bless those that bless Her, and I will curse those who curse Her.'"[68] A literal reading of the Bible continued to find its way into what was essentially a secular political issue.

There were an almost equal number of statements on the other side of the issue. One of the more articulate opponents of the legislation was David Sadd, executive director of the National Association of Arab Americans. He warned that "there is perhaps no other action which would have a more damaging effect on U.S. relations with the Arab and Islamic world or on the search for peace in the Middle East, than the transfer of the U.S. Embassy to Jerusalem. . . . We support the position of the United States . . . that the final status of Jerusalem should only be determined through negotiation." He read into the record a statement by the Jerusalem Committee of the Organization of the Islamic Conference: "The transfer of the Embassy would alter the universal character and sanctity of the Holy City. This transfer would be a serious violation of international law and U.N. resolutions and would irreparably damage the feeling, spiritual sensitivities and interests of the Arab states as well of the larger Islamic community worldwide."[69]

The National Council of Churches also opposed the legislation, but from a more balanced position. The Rev. Charles Kimball, director of its Middle East office, testified that "the National Council of Churches' position is clear and consistent in support of Israel, calling upon the Arab States and Palestinian Arabs to recognize the state of Israel . . . within secure, defined and recognized borders. At the same time, [it] has been consistent in support of the rights and security of the Palestinian people, both Christians and Muslims. . . . We believe that justice and peace for both the Israelis and the Palestinians require peace and justice for both." Accordingly, the official policy statement of the National Council stated that "the future status of Jerusalem should be included in the official negotiations . . . for a comprehensive solution of the Middle East conflict. Unilateral actions by any one group in relation to Jerusalem will only . . . threaten the peace of the city and possibly of the region."[70]

Probably the most persuasive opposition came from Michael Armacost, undersecretary for political affairs in the Department of State. He reaffirmed America's long-standing support of Israel, but he pointed out that "the United States has consistently sought to encourage peace in the Middle East through negotiations. We have . . . opposed efforts to resolve Arab-Israeli differences through force or unilateral actions. This principled commitment of the United States has helped preserve our ability to serve as the only effective mediator between the parties. . . . A change in the U.S. position on the status of Jerusalem . . . would seriously impair our ability to play a constructive role when the parties resume the search for peace. . . . Moving our Embassy to Jerusalem would be interpreted by many as prejudging the outcome of negotiations, thereby eroding our ability to serve as an honest broker."[71] He pointed out that this had been the consistent position of succeeding Republican and Democratic administrations, and his arguments were reinforced by letters in opposition to the legislation included in the record from former presidents Richard Nixon, Gerald Ford, and Jimmy Carter.[72]

Testimony before the Senate Foreign Relations Committee in 1984 was in almost exact parallel with that before the House committees. Kenneth Bialkin, national chairman of the Anti-Defamation League of B'nai B'rith, argued that the "bill presents an opportunity to . . . recognize the reality of the change in circumstances that has occurred since 1947 . . . following the desecration of the city since 1948 under the occupation of the Jordanians. . . . We have the opportunity to recognize the loving care which has been lavished on this city and to guard it from future attack."[73] Calvin Thomas, vice president of the Moral Majority, complained that "Israel is the only nation on Earth which is denied official recognition of its capital city. It is not right. It is not fair."[74] Dr. David Lewis, an ordained minister of the Assemblies of God, and president of the National Christian Leadership Conference for Israel, testified that hundreds of verses in both the Old and New Testaments "could be cited to support the position that Israel's return to the land, and Jerusalem is a fulfillment of the will of God."[75] As noted earlier, the Assemblies of God had long been among the supporters of Israel on biblical grounds.

On the other side of the issue, David Sadd of the National Association of Arab Americans repeated his warning that no action "would have a more damaging effect on U.S. relations with the Arab and Islamic worlds or on the search for peace in the Middle East than the transfer of the U.S. Embassy to Jerusalem."[76] Charles Kimball of the National Council of Churches sent in a letter in which he reiterated the position of the Council that the future status of Jerusalem should be included in negotiations between "Israel and the Palestinian people for a comprehensive solution of the Middle East conflict."[77] Lawrence Eagleburger, undersecretary of state for political affairs, argued that "the location of our Embassy is intimately related to the efforts of the United States to secure a just and lasting peace in the Middle East. . . . A change in the U.S. position on the status of Jerusalem would seriously undermine our ability to play an effective role in the . . . peace process."[78]

Possibly because two key committee chairs, Lee Hamilton of the House Subcommittee on Europe and the Middle East and Charles Percy of the Senate Foreign Relations Committee, agreed with the State Department position, the issue did not come to the floor of the House or Senate for a vote in 1984. On the other hand, in congressional debate eleven years later, it was revealed that "according to the Israeli press, Prime Ministers Begin and Shamir, successively, asked key senators involved to desist, lest the ensuing political storm work to Israel's detriment."[79] Whatever the reason, the issue did not come to a vote in 1984, but it did not go away. It had become imbedded in the national political landscape.

Oblique references to the issue were contained in both the Democratic and Republican platforms of 1992. The Democratic platform stated that "Jerusalem is the capital of the state of Israel and should remain an undivided city accessible to people of all faiths."[80] The Republican platform said that "Jerusalem should remain an undivided city, with free and unimpeded access to all holy places by people of all faiths. No genuine peace would deny Jews the right to live anywhere in the special city of Jerusalem."[81] In 1992 the House and Senate unanimously adopted a Concurrent Resolution "to commemorate the 25th anniversary of the reunification of Jerusalem, and affirming congressional sentiment that Jerusalem remain an undivided city."[82]

In March 1995, ninety-three members of the Senate signed a letter to Secretary of State Warren Christopher "encouraging 'planning to begin now' for relocation of the United States Embassy to the city of Jerusalem."[83] And 257 members of the House sent a letter to Christopher stating that "the relocation of the United States Embassy 'should take place no later than ... 1999."[84] Members of the House and Senate considered it expedient to let their pro-Israel sentiments be known.

The convergence of two factors brought the issue to a head. One was the scheduled arrival of the prime minister of Israel and the mayor of Jerusalem for a ceremony in the rotunda of the Capitol on October 25 in anticipation of the 1996 celebration of the 3,000th anniversary of King David's entry into Jerusalem.[85] The other was the onset of campaigning for the presidential primaries of 1996. The frontrunner for the GOP nomination, Bob Dole (R-KS), had unveiled his intent to introduce such legislation in a speech to the annual convention of AIPAC in May. And it was noted in the House debate that five presidential candidates supported the legislation.[86] A New York Jewish newspaper, the Forward, observed, "Efforts by individuals to emerge as the 'greater champion of Israel' would be laughable, were it not so blatant a play for positioning in the coming primaries."[87] In this context, legislation that had been introduced in May by Senators Dole, Moynihan, Jon Kyl (R-AZ), and Daniel Inouye (D-HI) was brought up for a quick vote just in time to be announced in the rotunda ceremony. It received two days of debate in the Senate, on October 23 and 24, and one brief debate in the House on October 24. As one House member complained, "No hearings were held; no committee consideration occurred; the administration was not given a chance to state its case before the Members ... and no opportunity has been given to assess the impact of this bill on the peace process."[88] All of this notwithstanding, the legislation was passed by a vote of 93 to 5 in the Senate and 363 to 48 in the House.

The text of the legislation was interesting. Its operative clauses stated that Jerusalem should remain an undivided city, that it should be recognized as the capital of the State of Israel, and that the embassy should be established in Jerusalem no later than May 31, 1999. It required regular reports from the secretary of state regarding progress toward that move, and dictated that a percentage of acquisition and maintenance funds for the State Department be allocated toward that end each year. It did, however, provide an escape clause. It said that the president could suspend the provisions of the law in six-month intervals if such suspension were deemed "necessary to protect the national security interests of the United States."[89] President Clinton had previously indicated his opposition to the legislation, and faced with a veto-proof majority in both Houses, he let the bill become law without his signature.[90] But he regularly invoked the waiver clause and suspended implementation indefinitely. The bill, therefore, became a purely symbolic gesture for domestic political purposes.

With such overwhelming votes in favor of the measure, it is a challenge to attempt a determination of which party, region, or religious denomination was the principal supporter of the action. Rather than an examination of voting records, it could be somewhat informative to look at who spoke on the floor of both houses and to see what they said. But the record of the Senate debate is of little help. The thirty-one speakers in support of the legislation and the two opponents rehashed the same secular arguments pro and con from the hearings of 1984, and there was an even spread of supporters across both parties, all regions of the country, and senators of virtually all religious denominations. No biblical arguments were brought to bear.

The debate on the floor of the House was a bit more revealing. Only forty minutes were allowed for debate, and a number of members obtained permission for their written remarks to be added to the record after the fact. The pro and con arguments were also a rehash of the secular arguments of 1984, with no mention made of the Bible. But the debate revealed an interesting split between the opinions of pro-Israel American Jews (who were more hawkish) and the government of Israel (which was more cautious). Ten out of the twenty House speakers who supported the legislation were Jewish, mostly from the Northeast. But it was revealed that two members of the Israeli government, Shimon Peres, the foreign minister, and Shulamit Aloni, the minister of communications, had indicated informally that "there is no need for [American] involvement at this time"; it would be "liable to cause tensions, which we don't need."[91] This was further confirmation that this had become an internal American political issue.

What had begun as a move by the American Zionist Organization and AIPAC, with strong support from the Religious Right, had been transformed into a political litmus test for politicians of both parties. While the final debates were on secular issues, the lack of serious opposition was derived in part from the fact that the general public was generally supportive of Israel's right to the land. As Robert Trice had concluded, "The pro-Israel sentiments of major segments of the articulate public [were] at least as important in determining congressional support as the electoral and financial strength of the Jewish community."[92]

The Arab Reaction

The Arab and Islamic world reacted to the congressional action with considerable anger. Jerusalem was a sensitive issue. The more moderate Arab American Institute in Washington observed that "the actions taken by the 105th Congress have pressed the Administration to violate the essence of the Israeli-Palestinian accords by unilaterally accepting the Israeli claim to exclusive control over Jerusalem."[93] In East Jerusalem, most Arabic dailies devoted their editorials to the "repulsive and hostile American step."[94] A highly respected Palestinian, Faisal Husseini, in a radio interview from East Jerusalem, attacked the move as "a grave act that could corrode the entire peace process." Nabil Amra, editor-in-chief of the daily *al-Haya al-Jadida*, described the bill as "a shameful interference in the peace process for short-term political expediency." The Palestinian Islamist leader, Shaikh Yusuf Hasan, said that it constituted "a disgraceful capitulation to the dictates of the Jewish lobby."

The Egyptian foreign minister, Amr Musa, speaking in Amman, Jordan, attacked the congressional action and rebuked those "regimes that are hurrying to make peace with Israel while Jerusalem is still occupied." The Iranians pointed out the "utter superficiality of the peace process as evidenced by [this] provocative American decision." The Jordanian Parliament issued a statement decrying the "pushing of this very delicate and sensitive matter in[to] the American Presidential elections battle at the cost of ... peace and stability in the area." Damascus warned that the action would "badly affect Washington's role as an intermediary in the peace process." And the minister of state for foreign affairs in the United Arab Emirates condemned the action as an "obvious siding with Israel which weakens ... the United States ... as one of the protectors of the peace movement in the Middle East." Of special concern was the view of Crown Prince Abdullah of Saudi Arabia that the bill was "null and void because Jerusalem is an Arab-Muslim town where the third-holiest Muslim shrine is located." In short, there was a widespread negative reaction from Arab countries of the Middle East.

The significance of this reaction for long-term American interests in the Middle East should not be underestimated. While it is true that an uneasy equilibrium has been maintained for a long time, the regimes that have participated in that equilibrium are not guaranteed to be in place forever. Fred Khouri, professor of political science at Villanova University, has argued that "lasting American security can be based only on the support of the people themselves, and not merely on some transitory and unpopular regimes." He notes that "while leaders come and go, the people stay forever; and that while repressive regimes (especially with U.S. aid) can maintain their rule" for a time, sooner or later the situation can explode.[95] This view may be overly pessimistic, but it is a concern that appears to have been overlooked in the domestic American politics of 1995.

Summation

Much had occurred in the years that elapsed between Truman's recognition of Israel and the symbolic congressional vote on moving the embassy. The cold war had come and gone, but it had left a perception that Israel was a strategic partner in a critical area of the world, and Israel had been seen as sharing in the same cultural, religious, and political values as the United States. In the general population, at least a part of this outlook was derived from biblical teachings, and it had been fostered by a de facto alliance between the pro-Israel lobby and the Religious Right. In political terms, this translated into a sense on the part of members of Congress that much was to be gained by demonstrating support for the State of Israel, and nothing was to be gained by opposition. This despite warnings from the Department of State that too strong a tilt toward Israel could seriously undermine the American role as a peacemaker and jeopardize its other interests in the area.

Epilogue

The al-Aqsa Intifada, September 11, and the Dynamics of Policy

The foregoing study was completed just prior to September 11, 2001, and this epilogue has been expanded as a consequence of the events of that day. The terrorist attack on the World Trade Center by Osama bin Laden's al-Qaeda network profoundly altered many of the dynamics of world politics. But not all of them. The forces at work in the Arab/Israeli conflict and the determinants of American policy toward that conflict remained unchanged—albeit in a much more complicated environment. At one level, the Palestinian issue appeared inextricably linked with bin Laden's challenge to the United States—as least in his inflammatory rhetoric and some of the reactions on the "Arab street." But at another level, the two issues should be dealt with separately, each in its own terms. The bin Laden challenge really appears to have been aimed at the Saudi and Egyptian governments and at the United States for its support of those governments. Israel's treatment of the Palestinians and American support of Israel was apparently added to gain support from the Arab masses. With this in mind, we will first examine Jerusalem and the al-Aqsa intifada (as it had evolved prior to September 11) and then the bin Laden challenge and the initial American response.

Jerusalem and the al-Aqsa Intifada

In many ways, the issues surrounding Jerusalem are symbolic of the entire Arab/Israeli dispute. Jews, seeking a homeland safe from anti-Semitism and the horrors of the Holocaust, have progressively occupied more and more Palestinian land—in the Mandate period, in the wars of 1948–49 and 1967, and in the settlement movement in the West Bank and Gaza. And Palestinians have consistently resisted—in the riots of 1920, 1929, 1936, the war of 1948–49, the intifada of 1987, and the al-Aqsa intifada of 2000. In the case of Jerusalem, after the war of 1967 the Israeli government expanded the boundary of the city eastward to include considerable Arab areas and created a semicircle of Jewish settlements around that area. It then declared Jerusalem to be the undivided capital of Israel. The most sensitive part of Jerusalem, of course, has been the site within the old walled city known as the Temple Mount by Jews and the Haram al-Sharif (Noble Sanctuary) by Arabs. Jews believe that its Western Wall is a remnant of the Second Temple, and Muslims consider Jerusalem to be their third most holy city, in part because of the tradition that Muhammad made a night ride to heaven from the Haram al-Sharif. The fighting of 1929 and 2000 was ignited over clashes between Arabs and Jews at the Western Wall and on the Temple Mount/Haram al-Sharif.

The issue of Jerusalem has resonance in much of the Arab and Islamic world, especially among the common people of Egypt and Saudi Arabia, the ruling family of Saudi Arabia, and the Muslim clerics of Iran. Although lip service is given to the plight of the Palestinian people by most of the surrounding Arab states, the question of actual support is much more complex. But on the question of Jerusalem, there is a well nigh unanimous belief that Jerusalem, or at least the Haram al-Sharif, should be under unquestioned Muslim control. Until recently, that issue has been dealt with by giving Muslims de facto control of the top of the site, where the Dome of the Rock and al-Aqsa Mosque are located, and Jews control of the Western Wall. Any tampering with that arrangement, or the appearance of tampering with it, can create severe reactions in many quarters.

With all of this in mind, a long line of American administrations had resisted the symbolic gesture of moving the American embassy from Tel Aviv to Jerusalem, because it would appear to take the side of Israel in advance of a negotiated settlement. But within the framework of domestic American politics, that question had become a litmus test of support for Israel. The arguments pro and con had been clearly reflected in the congressional hearings of 1984. Tom Dine of AIPAC had argued that Jerusalem was the undivided capital of the State of Israel, and no Israeli government that so much as implied relinquishing Jerusalem would survive in power for more than a day. David Sadd of the National Association of Arab Americans had warned that altering the universal character and sanctity of the Holy City would irreparably damage the feelings, spiritual sensitivities, and interests of the Arab states as well as the larger Islamic community worldwide. With so much intense feeling on both sides, the question of the final status of Jerusalem had consistently been left for projected "final status negotiations" sometime in the future.

In retrospect, the reaction to the offer made in 2000 by Israeli Prime Minister Ehud Barak, with the backing of President Clinton, should have come as no surprise. Barak offered to give the Palestinians sovereignty over parts of East Jerusalem and the Christian and Muslim quarters of the old city—but not the Temple Mount/Haram al-Sharif.[1] And when hard-liner Ariel Sharon made a highly publicized tour of the Temple Mount with an armed escort to demonstrate ultimate Israeli control, angry youths poured out of al-Aqsa Mosque and began throwing stones at the Sharon escort. That confrontation appears to have ignited the new intifada. There were, of course, a host of other issues involved, including the Right of Return, Settlements, and Borders, but the emotionally charged symbolism of the Haram al-Sharif was clearly a factor. What followed was a rapid escalation of violence, with charges and countercharges from both sides as to who was the most responsible. After months of angry confrontations and many deaths, by September 11 it appeared that the peace process was profoundly damaged, almost beyond repair. One casualty had been the government of Ehud Barak and his replacement as prime minister by Ariel Sharon, almost as Dine had predicted.

The Arab reaction was also highly predictable. One Arab newspaper warned that "the Arab world is witnessing unprecedented levels of public anger. . . . Ordinary Arabs just cannot stay silent while their brethren in the occupied territories are confronting the tanks and bullets of the Israeli army."[2] The Saudi-based Islamic Conference issued a statement following a meeting in November expressing "solidarity with the just struggle of the Palestinian people to recover their inalienable national rights, including the right to return to their homes and property and establish [an] independent state with Noble Jerusalem as its capital." They called for the Palestinians to have "undiminished sovereignty over East Jerusalem, including the holy places."[3] James Zogby, president of the Washington-based Arab American Institute, writing in the Saudi daily *Asharq al-Awsat*, warned that there is "growing Arab anger at the appearance that the United States has sided with Israel's position. . . . The result has been an unraveling of Arab attitudes toward both the prospects for regional peace and the very fabric of the U.S.–Arab relationship. At risk are U.S. interests in the broader Middle East and ties with several important Arab allies."[4] This is where matters stood in September 2001.

Osama bin Laden and September 11

The Osama bin Laden phenomenon did not originate with the Arab/Israeli dispute, although he did attempt to link with it in much of his rhetoric. The roots of that dispute go far back. Seeds of discontent in the Middle East and South Asia were sown by bitter memories of the Crusades; by resentment of colonial occupation by Britain and France in the nineteenth and twentieth centuries; by relative poverty by many compared with Western riches; by perceptions of authoritarian and corrupt regimes linked with the morally decadent West; and by fear of modernity in the traditional societies of that region. Modern attempts at reform of Islam to cope with all this originated in the nineteenth century with the writings and teachings of Jamal al-Din al-Afghani, grew into the formation of the Muslim Brotherhood in Cairo in 1928 and the Jamaat-i-Islami in Lahore in 1941, and threw off increasingly radical groups in the last half of the twentieth century. Among others, these included Hamas in Palestine and Islamic Jihad in Egypt (responsible for the assassination of Anwar al-Sadat and the murder of tourists at Luxor in Egypt).[5] The stage was thus set for the emergence of Osama bin Laden and al-Qaeda.

Osama bin Laden grew up in an exceedingly wealthy family in Saudi Arabia and became a devout, almost fanatical, follower of the Wahabbi version of Islam—by far the most conservative branch of the Sunni tradition, which is dominant in Saudi Arabia. He joined the Afghan resistance to Soviet occupation, moved to Sudan after the Soviets withdrew from Afghanistan, was forced by American pressure on the Sudanese government to leave Sudan, and then set up the al-Qaeda operation in Afghanistan. He was disowned by his family and rejected by the Saudi government, but continued to receive funding from a number of wealthy Saudis, ostensibly for charitable work in Afghanistan.[6] In February 1998 he joined with Dr. Ayman al-Zawahiri, head of the Egyptian Islamic Jihad, and others from Egypt, Pakistan, and Bangladesh to issue a "World Islamic Front" statement of "Jihad against Jews and Crusaders," which clearly outlined his mission. It read in part:

> First, for over seven years the United States has been occupying the lands of Islam in the holiest of places, the Arabian Peninsula, plundering its riches, dictating to its rulers, humiliating its people, terrorizing its neighbors, and turning its bases in the Peninsula into a spearhead through which to fight neighboring Muslim peoples. . . .

Second, despite the great devastation inflicted on the Iraqi people by the crusader-Zionist alliance, and despite the huge number of those killed, . . . Americans are once again trying to repeat the horrific massacres, as though they are not content with the protracted blockade imposed after the ferocious war. . . .

Third, if the Americans' aims behind these wars are religious and economic, the aim is also to *serve the Jews' petty state and divert attention from its occupation of Jerusalem and murder of Muslims there.* . . .

On that basis, and in compliance with God's order, we issue the following fatwa to all Muslims:

The ruling to kill the Americans and their allies—civilian and military—is an individual duty for every Muslim who can do it in any country in which it is possible to do it, in order to liberate the al-Aqsa Mosque and the holy mosque [Mecca] from their grip, and in order for their armies to move out of all the lands of Islam, defeated and unable to threaten any Muslim. [Emphasis added][7]

This was the call to arms behind the bombing of the two American embassies in Africa, the attack on the USS *Cole,* and the suicide mission that destroyed the twin towers of the World Trade Center in New York. It appears that bin Laden's real issue was with the ruling family of Saudi Arabia—both for not being sufficiently "Islamic" by his standards and for allowing American troops on the Arabian Peninsula. Dr. al-Zawahiri's real issue appears to have been with the Egyptian government—for not creating a full Islamic theocracy in Egypt and for suppressing his movement in that country. In both cases the United States was faulted for its support of those two governments, and the other issues were added to increase mass support. Responsible Muslims pointed out that bin Laden was not an Islamic scholar or mufti qualified to issue a fatwa; that the Qur'an clearly prohibits aggressive warfare;[8] and that the Prophet specifically had said that if fighting were necessary, "do not kill a woman, a child, an elderly person, those in retreat . . . and do not destroy buildings or destroy the land."[9] Bin Laden's statement was completely contrary to these basic teachings of Islam.

The American Response and the Question of Israel

The American reaction to September 11 was instant, swift, and forceful. President Bush and his administration rallied the American people; declared a war on terrorism; called for a worldwide coalition; launched a major military operation in Afghanistan—along with indigenous opponents of the Taliban—to root out bin Laden and his al-Qaeda network; declared as an enemy any government that provided support for terrorists; and moved to cut off worldwide funding for any terrorist organization *with global reach.* That phrase—"with global reach"—proved to be significant. It could be, and was, interpreted to exclude the three most significant terrorist organizations operating against Israel: Hamas, Islamic Jihad, and Hizbullah. And thus began a series of maneuvers within the United States to include those groups in order to clearly affirm American support for Israel, despite the difficulties that might cause with America's Arab allies—notably Saudi Arabia and Egypt.

This issue requires a bit of explanation. For several years, the Department of State had maintained a list of foreign terrorist organizations whose funds were blocked in financial institutions *in the United States.* Hamas (the "Islamic Resistance Movement" operating in Gaza and the West Bank) and Hizbullah (operating out of Lebanon) were on that list.[10] Following the September 11 attack, President Bush issued an Executive Order on September 23, aimed primarily at bin Laden and al-Qaeda, which made it theoretically possible for the Treasury Department to seize the assets in the United States of any foreign bank not cooperating in blocking terrorist funds elsewhere in the world. *Hamas and Hizbullah were not on that initial list,* apparently because they were not deemed to have "global reach," but more probably because their inclusion could create friction with America's Arab allies.[11]

The drumbeat from supporters of Israel to add the two groups was prompt. On September 25, former congressman Newt Gingrich wrote to Secretary of State Colin Powell, noting that "both Hamas and Hesbollah have recently repeated their commitment to suicide bombing and to terrorism" and "to ignore them will be to weaken the moral basis of our efforts." Congressmen Tom Lantos (D-CA, ranking Democratic member of the International Relations Committee), and Tom DeLay (R-TX, majority whip) addressed a joint letter to Secretary Powell on October 12, urging that Hizbullah, Hamas, and Palestinian Jihad be added to the list since they "deserve to be a major focus of our international campaign against terrorism."[12]

On October 31, the State Department added Hamas, Hizbullah, and Islamic Jihad to its list of foreign terrorist organizations under Executive Order 13224. This, of course, meant that those groups were placed on an equal footing with al-Qaeda, and the Treasury Department could theoretically seize the assets in the United States of any foreign bank not cooperating by blocking their funds elsewhere in the world.[13] However, in his daily press briefing on November 2, State Department spokesman Richard Boucher indicated that the focus was still very much on al-Qaeda, inferring that action was not imminent against the American accounts of foreign financial institutions that handled funds overseas for Hamas and Hizbullah.[14] For the moment at least, the action was therefore primarily symbolic—similar to the symbolic issue of moving the American embassy from Tel Aviv to Jerusalem.

Symbolism notwithstanding, the reaction from the government of Lebanon, the home base of Hizbullah, was instant and angry. In separate statements, President Emile Lahoud and the cabinet in Beirut retorted that the country was "not changing its policy that holds that Hezbollah is waging a legitimate campaign against Israeli occupation of Arab land." President Lahoud said Lebanon distinguishes "between terrorism, which we condemn, and [a] people's right to struggle for the liberation of their occupied territories." The cabinet added, "We wish that lists reaching us had included Israel as a terrorist state.... But, regretfully, there are double standards . . . that make doves out of occupiers of other people's lands and regard those who resist this occupation as terrorists."[15]

Pressure from Congress continued to mount. On November 16, a letter was addressed to President Bush by eighty-nine senators, urging full support of Israel as part of America's war on terrorism. It noted that the United States had "suffered firsthand the kind of terrorism that Israel has been subjected to since its birth ... [and] ... there is no excuse, no justification for terrorism. Whatever the grievance, the killing of innocent civilians to advance political goals can never be countenanced.... We are confident that you support Israel's efforts to defend itself."[16] The *New York Times* reported that the letter "stemmed from a meeting . . . between leaders of the American Jewish community and key senators," and had been proposed by Senator Christopher Bond (R-MO), with AIPAC being "particularly active in providing advice" on its content.[17]

As suicide bombings by Hamas and Islamic Jihad took more and more Israeli lives, the Israeli government escalated its retaliatory actions, and in this context President Bush made it increasingly clear that America supported "Israel's efforts to defend itself." This, in turn, evoked an Arab response. A senior columnist for the Saudi English-language *Arab News* decried the fact that the president had no word of criticism for "Israel's demolition of homes, . . . armored raids into Palestinian-controlled towns, the uprooting of orchards, the relentless checkpoints that have turned territories into a large prison, the destruction of the Palestinian economy, ... and ... the criminal policy of 'selective assassination,' a policy that no civilized nation in the world today would ever pursue."[18] In short, the Saudi columnist accused Bush of a total lack of even-handedness, a complaint widely heard in the Arab world.

There continued to be evidence that Christian fundamentalist support of Israel was alive and well in the United States. In November, the *New York Times* noted that Tim LaHaye and Jerry Jenkins's latest book in the Left Behind series had made the *Times* best-seller list and that it had an initial printing of 2.97 million copies.[19] A letter in the same month to supporters of the Friends of Israel Gospel Ministry reminded them, "We, as true Bible believers, must be steadfast in our commitment [to Israel].... God has said, 'Unto thy seed have I given this land' (Gen.15:18). The land is Israel; the people are the Jews ... [and] ... His word to us is, 'I will bless them that bless thee, and curse him that curseth thee' (Gen.12:3)."[20] Gary Bauer, president of a research organization called American Values, was quoted as saying, "As an evangelical, I ... believe that the Bible is pretty clear that ... God made a covenant with the Jews that ... [Israel] ... would be their land." He continued to press "Israel's case in a daily e-mail message to 100,000 Christian conservatives."[21]

Andrew Kohut, director of the Pew Research Center, writing in the *New York Times* in May 2002, reported that a nationwide survey showed that 41 percent of Americans sympathized more with the Israelis and only 13 percent sympathized more with the Palestinians. He added that "among white evangelical Republicans—a sizable voting bloc and a center of power within the party—62 percent favored Israel, compared with only 8 percent for the Palestinians." Furthermore, he noted that a Gallup poll had confirmed the fact that "Israel's biblical claim to the land is an important factor in explaining the support of many Americans."[22]

Congress also continued its strong symbolic support of Israel. On May 2, 2002, in an effort led by House Majority Whip Tom DeLay, resolutions approving of Israel's tough stance against the Palestinians were passed in the House by a vote of 352 to 21 and in the Senate by 92 to 2.[23] But the Bush administration exhibited the same caution regarding Jerusalem that had characterized previous administrations. On October 2, 2002, it announced that it would ignore (this time on constitutional grounds) a new congressional mandate attached to a State Department authorization bill that the United States recognize Jerusalem as the capital of Israel.[24] In short, the underlying dynamics of American policy toward Israel remained basically unchanged in the aftermath of September 11 and the increasing violence in Israel, the West Bank, and Gaza.

A Final Comment

It is much too early to speculate on where America's war on terrorism and the Arab/Israeli conflict will lead. At this writing, the war in Afghanistan had wound down, the initial phase of the war in Iraq had been concluded, and the Arab/Israeli conflict continued unabated. No matter what happens next, that conflict will probably plague American foreign policy in one way or another for many years. Future historians will have to assess the degree to which the determinants of American policy described in this study continue into the future. But it is reasonable to assume that an American cultural predisposition to support the State of Israel, based in part on the influence of the Christian Bible, will continue to be one of the factors in the dynamics of policy formulation for a long time to come.

Notes

Prologue: A Synopsis of the Study

1. Moshe Davis, "Reflections on Harry S. Truman and the State of Israel," in *Truman and the American Commitment to Israel,* ed. Allen Weinstein and Moshe Ma'oz (Jerusalem: Magnes Press, Hebrew University, 1981), 83.

Chapter 1. Biblical Criticism and the Rise of Fundamentalism

1. This discussion of the challenges to biblical literalism is based on Nancy T. Ammerman, "North American Protestant Fundamentalism," in *Fundamentalism Observed,* ed. Martin E. Marty and R. Scott Appleby (Chicago: University of Chicago Press, 1991), 8–14; Raymond A. Eve and Francis B. Harrold, *The Creationist Movement in Modern America* (Boston: Twayne, 1991), 12–20; and George E. Webb, *The Evolution Controversy in America* (Lexington: University Press of Kentucky, 1994), 1–6.

2. John H. Hayes, *An Introduction to Old Testament Study* (Nashville: Abingdon Press, 1979), 107–11.

3. Phyllis A. Bird, "The Authority of the Bible," in *The New Interpreter's Bible* (Nashville: Abingdon Press, 1994), 1:56.

4. Hayes, *An Introduction to Old Testament Study,* 120.

5. Bird, "The Authority of the Bible," 1:57.

6. Norman K. Gottwald, *The Hebrew Bible: A Socio-Literary Introduction* (Philadelphia: Fortress Press, 1985), 51.

7. *The HarperCollins Study Bible: New Revised Standard Version* (New York: HarperCollins, 1993). The HarperCollins version contains extensive notes to the text, and the original 1983 copyright for the NRSV is held by the Division of Christian Education of the National Council of Churches of Christ in the USA in New York. The other translation currently in wide use is the *Holy Bible: New International Version* (Grand Rapids: Vondervan, 1984).

8. *HarperCollins Study Bible,* 287.

9. John H. Marks, "The Book of Genesis," in *The Interpreter's One-Volume Commentary on the Bible*, ed. Charles M. Laymon (Nashville: Abingdon Press, 1971), 1. See also E. A. Speiser, *Genesis: Introduction, Translation, and Notes*, 3rd ed. (New York: Doubleday, 1964), xvii–xxxvii; Gerhard von Rad, *Genesis: A Commentary*, trans. John H. Marks, rev. ed. (Philadelphia: Westminster Press, 1972), 13–31.

10. William F. Albright, *Yahweh and the Gods of Canaan: A Historical Analysis of Two Contrasting Faiths* (1968; reprint, Winona Lake, Ind.: Eisenbrans, 1994), 64. While widely respected, Albright's work has not been without challenge; see, e.g., Thomas L. Thompson, *The Historicity of the Patriarchal Narratives: The Quest for the Historical Abraham* (Berlin: Walter de Gruyter, 1974), and Niels Peter Lemche, *The Israelites in History and Tradition* (Louisville, Ky.: Westminster John Knox Press, 1998).

11. Marks, "The Book of Genesis," 1.

12. Ibid., 7. The story in the Gilgamesh epic is a minor digression, but it includes a directive by the god Ea to a "man of [the city of] Shuruppak" to build a boat and take aboard his family and "all the beasts and animals of the field." A flood follows for "six days and seven nights," whereupon a dove, a swallow, and a raven are sent out to find dry land. Tablet XI, lines 31–155; in Maureen G. Kovacs, ed., *The Epic of Gilgamesh* (Stanford: Stanford University Press, 1985), 99–102.

13. Magnus Magnusson, *Archaeology of the Bible* (New York: Simon and Schuster, 1977), 23.

14. *Encyclopedia Britannica*, s.v. "Gilgamesh."

15. Magnusson, *Archaeology of the Bible*, 43. There is an excellent discussion of this issue in Nahum M. Sarna, "Israel in Egypt," in *Ancient Egypt: From Abraham to the Roman Destruction of the Temple*, ed. Hershel Shanks (Washington: Biblical Archeology Society and Prentice Hall, 1999), 33–54.

16. Magnusson, *Archaeology of the Bible*, 64.

17. Gerhard von Rad, *Old Testament Theology*, vol. 1, *The Theology of Israel's Historical Traditions*, 17–19. This is a fascinating hypothesis, well worth considering in more depth than is possible here.

18. Marks, "The Book of Genesis," 1–3. For a full discussion of these multiple sources, see Speiser, *Genesis*, xvii–xxxvii, and von Rad, *Old Testament Theology*, 24–28. The theory of multiple sources has been challenged by Herbert Chanan Brichto in *The Names of God: Poetic Readings in Biblical Beginnings* (New York: Basic Books, 1998). Brichto argues that the various names for God are more likely different poetic images used by a single author.

19. *The Interpreter's One-Volume Commentary on the Bible*, 1273. Scholarly debate on this subject continues unabated. For an interesting recent addition to the literature, see Israel Finkelstein and Neil Asher Silberman, *The Bible Unearthed: Archaeology's New Vision of Ancient Israel and the Origins of Its Sacred Texts* (New York: Free Press, 2001). They argue fairly persuasively that the books of Deuteronomy, Joshua, Judges, 1 and 2

Samuel, and 1 and 2 Kings were composed during the reign of King Josiah of Judah (639–609 B.C.E.) primarily to unify the Hebrew people around a strict monotheism and mythology of a glorious past. Among other things, they cast serious doubt on whether King David's reign was as glorious as described in the Bible.

20. For an interesting development of this theme, see Walter Brueggemann, *The Land: Place as Gift, Promise, and Challenge in Biblical Faith* (Philadelphia: Fortress Press, 1977).

21. Magnusson, *Archaeology of the Bible,* 41.

22. Karen Armstrong, *The Battle for God* (New York: Alfred A. Knopf, 2000), 144–45. Armstrong's study is an excellent account of fundamentalism in all three Abrahamic religions—Judaism, Christianity, and Islam.

23. Moody Bible Institute undergraduate catalog, 1999–2000, 17.

24. George M. Marsden, *Understanding Fundamentalism and Evangelicalism* (Grand Rapids: William B. Eerdmans, 1991), 38.

25. Armstrong, *The Battle for God,* 144.

26. Ibid., 171.

27. Ammerman, "North American Protestant Fundamentalism," 15–16.

28. Armstrong, *The Battle for God,* 171; *The Fundamentals: A Testimony to the Truth,* 12 vols. (Chicago: Testimony, 1910–15). There is an insightful commentary on the mixed quality of these articles in Mark A. Noll, *Between Faith and Criticism: Evangelicals, Scholarship, and the Bible in America* (San Francisco: Harper and Row, 1986), 38–47.

29. *The Fundamentals,* 1:90, 110–11.

30. *Dallas Theological Seminary, Seventy-fifth Anniversary* (Dallas Theological Seminary, n.d.), 2–3. The original name was Evangelical Theological College.

31. *We Believe: The Doctrinal Statement of Dallas Theological Seminary* (Dallas Theological Seminary, n.d.), 3.

32. Webb, *The Evolution Controversy in America,* 82.

33. Ibid., 81–93.

34. George Gallup Jr. and D. Michael Lindsay, *Surveying the Religious Landscape, Trends in U.S. Beliefs* (Harrisburg, Pa.: Morehouse, 1999), 38.

35. *Cincinnati Enquirer,* May 20, 2000, A11. The date most widely accepted for creation of the world by Creationists is 4004 B.C.E., calculated by Archbishop James Ussher of Ireland in the seventeenth century using inferences from statements in the Bible. See Eve and Harrold, *Creationist Movement,* 15.

36. Niles Eldredge, *The Triumph of Evolution and the End of Creationism* (New York: W. H. Freeman, 2000).

37. Ammerman, "North American Protestant Fundamentalism," 5.

38. Ibid., 2. In *Baptist Battles: Social Change and Religious Conflict in the Southern Baptist Convention* (New Brunswick: Rutgers University Press, 1990), Ammerman de-

scribes how the Southern Baptist Convention has been split internally between liberals and conservatives on the question of biblical inerrancy, with the fundamentalist wing arguing that "whether we live or die [as a denomination] lies in our dedication to the infallible Word of God" (81).

39. Gallup and Lindsay, *Surveying the Religious Landscape*, 35.

40. Telephone conversation with Tom W. Smith of the National Opinion Research Center at the University of Chicago, December 14, 1998, regarding his 1996 study, "The Religious Right."

41. This discussion of dispensational premillenialism is based on Robert G. Clouse, Robert N. Hosack, and Richard V. Pierard, *The New Millennium Manual: A Once and Future Guide* (Grand Rapids: Baker Books, 1999), 56–70; Ammerman, "North American Protestant Fundamentalism," 6–7; and Yaakov Ariel, *On Behalf of Israel: American Fundamentalist Attitudes towards Jews, Judaism, and Zionism, 1865–1945* (New York: Carlson, 1991), 13–23.

42. *The Scofield Study Bible: King James Version*, 1917 ed. (New York: Oxford University Press, 1945), 5.

43. Clouse, Hosack, and Pierard, *The New Millennium Manual*, 59. This particular sequence is the one developed by Cyrus Scofield.

44. There has been considerable controversy as to whether or not Jesus actually made the statements about his Second Coming attributed to him in the chapters cited. A basic work on this subject is *The Five Gospels: The Search for the Authentic Words of Jesus*, New Translation and Commentary by Robert W. Funk, Roy W. Hoover, and the Jesus Seminar (New York: Macmillan, 1993). Much of the debate is described in Marcus J. Borg and N. T. Wright, *The Meaning of Jesus: Two Visions* (San Francisco: Harper, 1999). One of the best analyses of the material is Marcus J. Borg, *Meeting Jesus Again for the First Time: The Historical Jesus and the Heart of Contemporary Faith* (San Francisco: Harper, 1994). Discussion of the debate has been omitted here because development of it would consume considerable space, and it is not really necessary for the thesis of this study.

45. Clouse, Hosack, and Pierard, *The New Millennium Manual*, 62–64; Ariel, *On Behalf of Israel*, 20–21.

46. Hal Lindsey, with C. C. Carlson, *The Late Great Planet Earth* (Grand Rapids: Zondervan, 1970), 40–43.

47. It is interesting to note that the 1993 New Revised Standard Version of the Bible translates this word as "but," while the 1984 New International Version translates the word as "and." The word "and" makes the passage more coherent, and it is used here as more likely to have been the version used by fundamentalist interpreters.

48. The spelling in the New International Version is the more commonly used "Armageddon."

49. Morton S. Enslin, "The Apocalyptic Literature," in *The Interpreter's One-Volume Commentary on the Bible*, 1106–9. There is an extended discussion of this genre in the *Anchor Bible Dictionary* (New York: Doubleday, 1992), 1:279–92; and a lengthy expo-

sition of the scholarly debates that have led to the recent understanding of this material is in John J. Collins, *Daniel: A Commentary on the Book of Daniel* (Minneapolis: Fortress Press, 1993), 24–71.

50. William Hugh Brownlee, "The Book of Ezekiel," in *The Interpreter's One-Volume Commentary on the Bible,* 411–35.

51. George A. F. Knight, "The Book of Daniel," in *The Interpreter's One-Volume Commentary on the Bible,* 436–50. There is a full discussion of Daniel in John J. Collins, *Daniel: With an Introduction to Apocalyptic Literature* (Grand Rapids: William B. Eerdmans, 1984).

52. This discussion of the historical/critical view of Revelation is based on Dennis C. Duling and Norman Perrin, *The New Testament: Proclamation and Parenesis, Myth and History,* 3d ed. (Fort Worth, Tex.: Harcourt Brace College, 1994), 447–69; David L. Barr, *New Testament Story: An Introduction,* 2d ed. (Belmont, Calif.: Wadsworth, 1995), 378–417; and S. MacLean Gilmore, "The Revelation to John," in *The Interpreter's One-Volume Commentary on the Bible,* 945–68.

53. There is an excellent study of this subject in Eugen Weber's *Apocalypses: Prophesies, Cults, and Millennial Beliefs through the Ages* (Cambridge: Harvard University Press, 1999).

54. Clouse, Hosack, and Pierard, *The New Millennium Manual,* 73.

55. Ibid., 81.

56. Ibid., 86.

57. Ibid., 90–91.

58. Yaakov Ariel, *On Behalf of Israel,* 12.

59. Ibid., 13.

60. John P. Newport, *The Lion and the Lamb: A Commentary on the Book of Revelation for Today* (Nashville: Broadman Press, 1986), 99–100.

61. Clouse, Hosack, and Pierard, *The New Millennium Manual,* 94–95.

62. Mayir Verete, "The Idea of the Restoration of the Jews," in *From Palmerston to Balfour: Collected Essays,* ed. Norman Rose (London: Frank Cass, 1992), 78–140.

63. Barbara W. Tuchman, *Bible and Sword: England and Palestine from the Bronze Age to Balfour* (New York: Funk and Wagnalls, 1956), 175–207.

64. Verete, "Why Was a British Consulate Established in Jerusalem?" in *From Palmerston to Balfour,* 45–77. Verete has meticulously examined the record on this point, and he gives most of the credit to Palmerston's strategic interests.

65. Tuchman, *Bible and Sword,* 207.

66. This description of Blackstone's career is based on the superb account in Ariel, *On Behalf of Israel,* 55–96.

67. *Jesus Is Coming* was intended for gratuitous distribution to ministers, missionaries, and theological students, especially in Blackstone's "dearly beloved Methodist Episcopal Church."

68. Ariel, *On Behalf of Israel,* 58–59.

69. Quoted in Ariel, *On Behalf of Israel*, 72.

70. Ibid., 72–74.

71. Ibid., 85.

72. Clouse, Hosack, and Pierard, *The New Millennium Manual*, 97–98.

73. Ibid., 98.

74. Moody Bible Institute undergraduate catalog, 1999–2000, 17.

75. Excel Omnibus Study #928 of July 11–15, 1997, done for the Associated Press, 1–2.

76. Tom W. Smith, "The Religious Right: Faith, Politics, Traditional Values, and Tolerance in Contemporary America," typescript, National Opinion Research Center, University of Chicago, July 14, 1996, 7.

Chapter 2. The Promised Land and Armageddon Theology

1. *Christian World*, November 15, 1917, 2, copy in the Dr. Williams Trust and Library in London. This was a multidenominatial newspaper, but heavily influenced by the Congregational Church.

2. Telephone conversation with Tom W. Smith of the National Opinion Research Center at the University of Chicago, December 14, 1998.

3. See, e.g., the Presbyterian Book of Common Worship (Westminster John Knox Press, 1993), 468; the Episcopal Book of Common Prayer (Church Hymnal Corporation, 1979), 891; and the Catholic Lectionary (Catholic, 1970), 49. The lectionaries are lists of Bible verses deemed appropriate for each day of the year, including Sundays, rotated through two or three years, as guides for personal reading, homilies, or sermons.

When used for homilies or sermons, the priest or minister attempts to develop a theme appropriate to the verses that he or she has selected from those suggested for that date. The pages in the three examples cited list verses from the book of Genesis for use on Sunday to describe God's promise of the land to Abraham and his descendants.

4. Telephone conversation with Dr. James W. Fowler on January 4, 1999. His works include *Faith Development and Pastoral Care* (Philadelphia: Fortress Press, 1987) and *Stages of Faith: The Psychology of Human Development and the Quest for Meaning* (San Francisco: Harper and Row, 1981, 1995).

5. In all fairness, it should be noted that the Rev. Dr. Philip B. Cliff of Birmingham, past president of the British National Christian Education Council and author of the definitive study of the English Sunday school noted below, did not agree that stories of Abraham, Joshua, and the Promised Land influenced people in England to support the return of the Jews to Palestine, the evidence presented here notwithstanding.

In lengthy correspondence and telephone conversations in 1999 and 2000, we agreed that no Sunday school lessons ever called explicitly for support of the State of Israel, but I argued that the biblical story of God's promise of the land to Abraham had been well known to many people in England and that Sunday school lessons were one of many sources of this knowledge.

6. Philip B. Cliff, *The Rise and Development of the Sunday School Movement in England, 1780–1980* (Nuffield, Redhill, Surrey: National Christian Education Council, 1986), 1–5; and Thomas Walter Laqueur, *Religion and Respectability: Sunday Schools and Working-Class Culture, 1780–1850* (New Haven: Yale University Press, 1976), 21–24, 160. Gloucester is in southwest England, between Birmingham and Bristol.

7. Cliff, *Sunday School Movement*, 5.

8. The Church of England Sunday School Institute was founded in 1811. Henry James Burgess, *Enterprise in Education: The Story of the Work of the Established Church in the Education of the People prior to 1870* (London: National Society, 1958), 23.

9. Marjorie Cruickshank, *Church and State in English Education, 1870 to the Present Day* (London: Macmillan, 1963), 1–37.

10. Cliff, *Sunday School Movement*, 147–53.

11. Laqueur, *Religion and Respectability*, 246.

12. Thiselton Mark, *For Childhood and Youth: Ideals of the Modern Sunday School* (London: James Clarke, 1913), 11. The inclusion of the Bible in the curricula of the English public schools in the late nineteenth and early twentieth centuries was confirmed in an interview with Rev. David F. Tennant, former head of religious education at Westhill College (now part of the University of Birmingham) at his home in Birmingham, May 8, 2001.

13. Robert W. Lynn and Elliott Wright, *The Big Little School: Two Hundred Years of the Sunday School*, 2d ed. (Nashville: Abingdon Press, 1980), 32, 33, 36.

14. *125th Celebration: Our Heritage in the Uniform Series, 1872–1997*, pamphlet (Committee on the Uniform Series, Division of Christian Education, National Council of Churches of Christ in the USA, n.d.), 6.

15. Ibid., 6.

16. Ibid., 8.

17. Ibid., 9.

18. *Church of England Sunday School Institute, Kensington Centre, 1885*, flyer in the Lambeth Palace Library, London.

19. Letter from Liam Purcell, design and production editor of the National Christian Education Council in Birmingham, February 18, 1999. When this research was done, the archives of the NCEC were temporarily unavailable for more in-depth study due to transfer of the material to a new location at the Orchard Learning Resource Center in Birmingham. Purcell and Elizabeth Bruce of the NCEC were able to glean the information quoted from limited material available to them.

20. Cliff, *Sunday School Movement*, 186. The text is Joshua's last speech before his death, and the quote is from Joshua 24:13. The theme of the speech is citing all that God has done for the people and obtaining a commitment from them to worship God, but the gift of the land is clearly included.

21. Tennant interview.

22. *Sunday School Chronicle*, June 28, 1878, 341.

23. *Sunday School Chronicle,* January 21, 1887, 29.

24. *Sunday School Chronicle,* January 3, 1890, 3.

25. *Ninety-fifth Annual Report, 1906, of the Incorporated National Society for Promoting the Education of the Poor in the Principles of the Established Church throughout England and Wales* (London: National Society, n.d.), 124; copy in the Church of England archives in South Bermondsey.

26. Laqueur, *Religion and Respectability,* 246. Cliff (*Sunday School Movement,* 165) gives the number as slightly under 6 million.

27. Robert Currie, Alan Gilbert, and Lee Horsley, *Churches and Church Goers: Patterns of Church Growth in the British Isles since 1700* (Oxford: Clarendon Press, 1977), 128, 133, 142, 149. Active members in 1900 were reported as 2,205,485 for the Church of England, 1,697,252 for the Presbyterians, 583,940 for the Methodists, 435,118 for the Congregationalists, and 362,479 for the Baptists. The apparent discrepancy between active members (about 3 million) and Sunday school participants (about 6 million) is probably accounted for by the fact that many children were not counted as church members. The reported Catholic total was 1,865,000 for 1894 (153).

28. Minutes of the Synod of the Presbyterian Church of England meeting in London, May 8, 1918, 846; copy in the archives of Westminster College, Cambridge.

29. *125th Celebration: Our Heritage in the Uniform Series,* 11.

30. The cycle of recommended topics consistently included the stories of Abraham and Joshua. *Uniform Series, 1992–98: International Sunday School Lessons [and] International Bible Lessons for Christian Teaching,* 3.

31. Telephone conversation with Dr. Amy Geary, professor of Christian education at Virginia Theological Seminary, on June 13, 2000.

32. Lynn and Wright, *The Big Little School,* 133.

33. *Yearbook of American and Canadian Churches* (New York: National Council of Churches of Christ in the United States of America, 1998), 6–7.

34. Sunday school lessons could not be obtained from the Churches of Christ.

35. Janaan Manternach and Carl Pfeifer, *This Is Our Faith* (Silver Burdett Ginn, 1998), 49, 130, 131. There is an interesting sidebar on p. 131: "Archeological evidence suggests that during the time most likely for an Israelite invasion (1200–1100 B.C.E.) Jericho was not an occupied city. Some scholars have even suggested that its walls were destroyed by an earthquake, rather than an invasion" (131).

36. Gerald F. Baumbach, *Coming to God's Word* (William H. Sadlier, 1998), 76, 79, 85, 116, 294, 295.

37. Telephone conversation with Tina Frazier of the National Missionary Baptist Convention of America, March 2, 1999.

38. *Bible Searchers Teacher—Grades 5 and 6* (LifeWay Christian Resources of the Southern Baptist Convention, 1986) lessons for October–December 1986, 37, and lessons for January–March 1987, 16, 18, 19, and 20.

39. Letter from Douglas C. Schmidt, senior editor, Bible-in-Life Curriculum, Cook Communication Ministries, Colorado Springs, Colo., June 14, 2000.

40. Telephone conversation with Dr. David Hall, Church of God in Christ Publishing House, Memphis, January 22, 1999; telephone conversation with Dr. Richard A. Rollins, National Baptist Convention of America, Dallas, December 10, 1998; telephone conversation with Grace Luis, Progressive National Baptist Convention, Washington, D.C., December 10, 1998.

41. Schmidt letter, June 14, 2000.

42. *Echoes: Upper Elementary Teacher's Commentary* (David C. Cook, 1998), 71, 74.

43. *New Invitation: Teacher* (Cokesbury) Issues for Grades 1 and 2, Fall 1997, 40; Grades 3 and 4, Fall 1996, 80, 87; Grades 3 and 4, Fall 1997, 40 and 46; Grades 5 and 6, Fall 1996, 100; Grades 5 and 6, Fall 1997, 60, 68.

44. Telephone conversation with a Ms. Perry, secretary at the National Baptist Convention Publishing Board in Nashville, June 13, 2000.

45. Lynn and Wright, *The Big Little School*, 140–41.

46. *Leader's Guide: Living the Word, Fall 1978 for Grades 5–6/6–7* (United Church Press, 1968), 12; and centerpiece in the *Student's Book* for the same lesson. Copies in the Presbyterian Church (USA) archives in Louisville, Ky.

47. *Bible Discovery, Grades 3–4, Fall 1988, Teacher's Guide* (Presbyterian Publishing House, 1988), 11. Copy in the Presbyterian Church (USA) archives in Louisville, Ky.

48. *Witness Sunday School Curriculum* (Augsburg Press, 1998), 37.

49. Thomas J. Doyle, *Our Life in Christ Teachers Guide* (Concordia), Issues for Kindergarten, September–November 1998, 45–48; Grades 1 and 2, September–November 1997, 41, 44; Grades 1 and 2, September–November 1998, 44 and 47; and Grades 3 and 4, September–November 1997, 35.

50. *Primary Teacher's Guide, Episcopal Children's Curriculum* (Morehouse, 1993), 39–40.

51. African Methodist Episcopal Church, *Junior Scholar Sunday School Quarterly,* Winter 1998/99, i.

52. Memo from Linda L. Zinn of the General Council of the Assemblies of God in Springfield, Mo., December 9, 1998.

53. *Primary Teacher Guide, March–May 1998: God's People Enter the Promised Land* (Gospel Publishing House, 1997), i.

54. *Primary 6: Old Testament: For Teaching Children Ages Eight through Eleven* (Church of Latter-day Saints, n.d.), 35, 101.

55. Ariel, *On Behalf of Israel,* 4.

56. *The Ministries of the Moody Bible Institute,* undated Moody Bible Institute flyer, and reprint of an article from the *Chicago Tribune* of July 23, 1994, provided by the Institute.

57. Moody Bible Institute undergraduate catalog, 1999–2000, 17.

58. Edgar C. James, *Arabs, Oil, and Armageddon* (Chicago: Moody Press, 1991).

59. Telephone conversation with Tyndale Marketing, April 22, 2004.

60. *New York Times,* June 8, 2000, C13.

61. *New York Times Book Review,* June 25, 2000, 26.

62. Flyers provided by Dallas Theological Seminary, April 4, 2000.

63. Ibid.

64. John F. Walvoord, *Israel in Prophecy* (Grand Rapids: Zondervan, 1962), 115.

65. John F. Walvoord, *Armageddon, Oil, and the Middle East Crisis: What the Bible Says about the Future of the Middle East and the End of Western Civilization,* rev. ed. (Grand Rapids: Zondervan, 1990), back cover.

66. Hal Lindsey, *Vanished into Thin Air: The Hope of Every Believer* (Beverly Hills: Western Front, 1999), 395.

67. Library of Congress Web site: www.loc.gov, query for "Hal Lindsey" July 11, 2000.

68. Lindsey, *Vanished into Thin Air,* 395.

69. Stephen R. Sizer, "Christian Zionism: Its History, Theology, and Politics," doctoral dissertation available on Rev. Dr. Sizer's Web site: www.virginiawater.org.uk/christchurch, chapter on "Hal Lindsey (born 1929): The Father of Apocalyptic Christian Zionism," 1–77.

70. Lindsey, *The Late Great Planet Earth,* 40–41.

71. *You Are Invited to Partner with the International Christian Embassy Jerusalem in Support of Israel,* flyer provided by ICEJ's Washington office, November 18, 1999.

72. Yaakov Ariel, "A Christian Fundamentalist Vision of the Middle East: Jan Willem van der Hoeven and the International Christian Embassy," in *Spokesmen for the Despised: Fundamentalist Leaders of the Middle East,* ed. R. Scott Appleby (Chicago: University of Chicago Press, 1977), 363–97.

73. *Building Bridges to Lasting Change,* flyer provided by the International Fellowship of Christians and Jews, January 24, 2000, 4.

74. Jennifer Moorehead, "End of Days: Israel, Christian Zionists, and Palestinian Rights," *AAUG Monitor* 14, no. 2 (July 1999): 8, citing an article by Arye Dean Cohen, "Evangelical Christians Supply Major Source of UJA [United Jewish Appeal] Donations," *Jerusalem Post,* November 13, 1997.

75. Timothy P. Weber, "How Evangelicals Became Israel's Best Friend," *Christianity Today,* October 5, 1998, 48.

76. Moorehead, "End of Days," 8, citing "Why Do Christian Friends of Israeli Communities Support Settlements?" and position statement from CFIC, www.cficdf.org/moreinfo.htm, which could not be retrieved again in July 2000

77. Ariel, "A Christian Fundamentalist Vision," in *Spokesman for the Despised,* ed. Scott Appleby, 371.

78. Clarence H. Wagner Jr., "Twelve Keys to Understanding Israel in the Bible,"

Bridges for Peace Israel Teaching Letter, October 1999, 2, and *Dispatch from Jerusalem* 24, no. 4 (July/August 1999): 20.

79. Clarence H. Wagner Jr., *Lessons from the Land of the Bible: Revealing More of God's Word* (Jerusalem: Bridges for Peace, 2000).

80. *A Mission with a Mission: What You Should Know about the Friends of Israel Gospel Ministry, Inc.,* flyer published by the Friends of Israel, 2, 7, 8.

81. *Loving Jewish People to Life . . . Helping Them in Time of Crisis . . . Teaching Christians Their Jewish Heritage . . . Introducing: The Friends of Israel Gospel Ministry,* flyer published by the Friends of Israel, 2.

82. Elwood McQuaid, *There Is Hope* (Bellmawr, N.J.: Friends of Israel Gospel Ministry, 1996), 113–14.

83. Grace Halsell, *Prophecy and Politics: The Secret Alliance between Israel and the U.S. Christian Right* (Chicago: Lawrence Hill Books, 1986), 14.

84. Clouse, Hosack, and Pierard, *The New Millennium Manual,* 130–34.

85. Merrill Simon, *Jerry Falwell and the Jews* (Middle Village, N.Y.: Jonathan David, 1984), 62–63.

86. Halsell, *Prophecy and Politics,* 15.

87. Clouse, Hosack, and Pierard, *The New Millennium Manual,* 99–104.

88. Gallup and Lindsay, *Surveying the Religious Landscape,* 61.

89. Ibid., 50.

90. Ibid., 35.

91. Tom Smith, telephone conversation, December 14, 1998.

92. Fax from ICR Survey Research Group in Media, Pa., December 30, 1999.

93. Fax from Rob Persons of the Gallup organization, May 25, 1999.

94. John C. Green et al., *Religion and the Culture Wars,* 332–33.

Chapter 3. The Balfour Declaration and the Palestine Mandate

1. Paul L. Hanna, *British Policy in Palestine* (Washington, D. C.: American Council on Public Affairs, 1942), 36. While long out of print, this is one of the best overall accounts available of British policy in Palestine from World War I to World War II. Others have refined details, but Hanna provides a well-researched overview.

2. Ibid., vii. The introduction to Hanna's book was written by Josephus Daniels, who had been the secretary of the navy in Woodrow Wilson's cabinet at the time of the declaration.

3. Joseph Gorny, *The British Labour Movement and Zionism, 1917–1949* (Totowa, N.J.: Frank Cass, 1983). This is an excellent analysis of that relationship by a professor at Tel Aviv University.

4. Stephen Mayor, *The Churches and the Labour Movement* (London: Independent

Press, 1967), 334–35, and Robert W. Wearmouth, *Methodism and the Working-Class Movements in England, 1800–1850* (Clifton, N.J.: Augustus M. Kelley, 1972), 13.

5. Mayor, *The Churches and the Labour Movement,* 361–63.

6. *Encyclopedia Britannica,* s.v. "John Wesley." For a more detailed account of Wesley's background, conversion experience, and early ministry, see Henry Carter, *The Methodist Heritage* (Nashville: Abingdon-Cokesbury Press, 1951).

7. David Hempton, *Methodism and Politics in British Society, 1750–1850* (Stanford: Stanford University Press, 1984), 232.

8. Ibid., 233.

9. The similarity is not surprising. Marxism has been called "a Christian heresy" in which Marx appeared to some to have modeled his ideal after the communal practices of the early church but replaced God with economics as the driving force toward that end.

10. Currie, Gilbert, and Horsley, *Churches and Churchgoers,* 139.

11. Chris Wrigley, *Arthur Henderson* (Cardiff: University of Wales Press, 1990), 2–3, 40–71.

12. Carl F. Brand, *The British Labour Party: A Short History,* rev. ed. (Stanford, Calif.: Hoover Institution Press, 1974), 10–11.

13. Andrew Thorpe, *A History of the British Labour Party* (London: Macmillan Press, 1997), 243.

14. Brand, *British Labour Party,* 29–53.

15. Ibid., 49.

16. Minutes of a joint meeting of the [National] Executive Committee and the Parliamentary Party, August 14, 1917, and Inter-Allied Labour and Socialist Conference, *Memorandum on War Aims: Agreed Upon . . . February 20th to 24th, 1918,* both in the National Museum of Labour History, Manchester.

17. Brand, *British Labour Party,* 51.

18. *Memorandum on War Aims,* 12. The version quoted here was approved by the Inter-Allied Labour and Socialist Conference. The version approved by the National Labor Conference on War Aims in December 1917 has only a few minor differences in wording: National Labor Conference on War Aims, *British Labor's War Aims* (American Association for International Conciliation, 1918).

19. Gorny, *The British Labour Movement and Zionism,* 12–46.

20. The basic work is Leonard Stein, *The Balfour Declaration* (Jerusalem: Magnes Press of the Hebrew University, 1961), but it should be supplemented with Jehuda Reinharz, "The Balfour Declaration and Its Maker: A Reassessment," *Journal of Modern History* 64, no. 3 (September 1992): 455–99; and Richard Ned Lebow, "Woodrow Wilson and the Balfour Declaration," *Journal of Modern History* 40, no. 4 (December 1998): 501–23. Hanna's previously cited study, *British Policy in Palestine,* has a useful summary, 14–38. A view that Weizmann's role was secondary to British interest in excluding

French influence from Palestine is expressed in Mayir Verete, "The Balfour Declaration and Its Makers" and "Further Reflections on the Makers of the Balfour Declaration," in *From Palmerston to Balfour*, 1–38, 204–26. Other relevant studies include Isaiah Friedman, *The Question of Palestine: British-Jewish-Arab Relations, 1914–1918*, 2d ed. (New Brunswick, N.J., 1992) and Ronald Sanders, *The High Walls of Jerusalem: A History of the Balfour Declaration and the Birth of the British Mandate for Palestine* (New York: Holt, Rinehart and Winston, 1983).

21. *Encyclopedia Britannica*, s.v. "Zionism," 1963, 23:956A.

22. Hanna, *British Policy in Palestine*, 30–31.

23. George Lenczowski, *The Middle East in World Affairs*, 4th ed. (Ithaca, N.Y.: Cornell University Press, 1980), 77.

24. T. G. Fraser, *The Middle East, 1914–1979* (New York: St. Martin's Press, 1980), 12–13.

25. This theme is woven throughout Stein, *Balfour Declaration*.

26. Earl Lloyd George, *My Father, Lloyd George* (New York: Crown, 1961), 20–21.

27. Stein, *Balfour Declaration*, 143.

28. *Encyclopedia Britannica*, s.v. "A. J. Balfour.".

29. Blanche Dugdale, *Arthur James Balfour: First Earl of Balfour* (London: Hutchinson, 1936), 1:433.

30. Ibid., 2:217.

31. Hanna, *British Policy in Palestine*, 32.

32. Ibid., 34.

33. A number of individuals both in the government and among the Zionists were involved in the drafting and redrafting of the document to respond to various objections and to make it acceptable to both the Allies and Jews in various parts of the world. See especially Reinharz, "The Balfour Declaration and Its Maker."

34. Lebow, "Woodrow Wilson and the Balfour Declaration," 509.

35. Hanna, *British Policy in Palestine*, 35.

36. Lebow, "Woodrow Wilson and the Balfour Declaration," 520–23.

37. Ibid., 523.

38. Paul Charles Merkley, *The Politics of Christian Zionism, 1891–1948* (London: Frank Cass, 1998), 89–90.

39. Reinharz, "The Balfour Declaration and Its Maker," 470–88.

40. Hanna, *British Policy in Palestine*, 37. See also *Times* (London), November 9, 1917, 7, and November 10, 1917, 7, and the *Manchester Guardian*, November 9, 1917, 5, and November 10, 1917, 4.

41. *Christian World*, November 15, 1917, 2, in the Dr. Williams Trust and Library, London.

42. *Baptist Times and Freeman*, December 14, 1917, 755, in the Angus Library, Regent's Park College, Oxford.

43. *Methodist Recorder,* November 15, 1917, in the John Rylands Library, Manchester.

44. *Church Times,* November 16, 1917, in the Lambeth Palace Library, London.

45. Minutes of the Synod of the Presbyterian Church in England, May 8, 1918, in the archives of Westminster College, Cambridge.

46. 67th Cong., 2d sess., *Congressional Record* 62, pt. 10 (1922): 10210.

47. Merkley, *Politics of Christian Zionism,* 98–100. One of the young Zionist lobbyists was Emanuel Neumann, who had learned the value of an appeal to the biblical background of Christians from Brandeis's relationship with William Blackstone.

48. 67th Cong., 2d sess., *Congressional Record* 62, pt. 10 (1922): 9799. This was also a time of anti-immigrant and anti-Semitic sentiment in the United States, and some of the unspoken reasoning could have been a desire to deflect Jewish immigration away from the United States and toward Palestine.

49. Ibid., 10:9816–17. "Extended Remarks" were texts added to the *Congressional Record,* with permission from the House, without actually being presented during the debate itself. This was a fairly common practice that permitted documentation of the representative's position on an issue.

50. Ibid., 10:9812.

51. Hanna, *British Policy in Palestine,* 69–85.

52. Ibid., 82.

53. Great Britain, Parliament, House of Commons, *Parliamentary Debates* (Hansard) (London: H.M. Stationery Office, 1909–1981), July 4, 1922, cols. 263–336.

54. Hanna, *British Policy in Palestine,* 86. For an excellent description of events in Palestine during the Mandate period, see Tom Seger, *One Palestine Complete: Jews and Arabs under the British Mandate,* trans. Haim Watzman (New York: Henry Holt, 2000).

55. Ibid., 92–97.

56. Presbyterian Church in England, Synod and General Assembly Minutes of March 19, 1918, 56, and May 9, 1923, 390, in the archives of Westminster College, Cambridge; and Church of Scotland General Assembly Reports for 1929, 905–7, in the archives of the New College Library, Edinburgh.

57. *Methodist Recorder,* April 3, 1930, 3.

58. *Baptist Times,* August 29, 1929, 647.

59. *Church Times,* April 4, 1930, 411, in the Lambeth Palace Library, London.

60. Hanna, *British Policy in Palestine,* 99.

61. Ibid., 100.

62. Ibid., 102.

63. Ibid., 104, and Great Britain, *Parliamentary Papers,* 1930–31, Command 661.

64. Hanna, *British Policy in Palestine,* 105.

65. *Church Times,* October 24, 1930, 487.

66. Great Britain, *Parliamentary Debates, Commons,* 5th series, vol. 245, cols. 77–210.

67. Ibid., cols. 79–80.

68. Ibid., col. 113.

69. Ibid., cols. 121–22.

70. Ibid., col. 147.

71. Gorny, *The British Labour Movement and Zionism*, 96–107. The MacDonald letter, read into the proceedings of the House of Commons on February 13, 1931, "explains" sixteen points in some detail and clearly negates the spirit of the White Paper. Great Britain, Parliament, House of Commons *Parliamentary Debates*, 5th series, vol. 248, cols. 751–57.

72. *Parliamentary Debates*, 5th series, vol. 245, cols. 78–79.

73. In a thoroughly researched study, Kenneth Stein has concluded that after 1930, many of the Jewish land purchases were from Palestinian Arab notables who needed the money, having lost their access to the privileges through which they had accumulated wealth under Ottoman rule. Stein, *The Land Question in Palestine, 1917–1939* (Chapel Hill: University of North Carolina Press, 1984).

74. Hanna, *British Policy in Palestine*, 4–5, 111, 120–24.

75. Great Britain, *Parliamentary Papers*, 1936–37, Command 5513.

76. Hanna, *British Policy in Palestine*, 124–31.

77. Ibid., 131–47.

78. Great Britain, *Parliamentary Papers*, 1938–39, Command 6019, p. 6.

79. Ibid., 6–12.

80. *Parliamentary Debates, Commons*, 5th series, vol. 312, cols. 1340–41.

81. Ibid., col. 1364.

82. Ibid., col. 1358.

83. *Baptist Times*, May 21, 1936, 395.

84. *Baptist Times*, October 22, 1936, 803.

85. *Baptist Times*, January 14, 1937, 27.

86. *Church of Scotland: Reports to the General Assembly, 1939*, 717, in the New College Library, Edinburgh.

87. Society of Friends, *London Yearly Meeting Proceedings*, 1937, 107 and 296, Friends House, London.

88. *Methodist Recorder*, July 22, 1937, 3.

89. Muhammad Y. Muslih, *The Origins of Palestinian Nationalism* (New York: Columbia University Press, 1988).

Chapter 4. Truman, the Bible, Israel, Oil, and the Soviet Union

1. Several works deal specifically with Truman's decision, including Michael J. Cohen, *Truman and Israel* (Berkeley: University of California Press, 1990); Bruce J. Evensen, *Truman, Palestine, and the Press: Shaping Conventional Wisdom at the Beginning of the Cold War* (New York: Greenwood Press, 1992); John Snetsinger, *Truman, the*

Jewish Vote, and the Creation of Israel (Stanford: Stanford University Press, 1974); and Evan W. Wilson, *Decision on Palestine: How the United States Came to Recognize Israel* (Stanford: Hoover Institution Press, 1979). Others contain especially useful sections related to the decision, including Peter L. Grose, *Israel in the Mind of America* (New York: Knopf, 1984); Michael J. Pragai, *Faith and Fulfillment: Christians and the Return to the Promised Land* (London: Vallentine Mitchell, 1985); and especially Paul Charles Merkley, *The Politics of Christian Zionism, 1891–1948.* Additional insight is offered in Kathleen Christison, *Perceptions of Palestine: Their Influence on U.S. Middle East Policy* (Berkeley: University of California Press, 1999); Richard H. Curtiss, *A Changing Image: American Perceptions of the Arab-Israel Dispute* (Washington, D.C.: American Educational Trust, 1986); and Cheryl A. Rubenberg, *Israel and the American National Interest: A Critical Examination* (Urbana: University of Illinois Press, 1986).

2. Lawrence J. Epstein, *Zion's Call: Christian Contributions to the Origins and Development of Israel* (Lanham, Md.: University Press of America, 1984), 123, and Merkley, *Politics of Christian Zionism,* 100–106. Epstein and Merkley give quite different accounts of the origin of the pro-Zionist organization, but Merkley's version appears to be the most thoroughly researched.

3. Pragai, *Faith and Fulfillment,* 130.

4. Except as otherwise noted, the following discussion of Emanuel Neumann, the American Palestine Committee, Reinhold Niebuhr, and the Christian Council on Palestine is based on Merkley, *Politics of Christian Zionism,* 100–106, 128–54, and Hassan S. Haddad, "Christian Zionism in America: The Religious Factor in American Middle East Policy," in *American Church Politics and the Middle East,* ed. Basheer K. Nijim (Belmont, Mass.: Association of Arab-American University Graduates, 1982), 107–33.

5. Merkley, *Politics of Christian Zionism,* 102.

6. Pragai, *Faith and Fulfillment,* 131.

7. Merkley, *Politics of Christian Zionism,* 102.

8. Ibid., 132.

9. Ibid., 142.

10. Grose, *Israel in the Mind of America,* 169.

11. Ibid., 170–71.

12. Pragai, *Faith and Fulfillment,* 132–33.

13. Grose, *Israel in the Mind of America,* 174.

14. 78th Cong., 2d sess., vol. 90, pt. 1 *Congressional Record* 963.

15. Copy of letter from Stimson dated March 17, 1944, in House Reports, 78th Cong., 2d sess., Miscellaneous, 5:2. The War Department appears to have been reacting to growing Arab concern over increasing Zionist influence in the United States: J. C. Hurewitz, *The Struggle for Palestine* (New York: W. W. Norton, 1950), 212–23.

16. U.S. Congress, House, Office of the Clerk, *Platforms of the Two Great Political Parties, 1932 to 1944* (Washington, D.C.: U.S. Government Printing Office, n.d.), 424.

17. Ibid., 410.

18. Copy of letter from Stimson dated October 10, 1944, in House Reports, 78th Cong., 2d sess., Miscellaneous, 5:2.

19. Grose, *Israel in the Mind of America*, 174.

20. 79th Cong., 1st sess., vol. 91, pt. 9 *Congressional Record*, 12396.

21. Ibid., 12165–89.

22. Data provided by the Roper Center at the University of Connecticut.

23. Ickes to Roosevelt, December 1, 1941, folder "Correspondence with the President," box 666, item 11, RG 253, Records of the Petroleum Administration for War, National Archives.

24. Memorandum by Ralph K. Davies, deputy petroleum administrator, October 15, 1941, attached to letter, Ickes to Roosevelt, October 18, 1941, folder "Correspondence with the President," box 666, item 11, RG253.

25. *Petroleum Facts and Figures, 1971* (Washington, D.C.: American Petroleum Institute, 1971), 284–85.

26. For a full discussion of this issue, see my study on *Aramco, the United States, and Saudi Arabia: A Study of the Dynamics of Foreign Oil Policy, 1933–1950* (Princeton: Princeton University Press, 1981).

27. Vice Chief of Naval Operations to Joint Chiefs of Staff, May 31, 1943, folder CCS463.7 (5–31–43), JCS Decimal Files, 1942–45, RG 218, Records of the Joint Chiefs of Staff, National Archives. The estimated reserves for Iran were 17.7 billion barrels, Iraq 14.5 billion barrels, and Kuwait 2.0 billion barrels.

28. This account of ʿAbd al-ʿAziz's career is based on Jacques Benoist-Mechin, *Arabian Destiny*, translated from the French by Denis Weaver (London: Elek Books, 1957); Harold C. Armstrong, *Lord of Arabia* (London: Arthur Barker, 1934), and Harry St. John Bridger Philby, *Saudi Arabia* (London: Ernest Benn, 1955), 237–58.

29. Benoist-Mechin, *Arabian Destiny*, 289.

30. Lenczowski, *The Middle East in World Affairs*, 582.

31. ʿAbd al-ʿAziz to President Roosevelt, March 10, 1945, copy in 79th Cong., 1st sess., *Appendix to the Congressional Record*, A 4813–15.

32. Ibid., A 4815.

33. This summary of developments in 1946 and 1947 is based on Louis J. Halle, *The Cold War as History* (New York: Harper and Row, 1967), 96–134.

34. Ibid., 121.

35. This description of American strategic planning is drawn from Irvine H. Anderson, *Aramco, the United States, and Saudi Arabia: A Study in the Dynamics of Foreign Oil Policy, 1933–1950* (Princeton: Princeton University Press, 1981), 163–78.

36. Cato D. Glover to Chief of Naval Operations, "Resume of PINCHER Planning," January 21, 1947, file A16–3(5) War Plans, OP30 files, CNO Records, National Archives.

37. R. L. Dennison to Secretary of the Navy, "Notes on the World Oil Situation," October 17, 1946, Politico-Military Division, Subject Files (2), 1946–47; Louis Denfield to Joint Chiefs of Staff, "Medium Range Emergency Plan," April 5, 1948, "Strategic Plans," OP30/21 files, and "War Plans," OP30A16–3 files, CNO Records, National Archives.

38. See, e.g., JCS 1833/1, "Preparation for Demolition of Oil Fields in the Middle East," April 7, 1948, and SNACC 398/4 (same title), May 25, 1948, file CCS600.6 Middle East (1–26–46), JCS General files, 1948, RG 218, National Archives.

39. JCS 1741, "Problem of Procurement of Oil for a Major War," January 29, 1947, 1–7, file CCS463.7 (9–6–45) Sec.6, JCS Decimal file, 1946–47, RG 218, National Archives.

40. State Department position paper prepared in advance of the "Pentagon Talks" with representatives of the British government in October and November 1947, *Foreign Relations of the United States* 5 (1947): 553. For further discussion of the State Department's position, see Anderson, *Aramco,* 169–70. It was argued that State's position was due to excessive corporate lobbying, but the full record says otherwise. Aramco and its parent companies kept a low profile on the subject of Zionism during this period, and there was more than ample reporting through diplomatic channels of ʿAbd al-ʿAziz's antipathy to Zionism. State's director of Near Eastern and African Affairs, Loy W. Henderson, was also sharply criticized as being anti-Semitic, a pawn of the oil companies, and a spokesman for the British Foreign Office. But the record is clear that Henderson's long service in Moscow and Eastern Europe had made him a confirmed cold warrior. He was opposed to anything that would alienate the Arab world and weaken support for the United States in an area critical to the containment of communism.

41. Unless otherwise noted, this discussion of Truman's biblical background is based on Merkley, *Politics of Christian Zionism,* 158–63; Cohen, *Truman and Israel,* 5–7; and David McCullough, *Truman* (New York: Simon and Schuster, 1992), 44, 83, 597.

42. *The Autobiography of Harry S. Truman,* ed. Robert H. Ferrell (Boulder: Colorado Associated University Press, 1980), 33–34.

43. Merlin Gustafson, "The Religion of a President," *Journal of Church and State* 10, no. 3 (Autumn 1968): 380. Gustafson's article also appeared under the title "Harry Truman as a Man of Faith" in *Christian Century* 90 (January 17, 1973): 75–78.

44. Clark Clifford, with Richard Holbrooke, *Counsel to the President: A Memoir* (New York: Random House, 1991), 8.

45. Quoted in Merkley, *Politics of Christian Zionism,* 165, as cited in Ferrell, ed., *Autobiography of Truman,* 136–37.

46. Merkley, *Politics of Christian Zionism,* 165–66.

47. This discussion of Britain's immediate postwar debate over Palestine is drawn from Ritchie Ovendale, "The Palestine Policy of the British Labour Government, 1947: The Decision to Withdraw," *International Affairs* 56, no. 1 (January 1980): 73–93. Ritchie's article is based primarily on records of the British Cabinet and Foreign Office during that period.

48. Ibid., 87 and 91.

49. Ibid., 77–78.

50. Merkley, *Politics of Christian Zionism,* 168–74.

51. Ibid., 173.

52. Ovendale, "Palestine Policy," 82–83.

53. Ibid., 88.

54. Grose, *Israel in the Mind of America,* 234–36.

55. Ibid., 244–45.

56. Ibid., 245, 256.

57. Ibid., 238.

58. Ibid., 248–54.

59. Merkley, *Politics of Christian Zionism,* 157, 176.

60. This account of Weizmann's meeting with Truman in 1947 is based on Merkley, *Politics of Christian Zionism,* 176, and Grose, *Israel in the Mind of America,* 246–48.

61. Merkley, *Politics of Christian Zionism,* 177.

62. This discussion of the partition plan and its implementation is drawn from Cohen, *Truman and Israel,* 199–221.

63. Unless otherwise noted, the discussion of events in the spring of 1948 is based on Merkley, *Politics of Christian Zionism,* 172–90, and Cohen, *Truman and Israel,* 133–49.

64. Merkley, *Politics of Christian Zionism,* 186.

65. Peter Grose cites circumstantial evidence that the line of argument in the second paper originated with Zionists who had targeted Clifford as the best avenue to Truman: Grose, *Israel in the Mind of America,* 270–71.

66. Grose, 269–70.

67. Ibid.

68. Clifford, *Counsel to the President,* 12.

69. See, e.g., Grose, *Israel in the Mind of America,* 289–93; McCullough, *Truman,* 614–17; Merkley, *Politics of Christian Zionism,* 188–89; Cohen, *Truman and Israel,* 212–15; Wilson, *Decision on Palestine,* 142–43; and Clifford's own recollections in *Counsel to the President,* 3–15.

70. Grose, *Israel in the Mind of America,* 290.

71. The quotations are from Grose, *Israel in the Mind of America,* 290–92.

72. Quoted in Clifford, *Counsel to the President,* 22.

Chapter 5. Christian Influence and Congressional Support of Israel

1. Christison, *Perceptions of Palestine,* 274, based on the work of Robert Jervis, *Perception and Misperception in International Politics* (Princeton: Princeton University Press, 1976), 146–55.

2. James L. Guth et al., "Religion and Foreign Policy Attitudes: The Case of Christian

Zionism," in John C. Green et al., *Religion and the Culture Wars: Dispatches from the Front* (Lanham, Md.: Rowman and Littlefield, 1996), 353.

3. The nine churches in the top sixteen that had not taken a position were the Southern Baptist Convention, the National Baptist Convention, USA, the Church of God in Christ, the African Methodist Episcopal Church, the National Baptist Convention of America, the Lutheran Church—Missouri Synod, the National Missionary Baptist Convention of America, the Progressive National Baptist Convention, and the Churches of Christ, as determined in telephone conversations with their central offices in 1999.

4. *The Baptist Faith and Mission,* adopted by the Southern Baptist Convention on June 14, 2000 (LifeWay Christian Resources, 2000), 7.

5. Don Peretz, *The Middle East Today,* 6th ed. (Westport, Conn.: Praeger, 1994), 136.

6. Resolution no. 1985–D135, "Increase Support for Refugees in the Diocese of Jerusalem," in *Journal of the General Convention of the Protestant Episcopal Church in the United States of America, 1985* (New York: General Convention, 1986), 268.

7. *A Resource on the Middle East* (Evangelical Lutheran Church in America, 1993), 8–9.

8. Telephone conversation with David Weaver, Middle East specialist with the National Council of Churches in New York, December 10, 1998.

9. *Minutes: 209th General Assembly, 1997, Part I, Journal* (Louisville, Ky.: Office of the General Assembly, n.d.), par. 35.0366, p. 564; and extracts from the 200th General Assembly (1988), from *Church and Society,* July/August 1988.

10. *Minutes of the General Assembly of the United Presbyterian Church in the United States of America, Part IA, 186th General Assembly, Louisville, Kentucky, June 17–26, 1974* (New York: Office of the General Assembly, 1974), 586.

11. Resolution no. 1988–DO53, "Affirm Goals of Justice, Peace, and Reconciliation for Israelis and Palestinians," *Journal of the General Convention of the Protestant Episcopal Church in the United States of America, 1988* (New York: General Convention, 1989), 293.

12. *Policy for Action VI: The Social Policies of the Episcopal Church* (Austin, Tex.: Archives of the Episcopal Church, 1998), 6.

13. Resolution no. 1985–B017, "Oppose Moving the United States Embassy from Tel Aviv to Jerusalem," *Journal of the General Convention of the Protestant Episcopal Church in the United States of America, 1985* (New York: General Convention, 1986), 130.

14. "A Message on the Israeli/Palestinian Conflict," affirmed by the 1989 ELCA Churchwide Assembly, appendix 5, in *A Resource on the Middle East* (Evangelical Lutheran Church in America, 1993), 23–24.

15. Copy of a resolution adopted by the third Churchwide Assembly of the Evangelical Lutheran Church in America on September 1, 1993, provided in a letter from Mark Brown of the Lutheran Office for Governmental Affairs in Washington, January 4, 1999.

16. *Yearbook of American and Canadian Churches* (New York: National Council of Churches of Christ in the United States of America, 1998), 7.

17. "Toward Peace in the Middle East: Perspectives, Principles, and Hopes: A Statement of the National Conference of Catholic Bishops, November 1989," *Pastoral Letters, 1987–1989* (Washington, D.C.: United States Catholic Conference, 1989), 136–61.

18. Letter to the author from Janelle R. Henderson, research assistant, and Susan J. Cohen, curator, of the United Methodist Archives Center at Ohio Wesleyan University in Delaware, January 19, 1998.

19. Articles in *World Outlook,* October 1949, 483–86; June 1950, 918–19; October 1958, 514–15; December 1958, 598–601; February 1963, 38–39.

20. Stephen B. L. Penrose Jr., "America and the Middle East," *World Outlook,* August 1948, 380–82.

21. Letter to the author from Josiah W. Douglas, manager, curriculum planning and development, Church of Jesus Christ of Latter-day Saints, Salt Lake City, February 10, 1999.

22. Steven Epperson, *Mormons and Jews: Early Mormon Theologies of Israel* (Salt Lake City: Signature Books, 1992), 213. For another interesting discussion of this affinity from a theological point of view, see Truman G. Madsen, *The Mormon Attitude toward Zionism.*

23. D. Kelly Ogden and David B. Galbraith, "What Are the Reasons behind the Long-standing Conflicts in the Holy Land, and How Should Latter-day Saints View Such Conflicts?" *Ensign,* September 1993, 52–53.

24. Letter to President Clinton from the Churches for Middle East Peace, Washington, D.C., October 1, 1998; copy provided by the Lutheran Office for Governmental Affairs in Washington, D.C.

25. For discussion of these points, see James L. Guth, "Response" [to Corwin Smidt, "Evangelical Voting Patterns, 1976–1988"], in *No Longer Exiles,* ed. Michael Cromartie (Washington, D.C.: Ethics and Public Policy Center, 1990), 119; and Paul Boyer, *Prophecy Belief in American Culture* (Cambridge: Harvard University Press, 1992), ix–xii. For an extreme version of the same motivations, see Eric Hoffer, *True Believer: Thoughts on the Nature of Mass Movements* (New York: Harper and Row, 1951), 61–82.

26. Andrew Kohut, John C. Green, Scott Keeter, and Robert C. Toth, *The Diminishing Divide: Religion's Changing Role in American Politics* (Washington, D.C.: Brookings Institution Press, 2000), 130–41. Their conclusions are based heavily on data collected by the Pew Research Center for the People and the Press in Washington, D.C., but they also utilize data from National Election Studies by the Center for Political Studies at the University of Michigan, Gallup polls available at the Roper Center for Public Opinion Research, a Citizen Participation Survey made available by the Inter-University Consortium for Political and Social Research, and a poll conducted by the Survey and Evaluation Research Laboratory at Virginia Commonwealth University in Richmond.

27. The summary did not single out "fundamentalists" within the category of "evangelicals." It should also be noted that, as reported earlier, belief that God promised the land to the Hebrew people and belief in a Second Coming both extend beyond the ranks of deeply committed evangelicals and fundamentalists.

28. William Martin, *With God on Our Side: The Rise of the Religious Right in America* (New York: Broadway Books, 1996), 1–23.

29. Cromartie, ed., *No Longer Exiles,* vii–viii.

30. *Pentecostal Evangel,* October 20, 1945, 4–5; copy provided by Joyce Lee of the Flower Pentecostal Heritage Center (Assemblies of God archives) in Springfield, Mo.

31. Weber, "How Evangelicals Became Israel's Best Friend," 42; Ruth W. Mouly, *The Religious Right and Israel: The Politics of Armageddon* (Cambridge, Mass.: Political Research Associates, 1985), 6.

32. Web site of the National Unity Coalition for Israel (www.israel-unitycoalition. com), downloaded October 23, 1999. The organization is based in Shawnee Mission, Kans., outside of Kansas City, but maintains an office in Silver Springs, Md. Esther Levens, president of the National Unity Coalition, in a telephone conversation on February 12, 2001, declined to provide a list of the "200 affiliated organizations," but confirmed that most of the organization's support came from small, intensely pro-Israel groups. The list of some of the supporting organizations was included in a press release by Americans for Peace Now, Washington, D.C., September 16, 1999, entitled "APN Report on 'Deceptive Proselytizing' in the National Unity Coalition for Israel."

33. *Congressional Record—Extension of Remarks* 143, no. 40 (April 8, 1997): E578.

34. Weber, "How Evangelicals Became Israel's Best Friend," 47.

35. Halsell, *Prophecy and Politics,* 72–75.

36. Simon, *Jerry Falwell and the Jews,* 62–64.

37. Halsell, *Prophecy and Politics,* 165–67.

38. Ibid., 75.

39. Mouly, *The Religious Right and Israel,* 28.

40. Donald Wagner, "Evangelicals and Israel: Theological Roots of a Political Alliance," *Christian Century,* November 4, 1998, 1023.

41. Mouly, *The Religious Right and Israel,* 40.

42. Except as otherwise noted, this discussion of AIPAC is based on J. J. Goldberg, *Jewish Power: Inside the American Jewish Establishment* (Reading, Mass.: Addison-Wesley, 1996), 197–226, with the modifications to Goldberg's interpretation expressed by Marshall J. Breger in his review of the book in *Commentary,* February 1997, 68–69. See also the review of Goldberg's book by Robert Leiter, of the Philadelphia weekly *Jewish Exponent,* in the *New York Times Book Review,* February 9, 1997, 25.

43. Paul Findley, *They Dare to Speak Out: People and Institutions Confront Israel's Lobby* (Westport, Conn.: Lawrence Hill, 1985), 317.

44. James M. Wall, "On Being 'Pro-Israel,'" *Christian Century*, January 20, 1993, 43–44.

45. Howard M. Sachar, *The Course of Jewish History* (New York: Vintage Books, 1990), 732.

46. Breger, *Commentary*, February 1997, 69.

47. Robert H. Trice, "Congress and the Arab-Israeli Conflict: Support for Israel in the U.S. Senate, 1970–1973," *Political Science Quarterly* 92, no. 3 (Fall 1977): 463.

48. Peter Beinart and Hanna Rosin, "AIPAC Unpacked," *New Republic*, September 20 and 27, 1993, 20–23.

49. Goldberg, *Jewish Power*, 199.

50. Ibid., 213.

51. Findley, *They Dare to Speak Out*, 109–13.

52. Flyer provided to the author by AIPAC in September 2000. The text goes on to compare the government and society of Israel with nineteen Arab states.

53. Jeffrey H. Birbaum, "Washington's Power 25," *Fortune*, December 8, 1997, 144.

54. Flyer provided to the author by Americans for a Safe Israel, New York City.

55. "Report on U.S. Assistance to the State of Israel," prepared by the staff of the U.S. General Accounting Office, released on June 24, 1983, p. 7. The quotation is from an "uncensored" copy of a draft of the report that was widely circulated in Washington at the time. The "uncensored" version includes a large number of sentences (not those quoted here) that were cut from the final version and that could be construed as critical of Israel in some way.

56. *CRS Issue Brief: Israel: U.S. Foreign Assistance* (Washington: Congressional Research Service, Library of Congress, October 28, 1999, Order Code IB85066), CRS-1.

57. Democratic Party Platform 1992, 14.

58. Republican Party Platform 1992, 61.

59. Ibid.

60. "Nations Maintaining Diplomatic Relations with Israel, 1984," in *Legislation Calling for a Move of the U.S. Embassy to Jerusalem, Hearings before the Committee on Foreign Relations of the House of Representatives*, 98th Cong., 2d sess., April 10–October 2, 1984, CIS-1985–H381–17, p. 336. By 1984, the countries maintaining diplomatic representation in Tel Aviv included Argentina, Australia, Austria, Belgium, Brazil, Burma, Canada, Denmark, Egypt, Finland, France, Germany, Greece, Italy, Japan, Liberia, Mexico, Norway, Peru, Philippines, Romania, South Africa, Sweden, Switzerland, Turkey, United Kingdom, and the United States. Those that were represented in Jerusalem but moved to Tel Aviv in 1980 were Bolivia, Chile, Colombia, Dominican Republic, Ecuador, El Salvador, Guatemala, Haiti, Netherlands, Panama, Uruguay, and Venezuela. Costa Rica and Zaire continued to maintain their embassies in Jerusalem in 1984.

61. Statement of Alleck A. Resnick, president, Zionist Organization of America, ibid., 182.

62. Statement of David J. Sadd, executive director of the National Association of Arab Americans, ibid., 110.

63. Remarks by Senator Daniel Patrick Moynihan, 104th Cong., 1st sess., *Congressional Record* 141 (October 23, 1995): S 15482. He refers to action he took in 1983.

64. *Legislation Calling for a Move of the U.S. Embassy in Israel to Jerusalem,* i.

65. Ibid., 182.

66. Ibid., 91–92.

67. Ibid., 85.

68. Ibid., 197, 199.

69. Ibid., 110–12.

70. Ibid., 128.

71. Ibid., 284.

72. Ibid., 449–53. The full record of the House hearings runs to 511 pages.

73. Senate Committee on Foreign Relations, *American Embassy in Israel,* 98th Cong., 2d sess., S 2031, 106.

74. Ibid., 113.

75. Ibid., 114, 123.

76. Ibid., 79.

77. Ibid., 137.

78. Ibid., 58–59.

79. 104th Cong., 1st sess., *Congressional Record* 141, no. 165 (October 24, 1995): H 10682.

80. Democratic Party Platform, 1992, 14.

81. Republican Party Platform, 1992, 62.

82. 104th Cong., 1st sess., *Congressional Record* 141, no. 165 (October 24, 1995): H 10680.

83 Ibid.

84. Ibid.

85. Ibid., H 10680, H 10682.

86. Ibid., H 10685.

87. Ibid.

88. Ibid., H 10682.

89. Ibid., H 10680.

90. "Bill to Relocate Embassy Heads to the President," *Congressional Quarterly,* October 28, 1995, 3318.

91. 104th Cong., 1st sess., *Congressional Record* 141, no. 165 (October 24, 1995): H 10685.

92. Trice, "Congress and the Arab-Israeli Conflict," 463.

93. *The 105th Congress and Middle East Peace* (Washington, D.C.: Arab American Institute, May 1998), 3.

94. This statement and all of the following ones regarding Arab reaction are taken from the English-language London-based newspaper *Middle East International,* November 3, 1995, 6; and the Beirut Arabic newspaper *Al-Nahar* of October 26, 1995, 1, with translation obtained with the assistance of Dr. Youssef T. Constandi of Cincinnati.

95. Fred J. Khouri, "The Challenge to U.S. Security and Middle East Policy," *Arab-American Affairs* 5 (Summer 1983): 12, 19.

Epilogue. The al-Aqsa Intifada, September 11, and the Dynamics of Policy

1. OpEd article by Robert Malley, special assistant for Arab-Israeli affairs to President Clinton from 1998 to 2001, *New York Times,* August 8, 2001. Malley was a participant in the 2000 Camp David meeting, and he reports that he, too, was frustrated by the failure of the Palestinians to really work toward a final settlement. But he points out that the timing was highly inauspicious from the Palestinian point of view due to inadequate preparatory work and that, while Barak's offer did not meet all of the long-stated expectations of the Palestinians, the Palestinians did make some concessions. He argues that it would have taken a real leap of faith to imagine that a conflict with "roots going back thousands of years [*sic*] ... with tens of thousands of victims along the way, could have been resolved in a fortnight without any of the core issues—territory, refugees, or the fate of Jerusalem—having previously been discussed by the leaders." For an interesting discussion of the breakdown of the peace process, see a long piece in the *New York Times,* July 26, 2001, A1, A12–A13.

2. *Mideast Mirror* (London), e-mail edition, November 20, 2000, reporting on an editorial in the Arab newspaper *al-Quds al-Arabi.*

3. *Mideast Mirror,* November 14, 2000, 14.

4. *Mideast Mirror,* e-mail edition, November 20, 2000.

5. For a discussion of these developments, see John L. Esposito, *Islam: The Straight Path* (New York: Oxford University Press, 1988), 116–202; Karen Armstrong, *Islam: A Short History* (New York: Modern Library, 2000), 140–87; and Bernard Lewis, "The Roots of Muslim Rage," *Atlantic,* September 1990, 47–53.

6. For a thorough discussion of bin Laden's background, see Peter L. Bergen, *Holy War, Inc.: Inside the Secret World of Osama bin Laden* (New York: Free Press, 2001).

7. Published in *al-Quds al-Arabi* on 23 February 1998, 3; English translation obtained on the web site of the World Islamic Front.

8. The phrase is "fight in God's cause against those who wage war against you, but do not commit aggression—for, verily, God does not love aggressors" (Qur'an 2:190).

9. Quotation provided by Dr. Baher Foad of Cincinnati.

10. "Foreign Terrorist Organizations," designations by Secretary of State Madeleine

K. Albright, October 8, 1999, 3. The designations are in accord with the provisions of the Antiterrorism and Effective Death Penalty Act of 1996. Hamas is an acronym for Islamic Resistance Movement in Arabic. It is an outgrowth of the Muslim Brotherhood, and its 1988 Covenant is filled with anti-Zionist invective and makes it clear that its objective is to drive Jews completely out of Palestine.

11. Executive Order 13224 of September 24, 2001, and *New York Times,* November 3, 2001, B1, B5.

12. Newt Gingrich to Secretary of State Colin Powell, September 25, 2001, and Congressmen Tom Lantos and Tom DeLay to Powell, October 12, 2001; copies provided by Lantos's office. The differences in the spelling of Hizbullah are as in the original documents.

13. Executive Order 13224 of September 23, 2001, as amended November 2, 2001.

14. State Department, daily press briefing, November 2, 2001.

15. *New York Times,* November 9, 2001, B3.

16. Eighty-nine senators to President George W. Bush, November 16, 2001; copy provided by the office of Senator Christopher Bond (R-MO).

17. *New York Times,* November 17, 2001, A5.

18. Fawaz Turki, "In Palestine, a Point of No Return," undated article downloaded from the *Arab View* Web site, December 24, 2001.

19. *New York Times,* November 23, 2001, A17.

20. William E. Sutter, executive director, The Friends of Israel, to "Dear Friend," November 2001.

21. *New York Times,* April 21, 2002, A14.

22. *New York Times,* May 14, 2002, A23.

23. *Congressional Quarterly Weekly,* May 4, 2002, 1136–37.

24. *New York Times,* October 2, 2002, A10.

Sources and Bibliography

With a subject that spans both religion and political history in two countries over a full century, the supply of potentially useful material is overwhelming. The task has been to narrow it down and focus on only the most relevant. This list of sources and bibliography is therefore not a comprehensive survey of the field but a condensed overview of what has proven to be the most valuable to this author. Of the available monographs, the most pertinent are the studies by Ammerman, Ariel, Feuerwerger, Grose, Guth, Halsell, Marsden, Merkley, Pragai, Sizer, Trice, Tuchman, and Wagner, listed in the bibliography that follows. Taken together, they present a useful survey of the influence of Christian Zionism on policy. But they must be woven together and supplemented with considerable data from other sources in order to present a coherent picture.

The most important other sources have been the archives of the major British and American denominations, as they related to church positions on public policy and the Sunday school movement. Archivists in Britain were exceedingly cordial and helpful, and the same was true of staffs of the major religious denominations in the United States. All of them were most forthcoming in locating and providing copies of relevant material. The research has been supplemented by material from government archives and government publications in both countries.

Primary Sources

British Archives

Baptist Archives, Angus Library, Regent's Park College, Oxford.
Church of England Archives, Lambeth Palace Library, Lambeth Road, London.
Church of England Record Center, South Bermondsey, London.
Church of Scotland Archives, New College Library, Edinburgh.

Congregational Church Archives, Dr. Williams Trust and Library, London.
Labour Party Archives, National Museum of Labour History, Manchester.
Methodist Archives, John Rylands Library, University of Manchester.
National Christian Education Council Archives, NCEC, Sally Oak, Birmingham.
Orchard Learning Resource Center, Westhill Campus, University of Birmingham.
Presbyterian Archives, Westminster College, Cambridge.
Society of Friends (Quaker) Archives, Friends House, London.

American Archives

National Archives, Washington, D.C. (Record Group 218, Records of the Joint Chiefs of Staff; Record Group 253, Records of the Petroleum Administrator for War; and OP30 Files, Records of the Chief of Naval Operations).

American Church Archives

African Methodist Episcopal Church, Washington, D.C.
Assemblies of God, Springfield, Mo.
Augsburg Press, Minneapolis.
Church of God in Christ Publishing House, Memphis.
Church of Jesus Christ of Latter-day Saints (Mormon), Salt Lake City.
Churches of Christ, Los Angeles.
Concordia Publishing House (Lutheran material), St. Louis.
David C. Cook Publishing Company, Colorado Springs, Colo.
Episcopal Archives, Austin, Tex.
Episcopal Office of Government Relations, Washington, D.C.
Evangelical Lutheran Church in America, Chicago.
Flower Pentecostal Heritage Center (Assemblies of God), Springfield, Mo.
General Convention of the Episcopal Church, New York.
Gospel Publishing House, Springfield, Mo.
LifeWay Christian Resources (Baptist), Nashville.
Lutheran Church—Missouri Synod, St. Louis.
Lutheran Office for Governmental Affairs, Washington, D.C.
Morehouse Group (publishers of Episcopal material), Harrisburg, Pa.
National Baptist Convention, USA, Nashville.
National Baptist Convention of America, Dallas.
National Council of Churches of Christ in the USA, New York.
National Missionary Baptist Convention of America, Nashville.
National Religion Research Center, University of Chicago
Presbyterian Church (USA), Louisville, Ky.
Progressive National Baptist Church, Washington, D.C.

Southern Baptist Convention, Nashville.

United Methodist Archives, Ohio Wesleyan University, Delaware.

United Methodist Publishing House, Nashville.

United States Catholic Conference, Washington, D.C.

Educational Institutions and Advocacy Groups

American Israel Public Affairs Committee, Washington, D.C.

Americans for a Safe Israel, New York.

Bridges for Peace, Tulsa, Okla.

Churches for Middle East Peace, Washington, D.C.

Dallas Theological Seminary, Dallas.

Friends of Israel Gospel Ministry, Westville, N.J.

International Christian Embassy Jerusalem, Washington, D.C., Office.

International Fellowship of Christians and Jews, Chicago.

Moody Bible Institute, Chicago.

National Unity Coalition for Israel, Shawnee Mission, Kans.

Government Publications

Great Britain. Parliament. *Parliamentary Debates*. London: H.M. Stationery Office, 1922–39.

———. *Parliamentary Papers, 1930–31* (Command 661). London: H.M. Stationery Office, 1932.

———. *Parliamentary Papers, 1936–37* (Command 5513). London: H.M. Stationery Office, 1938.

———. *Parliamentary Papers, 1938–39* (Command 6019). London: H.M. Stationery Office, 1940.

U.S. Congress. *Congressional Record*. 67th Cong., 2d sess., 1922.

———. 78th Cong., 2d sess., 1944.

———. 79th Cong., 1st sess., 1945.

———. 104th Cong., 1st sess., 1995.

———. *Congressional Record—Extension of Remarks*. 1997. Vol. 143, no. 40.

———. House Committee on Foreign Relations. *Hearings before the Committee on Foreign Relations of the House of Representatives on Legislation Calling for a Move of the U.S. Embassy to Jerusalem*. 98th Cong., 2d sess., 1984.

———. House Office of the Clerk. *Platforms of the Two Great Political Parties, 1932 to 1944*. Washington, D.C.: Government Printing Office, n.d.

———. *House Reports*. 78th Cong., 2d sess., 1944, Miscellaneous, vol. 5.

———. Senate Committee on Foreign Relations. *Hearings before the Committee on Foreign Relations on an American Embassy in Israel*. 98th Cong., 2d sess., 1984.

U.S. Congressional Research Service. *CRS Issue Brief: Israel: U.S. Foreign Assistance.* Washington, D.C.: Congressional Research Service, Library of Congress, 1999.

U.S. Department of Energy. *Annual Energy Review.* Washington, D.C.: Government Printing Office, annually.

———. *International Petroleum Monthly.* Washington, D.C.: Government Printing Office, monthly.

U.S. Department of State. *Foreign Relations of the United States.* Washington, D.C.: Government Printing Office, 1952–.

———. "Foreign Terrorist Organizations." Designation by Secretary of State Madeleine K. Albright, October 3, 1999.

U.S. General Accounting Office. "Report on U.S. Assistance to the State of Israel." Typescript. Released June 24, 1983.

Secondary Sources

Bibles and Reference Works

Anchor Bible. New York: Doubleday, 1985.

Anchor Bible Dictionary. New York: Doubleday, 1992.

Congressional Yellow Book: Who's Who in Congress. New York and Washington: Leadership Directories, Summer 1999.

HarperCollins Study Bible: New Revised Standard Version. New York: HarperCollins, 1993.

Holy Bible: New International Version. Grand Rapids: Vondervan, 1984.

The Interpreter's One-Volume Commentary on the Bible. Edited by Charles M. Laymon. Nashville: Abingdon Press, 1971.

The New Interpreter's Bible. Nashville: Abingdon Press, 1994.

The Scofield Study Bible: King James Version. 1917 ed. New York: Oxford University Press, 1945.

Study Helps to the Holy Bible: New Revised Standard Version. Nashville: Cokesbury, 1990.

Yearbook of American and Canadian Churches. New York: National Council of Churches of Christ in the United States of America, 1998.

Articles and Monographs

Ammerman, Nancy T. "North American Protestant Fundamentalism." In *Fundamentalism Observed: Volume 1 of the Fundamentalism Project,* ed. Martin E. Marty and R. Scott Appleby, 1–65. Chicago: University of Chicago Press, 1991.

Ariel, Yaakov. "A Christian Fundamentalist Vision of the Middle East: Jan Willem van der Hoeven and the International Christian Embassy." In *Spokesmen for the De-*

spised: Fundamentalist Leaders of the Middle East, ed. R. Scott Appleby, 363–97. Chicago: University of Chicago Press, 1977.

Beinart, Peter, and Hanna Rosin. "AIPAC Unpacked." New Republic, September 20 and 27, 1993, 20–23.

Birbaum, Jeffrey H. "Washington's Power 25." Fortune, December 8, 1997, 144.

"Conformism II: American Jewish Congress Silences Critics of Israel." Editorial. Tikkun 7, no. 3 (1992).

Excel Omnibus Study #928 (on beliefs regarding the Second Coming), done for the Associated Press, July 11–15, 1997. Typescript. International Communication Research, 605 West State Street, Media, Pa. 19063-2620.

"An Exclusive Interview with Clark Clifford." American Heritage, April 1977, 8–9.

Gustafson, Merlin. "Harry Truman as a Man of Faith." Christian Century 90 (January 17, 1973): 75–78.

———. "The Religion of a President." Journal of Church and State 10, no. 3 (Autumn 1968): 379–87.

Guth, James L. "Response" [to Corwin Smidt. "Evangelical Voting Patterns, 1976–1988"]. In No Longer Exiles: The Religious Right in American Politics. ed. Michael Cromartie, 119. Washington, D.C.: Ethics and Public Policy Center, 1990.

Guth, James L., Cleveland R. Fraser, John C. Green, Lyman A. Kellstedt, and Corwin Smidt. "Religion and Foreign Policy Attitudes: The Case of Christian Zionism." In John C. Green, James L. Guth, Corwin E. Smidt, and Lyman A. Kellstedt, Religion and the Culture Wars: Dispatches from the Front, 330–60. Lanham, Md.: Rowman and Littlefield, 1966.

Haddad, Hassan S. "Christian Zionism in America: The Religious Factor in American Middle East Policy." In American Church Politics and the Middle East, ed. Basheer K. Nijim, 107–33. Belmont, Mass.: Association of Arab-American University Graduates, 1982.

"Jihad against Jews and Crusaders," by the "World Islamic Front," published in the Arabic newspaper al-Quds al-Arabi of London, February 23, 1998, p. 3. Obtained from the Web site of the World Islamic Front.

Khouri, Fred J. "The Challenge to U.S. Security and Middle East Policy." Arab-American Affairs 5 (Summer 1983): 12 and 19.

Lebow, Richard Ned. "Woodrow Wilson and the Balfour Declaration." Journal of Modern History 40, no. 4 (December 1998): 501–23.

Lewis, Bernard. "The Roots of Muslim Rage." Atlantic, September 1990, 47–53.

Moorehead, Jennifer. "End of Days: Israel, Christian Zionists and Palestinian Rights." AAUG Monitor 14, no. 2 (July 1999): 1–12.

Ogden, D. Kelly, and David B. Galbraith. "What Are the Reasons behind the Longstanding Conflicts in the Holy Land, and How Should Latter-day Saints View Such Conflicts?" Ensign, September 1993, 52–53.

Ovendale, Ritchie. "The Palestine Policy of the British Labour Government, 1947: The Decision to Withdraw." *International Affairs* 56, no. 1 (January 1980): 73–93.

Penrose, Stephen B. L., Jr. "America and the Middle East." *World Outlook*, August 1948, 380–82.

Reinharz, Jehuda. "The Balfour Declaration and Its Maker: A Reassessment." *Journal of Modern History* 64, no. 3 (September 1992): 455–99.

Sarna, Nahum M. "Israel in Egypt." In *Ancient Egypt: From Abraham to the Roman Destruction of the Temple*, ed. Hershel Shanks, 33–54. Washington: Biblical Archeology Society and Prentice Hall, 1999.

Sizer, Stephen R. "Christian Zionism: Its History, Theology, and Politics." Doctoral thesis, 1999, available at www.virginiawater.org.uk/christchurch/.

Smith, Tom W. "The Religious Right: Faith, Politics, Traditional Values, and Tolerance in Contemporary America." Typescript. Chicago: National Opinion Research Center, University of Chicago, 1999.

Trice, Robert H. "Congress and the Arab-Israeli Conflict: Support for Israel in the U.S. Senate, 1970–1973." *Political Science Quarterly* 92, no. 3 (Fall 1977): 443–63.

Wagner, Donald. "Evangelicals and Israel: Theological Roots of a Political Alliance." *Christian Century*, November 4, 1998, 1020–26.

Wall, James M. "On Being 'Pro-Israel.'" *Christian Century*, January 20, 1993, 43–44.

Weber, Timothy P. "How Evangelicals Became Israel's Best Friend." *Christianity Today*, October 5, 1998, 39–49.

Books

Albright, William F. *Yahweh and the Gods of Canaan: A Historical Analysis of Two Contrasting Faiths.* 1968; reprint, Winona Lake, Ind.: Eisenbrans, 1994.

American Petroleum Institute. *Petroleum Facts and Figures, 1971.* Washington, D.C.: American Petroleum Institute, 1971.

Ammerman, Nancy T. *Baptist Battles: Social Change and Religious Conflict in the Southern Baptist Convention.* New Brunswick: Rutgers University Press, 1990.

Anderson, Irvine H. *Aramco, the United States and Saudi Arabia: A Study in the Dynamics of Foreign Oil Policy, 1933–1950.* Princeton: Princeton University Press, 1981.

Arab American Institute. *The 105th Congress and Middle East Peace.* Washington, D.C.: Arab American Institute, 1998.

Ariel, Yaakov. *On Behalf of Israel: American Fundamentalist Attitudes towards Jews, Judaism, and Zionism, 1865–1945.* New York: Carlson, 1991.

Armstrong, Harold C. *Lord of Arabia.* London: Arthur Baker, 1934.

Armstrong, Karen. *The Battle for God.* New York: Alfred A. Knopf, 2000.

———. *Islam: A Short History.* New York: Modern Library, 2000.

Barr, David L. *New Testament Story: An Introduction.* 2d ed. Belmont, Calif.: Wadsworth, 1995.

Benoist-Mechin, Jacques. *Arabian Destiny.* Translated from the French by Denis Weaver. London: Elek Books, 1957.

Bergen, Peter L. *Holy War, Inc.: Inside the Secret World of Osama bin Laden.* New York: Free Press, 2001.

B[lackstone], W[illiam] E. *Jesus Is Coming.* 1878. Reprint, Chicago: Fleming H. Revell and the Moody Bible Institute, 1917.

Book of Common Prayer. New York: Church Hymnal Corporation, 1979.

Book of Common Worship. Louisville, Ky.: Westminster John Knox Press, 1993.

Borg, Marcus J. *Meeting Jesus Again for the First Time: The Historical Jesus and the Heart of Contemporary Faith.* San Francisco: Harper, 1994.

Borg, Marcus J., and N. T. Wright. *The Meaning of Jesus: Two Visions.* San Francisco: Harper, 1999.

Boyer, Paul. *Prophecy Belief in American Culture.* Cambridge: Harvard University Press, 1992.

Brand, Carl F. *The British Labour Party: A Short History.* Rev. ed. Stanford, Calif.: Hoover Institution Press, 1974.

Brichto, Herbert Chanan. *The Names of God: Poetic Readings in Biblical Beginnings.* New York: Basic Books, 1998.

Brueggemann, Walter. *The Land: Place as Gift, Promise, and Challenge in Biblical Faith.* Philadelphia: Fortress Press, 1977.

Burgess, Henry James. *Enterprise in Education: The Story of the Work of the Established Church in the Education of the People prior to 1870.* London: National Society, 1958.

Carter, Henry. *The Methodist Heritage.* Nashville: Abingdon-Cokesbury Press, 1951.

Christison, Kathleen. *Perceptions of Palestine: Their Influence on U.S. Middle East Policy.* Berkeley: University of California Press, 1999.

Cliff, Philip B. *The Rise and Development of the Sunday School Movement in England, 1780–1980.* Nuffield, Redhill, Surrey: National Christian Education Council, 1986.

Clifford, Clark, with Richard Holbrooke. *Counsel to the President: A Memoir.* New York: Random House, 1991.

Clouse, Robert G., Robert N. Hosack, and Richard V. Pierard. *The New Millennium Manual: A Once and Future Guide.* Grand Rapids: Baker Books, 1999.

Cohen, Michael J. *Truman and Israel.* Berkeley: University of California Press, 1990.

Collins, John J. *Daniel: A Commentary on the Book of Daniel.* Minneapolis: Fortress Press, 1993.

———. *Daniel: With an Introduction to Apocalyptic Literature.* Grand Rapids: William B. Eerdmans, 1984.

Cruickshank, Marjorie. *Church and State in English Education, 1870 to the Present Day.* London: Macmillan, 1963.

Currie, Robert, Alan Gilbert, and Lee Horsley. *Churches and Church Goers: Patterns of Church Growth in the British Isles since 1700.* Oxford: Clarendon Press, 1977.

Curtiss, Richard H. *A Changing Image: American Perceptions of the Arab-Israeli Dispute.* Washington, D.C.: American Educational Trust, 1986.

Davidson, Lawrence. *America's Palestine: Popular and Official Perceptions from Balfour to Israeli Statehood.* Gainesville: University Press of Florida, 2001.

Dugdale, Blanche. *Arthur James Balfour: First Earl of Balfour.* 2 vols. London: Hutchinson, 1936.

Duling, Dennis C., and Norman Purrin. *The New Testament: Proclamation and Parenesis, Myth and History.* 3d ed. Fort Worth, Tex.: Harcourt Brace College, 1994.

Eldredge, Niles. *The Triumph of Evolution and the End of Creationism.* New York: W. H. Freeman, 2000.

Epperson, Steven. *Mormons and Jews: Early Mormon Theologies of Israel.* Salt Lake City: Signature Books, 1992.

Epstein, Lawrence J. *Zion's Call: Christian Contributions to the Origins and Development of Palestine.* Lanham, Md.: University Press of America, 1984.

Esposito, John L. *Islam: The Straight Path.* New York: Oxford University Press, 1988.

Eve, Raymond E., and Francis B. Harrold. *The Creationist Movement in Modern America.* Boston: Twayne, 1991.

Evensen, Bruce J. *Truman, Palestine, and the Press: Shaping Conventional Wisdom at the Beginning of the Cold War.* New York: Greenwood Press, 1992.

Ferrell, Robert H., ed. *The Autobiography of Harry S. Truman.* Boulder: Colorado Associated University Press, 1980.

Feuerwerger, Marvin C. *Congress and Israel: Foreign Aid Decision-Making in the House of Representatives, 1969–1976.* Westport, Conn.: Greenwood Press, 1979.

Findley, Paul. *They Dare to Speak Out: People and Institutions Confront Israel's Lobby.* Westport, Conn.: Lawrence Hill, 1985.

Finkelstein, Israel, and Neil Asher Silberman. *The Bible Unearthed: Archaeology's New Vision of Ancient Israel and the Origins of Its Sacred Texts.* New York: Free Press, 2001.

Fowler, James W. *Faith Development and Pastoral Care.* Philadelphia: Fortress Press, 1987.

———. *Stages of Faith: The Psychology of Human Development and the Quest for Meaning.* San Francisco: Harper and Row, 1981, 1995.

Fraser, T. G. *The Middle East, 1914–1979.* New York: St. Martin's Press, 1980.

Friedman, Isaiah. *The Question of Palestine: British-Jewish-Arab Relations, 1914–1918.* 2d ed. New Brunswick, N.J., 1992.

The Fundamentals: A Testimony to the Truth. 12 vols. Chicago: Testimony, 1910–15.

Funk, Robert W., Roy W. Hoover, and the Jesus Seminar. *The Five Gospels: The Search for the Authentic Words of Jesus.* New translation and commentary. New York: Macmillan, 1993.

Gallup, George, Jr., and D. Michael Lindsay. *Surveying the Religious Landscape: Trends in U.S. Beliefs.* Harrisburg, Pa.: Morehouse, 1999.

Goldberg, J. J. *Jewish Power: Inside the American Jewish Establishment.* Reading, Mass.: Addison-Wesley, 1996.

Gorny, Joseph. *The British Labour Movement and Zionism, 1917–1949.* Totowa, N.J.: Frank Cass, 1983.

Gottwald, Norman K. *The Hebrew Bible: A Socio-Literary Introduction.* Philadelphia: Fortress Press, 1985.

Grose, Peter. *Israel in the Mind of America: The Untold Story of America's 150-Year Fascination with the Idea of a Jewish State, and the Complex Role Played by This Country and Its Leaders in the Creation of Modern Israel.* New York: Alfred A. Knopf, 1984.

Halle, Louis J. *The Cold War as History.* New York: Harper and Row, 1967.

Halsell, Grace. *Prophecy and Politics: The Secret Alliance between Israel and the U.S. Christian Right.* Chicago: Lawrence Hill Books, 1986.

Hanna, Paul L. *British Policy in Palestine.* Washington, D.C.: American Council on Public Affairs, 1942.

Hayes, John H. *An Introduction to Old Testament Study.* Nashville: Abingdon Press, 1979.

Hempton, David. *Methodism and Politics in British Society, 1750–1850.* Stanford: Stanford University Press, 1984.

Hoffer, Eric. *True Believer: Thoughts on the Nature of Mass Movements.* New York: Harper and Row, 1951.

James, Edgar C. *Arabs, Oil, and Armageddon.* Chicago: Moody Press, 1991.

Jervis, Robert. *Perception and Misperception in International Politics.* Princeton: Princeton University Press, 1976.

Keay, John. *Sowing the Wind: The Seeds of Conflict in the Middle East.* New York: W. W. Norton, 2003.

Kohut, Andrew, John C. Green, Scott Keeter, and Robert C. Toth. *The Diminishing Divide: Religion's Changing Role in American Politics.* Washington, D.C.: Brookings Institution Press, 2000.

Kovacs, Maureen G., ed. *The Epic of Gilgamesh.* Stanford: Stanford University Press, 1985.

Laqueur, Thomas Walter. *Religion and Respectability: Sunday Schools and Working-Class Culture, 1780–1850.* New Haven: Yale University Press, 1976.

Lectionary. New York: Catholic, 1970.

Lemche, Niels Peter. *The Israelites in History and Tradition.* Louisville, Ky.: Westminster John Knox Press, 1998.

Lenczowski, George. *The Middle East in World Affairs.* 4th ed. Ithaca, N.Y.: Cornell University Press, 1980.

Lindsey, Hal. *Vanished into Thin Air: The Hope of Every Believer.* Beverly Hills: Western Front, 1999.

Lindsey, Hal, with C. C. Carlson. *The Late Great Planet Earth.* Grand Rapids: Zondervan, 1970.

————. *The Late Great Planet Earth.* New York: Harper Paperbacks, 1992.

Lloyd George, Earl. *My Father, Lloyd George.* New York: Crown, 1961.

Lynn, Robert W., and Elliott Wright. *The Big Little School: Two Hundred Years of the Sunday School.* 2d ed. Nashville: Abingdon Press, 1980.

Madsen, Truman G. *The Mormon Attitude toward Zionism.* Lecture at Haifa University, May 1980. Published as a 25-page booklet.

Magnusson, Magnus. *Archaeology of the Bible.* New York: Simon and Schuster, 1977.

Mark, Thiselton. *For Childhood and Youth: Ideals of the Modern Sunday School.* London: James Clarke, 1913. Uncataloged copy in Stock Room 1 of the Orchard Learning Resource Center, marked with call number 268.1 T1.

Marsden, George M. *Fundamentalism and American Culture: The Shaping of Twentieth-Century Evangelicalism.* New York: Oxford University Press, 1980.

————. *Understanding Fundamentalism and Evangelicalism.* Grand Rapids: William B. Eerdmans, 1991.

Martin, William. *With God on Our Side: The Rise of the Religious Right in America.* New York: Broadway Books, 1996.

Mayor, Stephen. *The Churches and the Labour Movement.* London: Independent Press, 1967.

McCullough, David. *Truman.* New York: Simon and Schuster, 1992.

McQuaid, Elwood. *There Is Hope.* Bellmawr, N.J.: Friends of Israel Gospel Ministry, 1996.

Merkley, Paul Charles. *Christian Attitudes towards the State of Israel.* Montreal: McGill-Queen's University Press, 2001.

————. *The Politics of Christian Zionism, 1891–1948.* London: Frank Cass, 1998.

Mouly, Ruth W. *The Religious Right and Israel: The Politics of Armageddon.* Cambridge, Mass.: Political Research Associates, 1985.

Muslih, Muhammad Y. *The Origins of Palestinian Nationalism.* New York: Columbia University Press, 1988.

Newport, John P. *The Lion and the Lamb: A Commentary on the Book of Revelation for Today.* Nashville: Broadman Press, 1986.

Noll, Mark A. *Between Faith and Criticism: Evangelicals, Scholarship, and the Bible in America.* San Francisco: Harper and Row, 1986.

Peretz, Don. *The Middle East Today.* 6th ed. Westport, Conn.: Praeger, 1994.

Philby, Harry St. John Bridger. *Saudi Arabia.* London: Ernest Benn, 1955.

Pragai, Michael J. *Faith and Fulfillment: Christians and the Return to the Promised Land.* London: Vallentine Mitchell, 1985.

Rad, Gerhard von. *Genesis: A Commentary.* Trans. John H. Marks. Rev. ed. Philadelphia: Westminster Press, 1972.

————. *Old Testament Theology,* vol. 1, *The Theology of Israel's Historical Traditions.* New York: Harper, 1962.

Rubenberg, Cheryl A. *Israel and the American National Interest: A Critical Examination.* Urbana: University of Illinois Press, 1986.

Sachar, Howard M. *The Course of Jewish History.* New rev. ed. New York: Vintage Books, 1990.

Sanders, Ronald. *The High Walls of Jerusalem: A History of the Balfour Declaration and the Birth of the British Mandate for Palestine.* New York: Holt, Rinehart and Winston, 1983.

Seger, Tom. *One Palestine Complete: Jews and Arabs under the British Mandate.* Translated by Haim Watzman. New York: Henry Holt, 2000.

Simon, Merrill. *Jerry Falwell and the Jews.* Middle Village, N.Y.: Jonathan David, 1984.

Snetsinger, John. *Truman, the Jewish Vote, and the Creation of Israel.* Stanford: Stanford University Press, 1974.

Speiser, E. A. *Genesis.* Garden City, N.Y.: Doubleday, 1964.

Stein, Kenneth. *The Land Question in Palestine, 1917–1939.* Chapel Hill: University of North Carolina Press, 1984.

Stein, Leonard. *The Balfour Declaration.* Jerusalem: Magnes Press of the Hebrew University, 1961.

Thompson, Thomas L. *The Historicity of the Patriarchal Narratives: The Quest for the Historical Abraham.* Berlin: Walter de Gruyter, 1974.

Thorpe, Andrew. *A Short History of the British Labour Party.* London: Macmillan Press, 1997.

Tuchman, Barbara W. *Bible and Sword: England and Palestine from the Bronze Age to Balfour.* New York: Funk and Wagnalls, 1956.

Verete, Mayir. *From Palmerston to Balfour: Collected Essays.* Edited by Norman Rose. London: Frank Cass, 1992.

Wagner, Clarence H., Jr. *Lessons from the Land of the Bible: Revealing More of God's Word.* Jerusalem: Bridges for Peace, 2000.

———. "Twelve Keys to Understanding Israel in the Bible." *Bridges for Peace Israel Teaching Letter,* October 1999, 2.

Wagner, Donald E. *Anxious for Armageddon: A Call to Partnership for Middle Eastern and Western Christians.* Waterloo, Ontario: Herald Press, 1995.

Walvoord, John F. *Armageddon, Oil, and the Middle East Crisis: What the Bible Says about the Future of the Middle East and the End of Western Civilization.* Rev. ed. Grand Rapids: Zondervan, 1990.

———. *Israel in Prophecy.* Grand Rapids: Zondervan, 1962.

Wearmouth, Robert W. *Methodism and the Working-Class Movements in England, 1800–1850.* Clifton, N.J.: Augustus M. Kelley, 1972.

Webb, George E. *The Evolution Controversy in America.* Lexington: University Press of Kentucky, 1994.

Weber, Eugen. *Apocalypses: Prophesies, Cults, and Millennial Beliefs through the Ages.* Cambridge: Harvard University Press, 1999.

Weinstein, Allen, and Moshe Maʻoz, eds. *Truman and the American Commitment to Israel.* Jerusalem: Magnes Press of the Hebrew University, 1981.

Wilson, Evan W. *Decision on Palestine: How the United States Came to Recognize Israel.* Stanford, Calif.: Hoover University Press, 1979.

Wrigley, Chris. *Arthur Henderson.* Cardiff: University of Wales Press, 1990.

Index

Passages from books of the Bible are in italics.

Irvine H. Anderson is a retired professor of American diplomatic history, having taught at Xavier University and the University of Cincinnati. He is the author of *Aramco, the United States, and Saudi Arabia: A Study of the Dynamics of Foreign Oil Policy, 1933–1950* and *The Standard-Vacuum Oil Company and United States East Asian Policy, 1933–1941.*